Journal and Practice Workbook

Contents

Journal and More Practice

UNIT 3 Transformations

UNIT 4 Triangle Congruence

Module 7 Congruent Triangles and Polygons

Module 8 Triangle Congruence Criteria

UNIT 5 Relationships Within Triangles

Module 9 Properties of Triangles

UNIT 6 Quadrilaterals, Polygons, and Triangle Similarity

Step It Out

Learn the Math

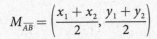 Given the points $A(-3, 2)$, $B(5, 8)$, $P(0, 1)$, and $Q(2, 9)$, find the midpoint M of $\overline{AB}$ and the midpoint R of $\overline{PQ}$. Do the segments intersect at one of the midpoints?

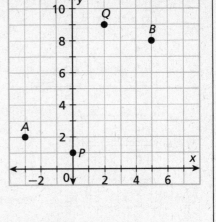

$M_{\overline{AB}} = \left(\dfrac{x_1 + x_2}{2}, \dfrac{y_1 + y_2}{2} \right)$ Midpoint Formula

$M_{\overline{AB}} = \left(\dfrac{-3 + 5}{2}, \dfrac{2 + 8}{2} \right)$ Substitute.

$M_{\overline{AB}} = \left(\dfrac{2}{2}, \dfrac{10}{2} \right)$ Add.

$M_{\overline{AB}} = (1, 5)$ Divide.

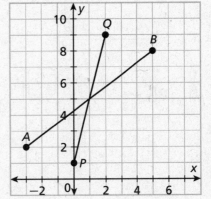

$M_{\overline{PQ}} = \left(\dfrac{x_1 + x_2}{2}, \dfrac{y_1 + y_2}{2} \right)$ Midpoint Formula

$M_{\overline{PQ}} = \left(\dfrac{0 + 2}{2}, \dfrac{9 + 1}{2} \right)$ Substitute.

$M_{\overline{PQ}} = \left(\dfrac{2}{2}, \dfrac{10}{2} \right)$ Add.

$M_{\overline{PQ}} = (1, 5)$ Divide.

Since they both have a midpoint at $(1, 5)$, they do intersect at their midpoint.

Do the Math

Given the points $S(-2, -4)$, $T(4, 6)$, $C(-6, 10)$, and $D(4, -8)$, find the midpoint M of $\overline{ST}$ and R of $\overline{CD}$. Do the segments intersect at one of the midpoints?

$M_{\overline{ST}} = \left(\dfrac{x_1 + x_2}{2}, \dfrac{y_1 + y_2}{2} \right)$ \qquad Midpoint Formula

$M_{\overline{ST}} = \left(\dfrac{\boxed{} + 4}{2}, \dfrac{-4 + \boxed{}}{2} \right)$ \qquad Substitute.

$M_{\overline{ST}} = \left(\dfrac{\boxed{}}{2}, \dfrac{\boxed{}}{2} \right)$ \qquad Add.

$M_{\overline{ST}} = \left(\boxed{}, \boxed{} \right)$ \qquad Divide.

$M_{\overline{CD}} = \left(\dfrac{x_1 + x_2}{2}, \dfrac{y_1 + y_2}{2} \right)$ \qquad Midpoint Formula

$M_{\overline{CD}} = \left(\dfrac{\boxed{} + 4}{2}, \dfrac{10 + \boxed{}}{2} \right)$ \qquad Substitute.

$M_{\overline{CD}} = \left(\dfrac{\boxed{}}{2}, \dfrac{\boxed{}}{2} \right)$ \qquad Add.

$M_{\overline{CD}} = \left(\boxed{}, \boxed{} \right)$ \qquad Divide.

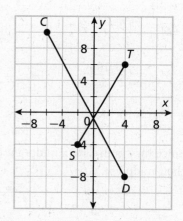

Since the segments have different midpoints, they do not intersect at their midpoints. You can graph the segments to see that they do not intersect at their midpoints.

ONLINE
Video Tutorials and
Interactive Examples

1. Name the ray. _____

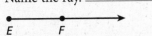

2. Name the plane in four different ways. _____

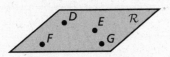

_____

_____

_____

3. Point B is on $\overline{AC}$. What is the length of $\overline{AB}$ if $AC = 22$ and $BC = 13$? _____

4. If T is the midpoint of $\overline{SU}$ and $ST = 17$, what is the length of $\overline{SU}$? _____

5. Use the figure to solve for x. _____

For Problems 6–9, use the graph to the right.

6. Find the midpoint of $\overline{AB}$. _____

7. Find the midpoint of $\overline{CD}$. _____

8. Find the midpoint of $\overline{EF}$. _____

9. Do $\overline{AB}$ and $\overline{CD}$ have the same length? _____

State each segment length.

$AB =$ _____

$CD =$ _____

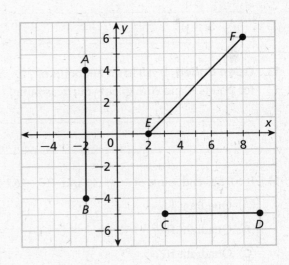

10. Point C is on the midpoint of a section of highway, represented by $\overline{AB}$. If $AB = 32$ miles, $AC = 4x$ miles, and $CB = 12 + x$ miles, explain three different ways that you could solve for x.

_____

_____

_____

_____

_____

11. Math on the Spot $\overline{CD}$ has endpoints $C(-3, 4)$ and $D(1, -2)$. Find the coordinates of its midpoint.

_____

_____

_____

_____

12. Critique Reasoning Kirsten's house is located at a point on the map that is 7 miles west and 2 miles south of the center of town. She drives to a movie theater, which is 5 miles east and 3 miles north of the center of town. If the image represents the road she drove, how far did she travel?

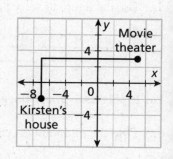

_____

_____

_____

13. Open Ended If $\overline{AB}$ has a midpoint of $M(-5, 4)$, what are possible coordinates for points A and B? Explain your reasoning.

_____

_____

14. If $\overline{ST}$ has endpoints $S(-3, -4)$ and $T(5, -6)$, in which quadrant does its midpoint lie?

(A) Quadrant I

(B) Quadrant II

(C) Quadrant III

(D) Quadrant IV

Step It Out

Learn the Math

EXAMPLE 1 Use a compass and straightedge to construct the angle bisector of ∠QRS.

Draw an angle and label it ∠QRS.	
Place the point of the compass on the vertex R. Draw an arc that intersects both sides of the angle. Label the intersections X and Y.	
Place the point of the compass on X and draw an arc.	
Place the point of the compass on Y and draw the same-sized arc.	
Label the intersection of the arcs T. Use a straightedge to draw $\overrightarrow{RT}$.	

Do the Math

Use a compass and straightedge to construct the angle bisector of ∠DEF.

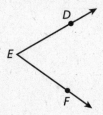

Learn the Math

EXAMPLE 2 Find the measures of $\angle FJG$ and $\angle GJH$, given that $m\angle FJH = 168°$.

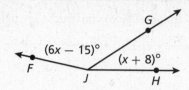

$m\angle FJH = m\angle FJG + m\angle GJH$	Angle Addition Postulate
$168 = (6x - 15) + (x + 8)$	Substitute.
$168 = (6x + x) + (-15 + 8)$	Commutative and Associative Properties
$168 = (7x - 7)$	Combine like terms.
$175 = 7x$	Simplify.
$25 = x$	Divide.

So $m\angle FJG = \left[(6 \times 25) - 15\right]° = 135°$ and $m\angle GJH = (25 + 8)° = 33°$.

Do the Math

Find the measures of $\angle WVY$ and $\angle YVZ$, given that $m\angle WVZ = 80°$.

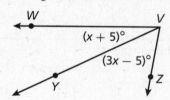

$m\angle \boxed{} = m\angle \boxed{} + m\angle \boxed{}$	Angle Addition Postulate
$80 = \boxed{} + \boxed{}$	Substitute.
$80 = \boxed{} + \boxed{}$	Commutative and Associative Properties
$80 = \boxed{}$	Combine like terms.
$\boxed{} = x$	Divide.

So, $m\angle WVY = \boxed{}$ and $m\angle YVZ = \boxed{}$.

Name _____

LESSON 1.2
More Practice

ONLINE
Video Tutorials and
Interactive Examples

1. Name each angle in three different ways.

A.

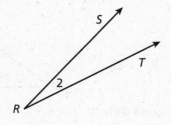

_____

B.

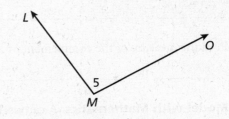

_____

2. Draw and label adjacent angles *LMN* and *NMO*.

3. **Math on the Spot** Use a protractor to measure the following angles.

A.

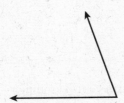

_____

B.

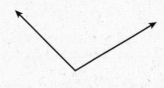

_____

4. Use a protractor to draw an angle for each of the given measures.

A. 60°   **B.** 115°   **C.** 76°

5. Angles *ABC* and *DEF* are complementary angles. If m∠*ABC* = 72°,
   what is m∠*DEF*?

_____

6. **Critical Thinking** $\angle RST$ is its own complement. What is the measure of the angle that is supplementary to $\angle RST$?

_____

7. Find the measure of the complement of $\angle M$.

_____

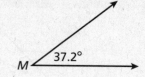

M 37.2°

8. **Model with Mathematics** A carousel measures 360 degrees around with 5 rows of horses evenly distributed. What is the measure of the angle formed by rays drawn from the center of the carousel through the middle of each of two rows of horses next to each other? Start by drawing a model of the carousel, showing each row of horses as a ray.

_____

9. Suppose $m\angle Z = (6x)°$. What is the range of the values of x? Explain your reasoning.

_____

_____

_____

10. **Critique Reasoning** $\overrightarrow{RT}$ bisects $\angle QRS$. Bailey is solving for $m\angle QRS$ when $m\angle QRS = (5x - 5)°$ and $m\angle QRT = (2x)°$. His work is shown. Describe and correct Bailey's error in solving for x.

$$2(5x - 5) = 2x$$
$$10x - 10 = 2x$$
$$10x - 10 - 10x = 2x - 10x$$
$$-10 = -8x$$
$$10 = 8x$$
$$x = \frac{5}{4}$$

_____

_____

_____

_____

11. $\angle STU$ and $\angle VWX$ are supplementary angles. If $m\angle STU = 34°$, what is $m\angle VWX$?

Ⓐ 156°

Ⓑ 146°

Ⓒ 56°

Ⓓ 46°

Step It Out

Learn the Math

EXAMPLE 1 The steps for constructing a square using a compass and ruler are shown.

Step 1		Draw a circle using a compass. Label the center point as M.
Step 2		Using a ruler, draw a diameter that passes through the center point M. Label the points on the circle A and C.
Step 3		Place the point of your compass on point C and draw an arc.
Step 4		Keeping the compass open to the same distance, place the point of your compass on point A and draw an arc.
Step 5		Draw a diameter through the center M and the intersection of the arcs. Label the points on the circle B and D.
Step 6		Use your ruler to connect the adjacent endpoints of the diameters.

Do the Math

Construct a hexagon following these steps using a compass and ruler.

Step 1	Draw a circle using a compass. Label the center point as M.
Step 2	Draw a small arc from any point on the circle using the radius as the length.
Step 3	Keeping the compass open to the radius, place the compass on the point of intersection of the circle and the arc and draw another arc to the right.
Step 4	Continue this pattern going in a clockwise direction until you reach the initial point.
Step 5	Use a ruler to draw segments connecting each of the segments.

Name _____

Step It Out

Learn the Math

EXAMPLE 2 Find the area of the picture of the rocket.

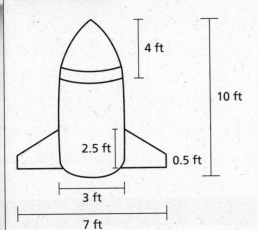

4 ft

10 ft

2.5 ft

0.5 ft

3 ft

7 ft

Step 1	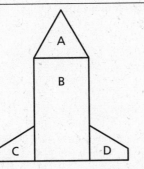 A B C D	Choose shapes to model the picture of the rocket. Then find the area of each shape.
Step 2	4 ft / 3 ft **A:** $A = \frac{1}{2}(4)(3) = \frac{1}{2}(12) = 6$	6 ft / 3 ft **B:** $A = 6(3) = 18$
	2.5 ft / 0.5 ft / 2 ft **C:** $A = 2\left(\frac{2.5 + 0.5}{2}\right) = 2\left(\frac{3}{2}\right) = 3$	2.5 ft / 0.5 ft / 2 ft **D:** $A = 2\left(\frac{2.5 + 0.5}{2}\right) = 2\left(\frac{3}{2}\right) = 3$
Step 3	Find the sum of the areas of each shape. $A = 6 + 18 + 3 + 3 = 30 \text{ ft}^2$	

The area of the picture of the rocket is about 30 square feet.

Do the Math

Find the area of the hexagon.

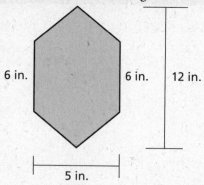

6 in.   6 in.   12 in.

5 in.

Learn the Math

EXAMPLE 3   Prove the Pythagorean Theorem based on the given diagram.

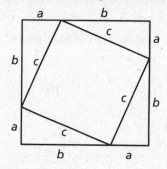

$A = (a + b)^2$ or $A = 4\left(\dfrac{1}{2}ab\right) + c^2$	Find the area of the square. Use the formula for a square, s^2, with $s = a + b$, or add the areas of the four triangles $\left(\dfrac{1}{2}ab\right)$ plus the area of the inside square (c^2).
$(a + b)^2 = 4\left(\dfrac{1}{2}ab\right) + c^2$	Use the Reflexive Property of Equality to set the formulas equal to each other.
$a^2 + 2ab + b^2 = 2ab + c^2$	Simplify.
$a^2 + b^2 = c^2$	Use the Subtraction Property of Equality to subtract $2ab$ from both sides. This gives the formula for the Pythagorean Theorem.

Do the Math

Use the diagram to present another proof of the Pythagorean Theorem.

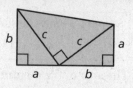

Name _____

LESSON 1.3
More Practice

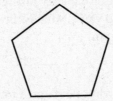
ONLINE
Video Tutorials and
Interactive Examples

1. Classify the polygon.

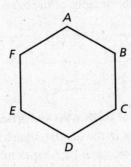

_____

2. Name the polygon in four different ways.

_____   _____

_____   _____

3. Draw a regular polygon with 8 vertices.

4. Draw a polygon with 5 sides that have five different lengths.

5. What is the height of a triangle with a base of 4 m and an area of 14 m²? _____

6. What is the area of a rectangle with a length of 4 ft and width of 6 ft? _____

7. What is the perimeter of a square with an area of 36 in²? _____

8. A fire marshal states that the maximum capacity of a school gym per square yard is 5 students. If the gym is 30 yards by 20 yards, what is the maximum number of students that can attend a dance held in the gym?

9. **Open Ended** A trapezoid has a height of 6 ft and a total area of 30 ft². What are possible lengths of the bases? Explain your reasoning.

10. **Model with Mathematics** The outline of a park is shown in the diagram. Each square on the grid represents a square yard. Use shapes to model the area of the park. Explain your reasoning and justify your calculations.

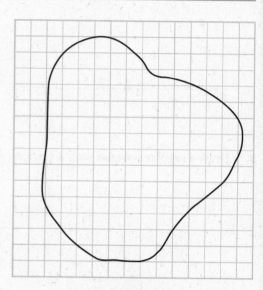

11. **Use Structure** Find the area of the trapezoid using the Pythagorean Theorem and the formula for a trapezoid. Then find the area by finding the areas of the two triangles and quadrilateral. Compare your answers. Are they the same? Explain.

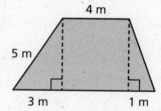

12. A building that is 195 feet tall casts a shadow that measures 28 feet long. Collin stands at the end of the shadow. How far are Collin's feet from the top of the building?

Ⓐ 223 ft

Ⓑ 197 ft

Ⓒ 193 ft

Ⓓ 167 ft

Step It Out

Learn the Math

EXAMPLE 1 ▶ Calculate the perimeter of the triangle. Round your answer to the nearest hundredth.

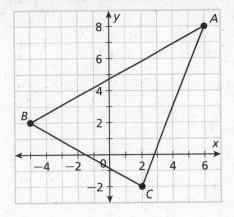

Find the length of each side.

$\overline{AB}$	$\overline{AC}$	$\overline{BC}$	
$d = \sqrt{(x_2 - x_1)^2 + (y_2 - y_1)^2}$	$d = \sqrt{(x_2 - x_1)^2 + (y_2 - y_1)^2}$	$d = \sqrt{(x_2 - x_1)^2 + (y_2 - y_1)^2}$	Distance Formula
$A(6,8)$ and $B(-5,2)$	$A(6,8)$ and $C(2,-2)$	$B(-5,2)$ and $C(2,-2)$	Identify points.
$d = \sqrt{(-5-6)^2 + (2-8)^2}$	$d = \sqrt{(2-6)^2 + (-2-8)^2}$	$d = \sqrt{(2-(-5))^2 + (-2-2)^2}$	Input values.
$= \sqrt{(-11)^2 + (-6)^2}$	$= \sqrt{(-4)^2 + (-10)^2}$	$= \sqrt{(7)^2 + (-4)^2}$	Subtract to simplify.
$= \sqrt{121 + 36}$	$= \sqrt{16 + 100}$	$= \sqrt{49 + 16}$	Square the differences.
$= \sqrt{157}$	$= \sqrt{116}$	$= \sqrt{65}$	Add.
≈ 12.53	≈ 10.77	≈ 8.06	Find the square root.

$d \approx 12.53 + 10.77 + 8.06 = 31.36$ Calculate the sum to find the perimeter.

Do the Math

Calculate the perimeter of the triangle. Round your answer to the nearest hundredth.

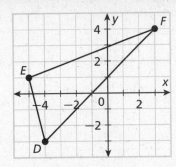

Learn the Math

EXAMPLE 2 ▸ The area of a lake can be calculated by modeling it on a coordinate plane. This lake roughly fits the shape of a parallelogram. What is the area of the lake if 1 unit on the grid represents 1 mile?

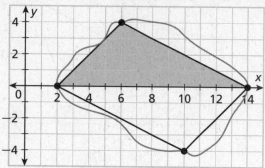

Divide the parallelogram into two triangles.

$14 - 2 = 12$ Find the length of the base of the triangles.

$4 - 0 = 4$ and $0 - (-4) = 4$ Find the height of the triangles.

$A = \frac{1}{2}(12)(4)$ and $A = \frac{1}{2}(12)(4)$ Use the formula for the area of a triangle.

$A = 24$ and $A = 24$ Simplify.

$24 + 24 = 48$ Add the area of the two triangles.

The lake is 48 square miles.

Do the Math

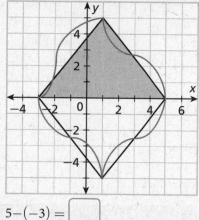

A landscaper needs to calculate the area of a yard. What is the area of the yard if each square on the coordinate plane represents 100 square feet?

Divide the parallelogram into two triangles.

$5 - (-3) = \boxed{}$ Find the length of the base of the triangles.

$5 - 0 = \boxed{}$ and $0 - \left(\boxed{}\right) = 5$ Find the height of the triangles.

$A = \frac{1}{2}\left(\boxed{}\right)\left(\boxed{}\right)$ and $A = \frac{1}{2}(8)(5)$ Use the formula for the area of a triangle.

$A = \boxed{}$ and $A = 20$ Simplify.

$\boxed{} + 20 = \boxed{}$ Add the area of the two triangles.

$\boxed{}(100) = \boxed{}$ square feet   Multiply the area by 100 square feet.

Name

LESSON 1.4
More Practice

ONLINE
Video Tutorials and
Interactive Examples

1. Use the figure shown.

   A. Which segments are congruent?

   _____

   B. What are the lengths of the congruent segments?

   _____

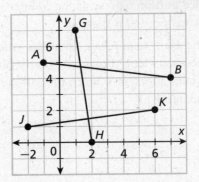

2. What is the area of the parallelogram?

   _____

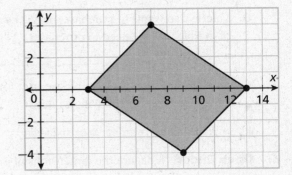

3. What is the perimeter of the parallelogram?

   _____

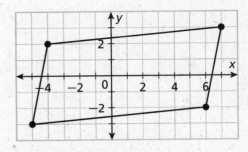

4. What are the area and perimeter of a polygon with vertices $(1, -2)$, $(1, 5)$, and $(7, -2)$?

   _____

   _____

   _____

5. Use Structure The blueprint shows Valerie's kitchen. The shaded portion represents the counter space, and the unshaded portion is the floor.

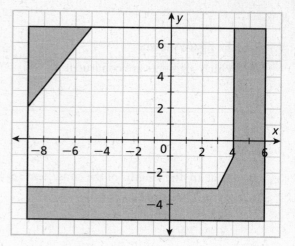

A. Valerie wants to purchase floor tile, which is sold by the square foot. If each unit on the blueprint represents a foot, how much tile will she need to purchase?

_____

_____

_____

B. Valerie also wants to purchase marble countertops. How many square feet of marble will she need to purchase?

_____

C. Finally, Valerie wants to purchase trim for the perimeter of her floors. How many feet of trim will she need?

_____

6. Open Ended What are the dimensions of a rectangle with an area equal to the parallelogram with vertices $(6, 21)$, $(14, 15)$, $(6, 0)$, and $(-2, 6)$? Explain.

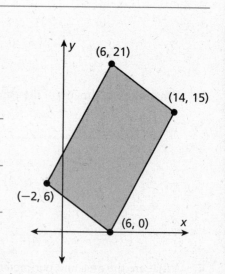

_____

_____

_____

7. What is the distance between the coordinates $(-12, -4)$ and $(-1, 56)$?

Ⓐ 53.2

Ⓑ 53.6

Ⓒ 61

Ⓓ 61.4

Step It Out

Learn the Math

EXAMPLE 1 ▸ The definition of a right angle is an angle with a measure of exactly 90 degrees. Write the definition of a right angle as a biconditional statement.

Hypothesis: An angle is a right angle.

Conclusion: The angle has a measure of 90 degrees.

Biconditional Statement:

<u>An angle is a right angle</u> if and only if <u>the angle has a measure of 90 degrees.</u>
        Hypothesis   Conclusion

Do the Math

A

The definition of an acute triangle is a triangle in which all angles have a measure less than 90 degrees.

Write the definition of an acute triangle as a biconditional statement.

Hypothesis: _____

Conclusion: _____

Biconditional Statement: _____

B

The definition of parallel lines is the lines never intersect.

Write the definition of parallel lines as a biconditional statement.

Hypothesis: _____

Conclusion: _____

Biconditional Statement: _____

C

The definition of a pentagon is a polygon with five sides.

Write the definition of a pentagon as a biconditional statement.

Hypothesis: _____

Conclusion: _____

Biconditional Statement: _____

Learn the Math

EXAMPLE 2 A billboard reads, "If you can read this, you have missed your exit." Write the converse, inverse, and contrapositive of this statement.

Converse: If you have missed your exit, then you can read this.

Inverse: If you cannot read this, then you have not missed your exit.

Contrapositive: If you have not missed your exit, then you cannot read this.

Do the Math

A

A sign in a restaurant reads, "If it is your birthday, you get free ice cream." Write the converse, inverse, and contrapositive of this statement.

Converse: _____

Inverse: _____

Contrapositive: _____

B

A label on a container reads, "If you are not 100% satisfied, we will refund your purchase price." Write the converse, inverse, and contrapositive of this statement.

Converse: _____

Inverse: _____

Contrapositive: _____

C

A movie poster says, "If you like action movies, then you will like this movie." Write the converse, inverse, and contrapositive of this statement.

Converse: _____

Inverse: _____

Contrapositive: _____

D

A sign at an amusement park ride says, "If you are at least four feet tall, you are allowed to take this ride." Write the converse, inverse, and contrapositive of this statement.

Converse: _____

Inverse: _____

Contrapositive: _____

Name _____

LESSON 2.1
More Practice

ONLINE
Video Tutorials and
Interactive Examples

1. For each definition below, identify the hypothesis and conclusion.
   Then write a biconditional statement that corresponds to the definition.

   A. Congruent angles are angles with the exact same measure.

   _____

   _____

   _____

   B. An octagon is a polygon with exactly eight sides and angles.

   _____

   _____

   _____

   C. An angle bisector is a line or ray that divides an angle into two congruent angles.

   _____

   _____

   _____

2. A biconditional statement says, "A polygon is a square if and only if the polygon has
   four equal sides and four right angles." Write the hypothesis and conclusion.

   _____

   _____

3. A statement says, "If the measure of $\angle J$ equals the measure of $\angle K$, the angles are
   congruent." Write the converse, inverse, and contrapositive of this statement.

   _____

   _____

   _____

4. What is the original statement if the converse of the original statement is "If a number
   is divisible by two, then it is an even number"? What is the inverse of the original
   statement?

   _____

   _____

5. Write the biconditional statement if the hypothesis is "This month is November," and
   the conclusion is "Next month is December."

   _____

6. In order to win a hockey game, a team must outscore its opponent. Write the hypothesis, conclusion, and biconditional statement that describe when a team wins a hockey game.

_____

_____

_____

7. Write the contrapositive of the statement, "If you make no mistakes in the exam, then you receive a score of 100%."

_____

_____

8. **Reason** A right triangle is a triangle that contains a right angle. Write the biconditional statement for the statement above. Also, write the converse of the statement. Is the converse a true statement? Explain.

_____

_____

_____

9. **Open Ended** If your original biconditional statement is true, would the contrapositive be true? Give an example to illustrate your reasoning.

_____

_____

_____

10. Which biconditional statement below is true?

Ⓐ An angle is obtuse if and only if the angle's measure is less than 90 degrees.

Ⓑ An angle is obtuse if and only if the angle's measure is greater than 90 degrees.

Ⓒ An angle is obtuse if and only if the angle's measure is equal to 90 degrees.

Ⓓ An angle is obtuse if and only if the angle's measure is greater than or equal to 90 degrees.

Name _____

Step It Out

Learn the Math

EXAMPLE 1 ▶ Write a two-column proof for the Midpoint Formula.

Given: (x_1, y_1) and (x_2, y_2) are two points in the coordinate plane.

Prove: The midpoint is $\left(\dfrac{x_1 + x_2}{2}, \dfrac{y_1 + y_2}{2} \right)$.

Statements	Reasons
1. (x_1, y_1) and (x_2, y_2) are two points in the coordinate plane.	1. Given
2. The distance between (x_1, y_1) and (x_2, y_2) is $\sqrt{(x_2 - x_1)^2 + (y_2 - y_1)^2}$.	2. Distance Formula
3. The distance between (x_1, y_1) and $\left(\dfrac{x_1 + x_2}{2}, \dfrac{y_1 + y_2}{2} \right)$ is $\sqrt{\left(\dfrac{x_1 + x_2}{2} - x_1 \right)^2 + \left(\dfrac{y_1 + y_2}{2} - y_1 \right)^2}$.	3. Substitute.
4. $\sqrt{\left(\dfrac{x_1 + x_2}{2} - x_1 \right)^2 + \left(\dfrac{y_1 + y_2}{2} - y_1 \right)^2} = \sqrt{\left(\dfrac{x_1 + x_2}{2} - \dfrac{2x_1}{2} \right)^2 + \left(\dfrac{y_1 + y_2}{2} - \dfrac{2y_1}{2} \right)^2}$	4. Common denominators
5. $\sqrt{\left(\dfrac{x_1 + x_2}{2} - \dfrac{2x_1}{2} \right)^2 + \left(\dfrac{y_1 + y_2}{2} - \dfrac{2y_1}{2} \right)^2} = \sqrt{\dfrac{(x_2 - x_1)^2}{4} + \dfrac{(y_2 - y_1)^2}{4}}$	5. Add and factor.
6. $\sqrt{\dfrac{(x_2 - x_1)^2}{4} + \dfrac{(y_2 - y_1)^2}{4}} = \dfrac{1}{2} \sqrt{(x_2 - x_1)^2 + (y_2 - y_1)^2}$	6. Square root
7. $\left(\dfrac{x_1 + x_2}{2}, \dfrac{y_1 + y_2}{2} \right)$ is the midpoint between (x_1, y_1) and (x_2, y_2).	7. Definition of midpoint

Do the Math

Given: △ABC

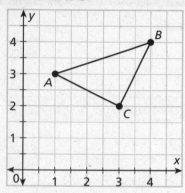

Prove that △ABC is a right triangle by writing a two-column proof.

Statements	Reasons
1. slope of $\overline{BC} = \dfrac{4-2}{4-3} = 2$	1.
2. slope of $\overline{AC} = \dfrac{2-3}{3-1} = \dfrac{-1}{2}$	2.
3. $\overline{AC}$ and $\overline{BC}$ are perpendicular.	3.
4. ∠BCA is a right angle.	4.
5. △ABC is a right triangle.	5.

1. Given: △*DEF*
Prove: △*DEF* is isosceles.

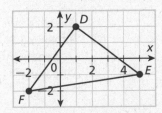

Statements	Reasons
1.	1.
2.	2.
3.	3.
4.	4.

2. Given: quadrilateral *HIJK*
Prove: Quadrilateral *HIJK* is a parallelogram.

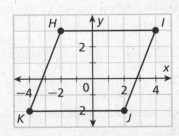

Statements	Reasons
1.	1.
2.	2.
3.	3.

3. **Math on the Spot** Use the given flowchart to write a two-column proof of the Alternate Interior Angles Theorem.

Given: $\ell \parallel m$
Prove: $\angle 1 \cong \angle 2$
Alternate Interior Angles Theorem

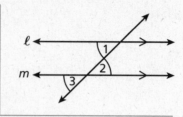

Flowchart Proof

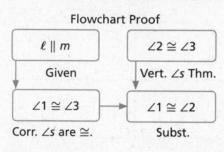

_____   _____
_____   _____
_____   _____
_____   _____

4. **Open Ended** Explain why the statement "It will always rain on my birthday" uses inductive reasoning.

_____
_____

5. Choose the appropriate reasons to fill in the proof below.

Given: $5t - 2 = 13$

Prove: $t = 3$

Statements	Reasons
1. $5t - 2 = 13$	**1.** Given
2. $5t - 2 + 2 = 13 + 2$	**2.**
3. $5t - 15$	**3.** Simplify.
4. $5t \div 5 = 15 \div 5$	**4.**
5. $t = 3$	**5.** Simplify.

Ⓐ 2. Addition Property of Equality, 4. Multiplication Property of Equality

Ⓑ 2. Addition Property of Equality, 4. Division Property of Equality

Ⓒ 2. Subtraction Property of Equality, 4. Multiplication Property of Equality

Ⓓ 2. Subtraction Property of Equality, 4. Division Property of Equality

Name _____

Step It Out

Learn the Math

EXAMPLE 1 ▶ The plans for a vegetable garden show a diagram of the garden layout. The boards used to make the garden are represented by $\overline{AB}$, $\overline{BC}$, $\overline{CD}$, $\overline{CI}$, $\overline{DJ}$, $\overline{AE}$, $\overline{EF}$, $\overline{BG}$, $\overline{GH}$, and $\overline{IJ}$.

To see how many boards of each size to cut, Jean arranges the segments from the plan into groups.

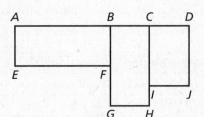

Group One consists of $\overline{AB}$ and $\overline{EF}$ because $\overline{AB} \cong \overline{EF}$.

Group Two consists of $\overline{BC}$, $\overline{GH}$, $\overline{AE}$, $\overline{CD}$, and $\overline{IJ}$ because $\overline{BC} \cong \overline{GH} \cong \overline{AE} \cong \overline{CD} \cong \overline{IJ}$.

Group Three consists of $\overline{BG}$ and $\overline{CH}$ because $\overline{BG} \cong \overline{CH}$.

Group Four consists of $\overline{CI}$ and $\overline{DJ}$ because $\overline{CI} \cong \overline{DJ}$.

Do the Math

Kit draws a design for a sculpture made of sticks glued together. Place the sticks into groups according to size.

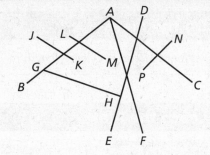

The first group has $\overline{DE}$ in it.

What other line segments belong in this group?

_____

Why do these segments belong together?

_____

The second group has $\overline{AB}$ in it.

What other line segments belong in this group?

_____ because _____.

The third group has $\overline{NP}$ in it. What other line segments belong in this group?

_____ and _____ because _____.

The fourth group has only $\overline{GH}$ in it. Explain why it is the only segment in this group.

_____

Learn the Math

EXAMPLE 2 ▶ Segment $\overline{KM}$ has a length of 18. Prove that $\overline{KL} \cong \overline{LM}$.

First, notice that the number marked on the figure tells you that $\overline{LM} = 9$.

Second, set up a two-column proof, beginning with the lengths that are given.

Statements	Reasons
1. $KM = 18$, $LM = 9$	1. Given
2. $KM = KL + LM$	2. Segment Addition Postulate
3. $18 = KL + 9$	3. Substitution
4. $18 - 9 = KL + 9 - 9$	4. Subtraction Property of Equality
5. $9 = KL$	5. Simplify.
4. $\overline{KL} \cong \overline{LM}$	6. Definition of congruent segments

Do the Math

Segment $\overline{MP}$ on $\overline{MQ}$ has a length of 7 and $PQ = 7$. Prove that $MQ = 14$.

Learn the Math

EXAMPLE 3 ▶ Given: In $\triangle ABC$, $AB = AC$ and $BC = AC$. Prove: $\overline{AB} \cong \overline{BC}$.

Statements	Reasons
1. $AB = AC$, $BC = AC$	1. Given
2. $AB = BC$	2. Transitive Property of Equality
3. $\overline{AB} \cong \overline{BC}$	3. Definition of congruent segments

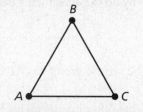

Do the Math

Given: $ABCD$ is a rectangle. Prove: $\overline{AB} \cong \overline{CD}$.

Learn the Math

EXAMPLE 4 ▶ What value of x will make $\overline{QR} \cong \overline{RS}$?

$$3x - 5 = 2x - 1$$
$$3x - 5 - 2x = 2x - 2x - 1$$
$$x - 5 = -1$$
$$x - 5 + 5 = -1 + 5$$
$$x = 4$$

Do the Math

What value of x will make $\overline{AB} \cong \overline{BC}$?

Name _____

**State the property of congruence that makes each statement true.
The first one is done for you.**

1. If $\overline{JK} \cong \overline{PQ}$ and $\overline{PQ} \cong \overline{TR}$, then $\overline{JK} \cong \overline{TR}$.
       Transitive Property of Congruence

2. $\overline{ST} \cong \overline{ST}$
   _____

3. If $\overline{PQ} \cong \overline{JK}$ and $\overline{JK} \cong \overline{LM}$, then $\overline{PQ} \cong \overline{LM}$.
   _____

4. If $\overline{ST} \cong \overline{LM}$, then $\overline{LM} \cong \overline{ST}$.
   _____

5. $\overline{HJ} \cong \overline{HJ}$
   _____

6. $\overline{PQ} \cong \overline{FG}$ so $\overline{FG} \cong \overline{PQ}$.
   _____

7. $\overline{AB} \cong \overline{FG}$ and $\overline{FG} \cong \overline{KL}$ so $\overline{AB} \cong \overline{KL}$.
   _____

8. Segment 1 $\cong$ Segment 2 so
   Segment 2 $\cong$ Segment 1.
   _____

Use the Segment Addition Postulate to find the missing lengths.

9. $AB = 2$, $BC = 8$, $AC = ?$

10. $AB = 7$, $BC = 7$, $AC = ?$

11. $AC = 19$, $AB = 17$, $BC = ?$

12. $AB = 3$, $AC = 11$, $BC = ?$

13. $BC = 7$, $AB = 14$, $AC = ?$

J, K, and L are points on the same segment, and K is between J and L.

14. $JK = 10$, $JL = 19$, $KL = ?$ _____

15. $JK = KL$ and $JL = 24$, $JK = ?$ _____

16. $JL = 30$, $JK = 3x + 4$, $KL = 10x$, $x = ?$, $JK = ?$ _____

17. $JL = 50 - 2x$, $JK = x + 7$, $KL = 3x + 1$, $JK = ?$ _____

18. Lee begins to build a model of a barn by arranging the framing sticks into three groups of congruent lengths. How should these sticks be grouped?

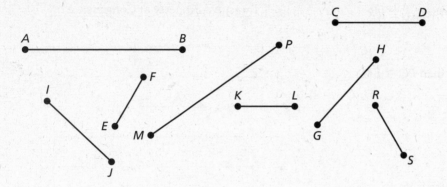

_____

_____

19. Open Ended Explain what AB means and what $\overline{AB}$ means. How are these two meanings related?

_____

_____

20. Critique Reasoning In a proof, Alex wrote the following step:

$AB = 7$ and $BC = 7$, so $\overline{AB} \cong \overline{BC}$.   Transitive Property of Congruence

Explain the error in Alex's proof. Then write the statements and reasons needed to get from $AB = 7$ and $BC = 7$ to $\overline{AB} \cong \overline{BC}$.

_____

_____

_____

21. A farmer plants trees in a straight row that is 21 feet long. The trees must be 7 feet from each other. How many trees can be planted in this row? Draw a sketch to explain your answer.

_____

22. The segment JL has midpoint M. $JM = 3x + 2$ and $ML = 14 - x$. What is the value of x?

Ⓐ 6   Ⓒ 16

Ⓑ 3   Ⓓ 12

Name _____

Step It Out

Learn the Math

EXAMPLE 1 ▶ Given: m∠JKM = 75°. Find m∠MKL. Justify each step.

First, write the angle measure from the Given on the figure.

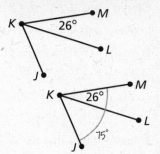

Then, use the information marked on the figure.

1. m∠JKM = 75°   **1.** Given

2. m∠JKL + m∠LKM = m∠JKM   **2.** Angle Addition Postulate

Substitute the angle measures you know.

3. m∠JKL + 26° = 75°   **3.** Substitute.

Subtract 26 from both sides of the equation.

4. m∠JKL + 26° − 26° = 75° − 26°   **4.** Subtraction Property of Equality

5. m∠JKL = 49°   **5.** Simplify.

Do the Math

m∠DEF = 122° and m∠DEG = 106°

Find m∠GEF. Justify your steps.

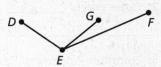

1. m∠DEF = 122°, m∠DEG = 106°   **1.** Given

2. m∠DEF = m∠DEG + ☐   **2.** Angle _____ Postulate

Substitute the angle measures you know.

3. ☐ = ☐ + m∠GEF   **3.** Substitute.

4. 122° − 106° = ☐   **4.** _____ Property of Equality

5. m∠GEF = ☐   **5.** Simplify.

Learn the Math

EXAMPLE 2 ▸ Prove the Congruent Supplements Theorem.

Given: $m\angle A = 65°$, $m\angle B = 115°$, $m\angle C + m\angle A = 180°$

Prove: $\angle B \cong \angle C$

1. $m\angle A = 65°$, $m\angle B = 115°$, $m\angle C + m\angle A = 180°$	1. Given
2. $m\angle A + m\angle B = 180°$ $65° + 115° = 180°$	2. Definition of supplementary angles
3. $m\angle A + m\angle B = m\angle A + m\angle C$	3. Transitive Property of Equality
4. $m\angle B = m\angle C$	4. Subtraction Property of Equality
5. $\angle B \cong \angle C$	5. Definition of congruent angles

Do the Math

Prove the Congruent Supplements Theorem.

Given: triangle with $\angle 1 \cong \angle 2$, $\angle 1$ and $\angle 4$ are supplements, $\angle 2$ and $\angle 3$ are supplements.

Prove: $\angle 4 \cong \angle 3$

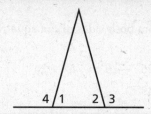

Statements	Reasons
1. $\angle 1 \cong \angle 2$, $\angle 1$ and $\angle 4$ are supplements, $\angle 2$ and $\angle 3$ are supplements.	1. Given
2. $m\angle 1 + m\angle 4 = 180°$ $m\angle 2 + m\angle 3 = 180°$	2. Definition of _____ angles
3. $\boxed{} + \boxed{} = m\angle 2 + m\angle 3$	3. Transitive Property of Equality
4. $m\angle 1 = \boxed{}$	4. Definition of _____ angles
5. $m\angle 1 + m\angle 4 - m\angle 1 = m\angle 2 + m\angle 3 - \boxed{}$	5. Subtraction Property of Equality
6. $m\angle 4 = m\angle 3$	6. Simplify.
7. $\boxed{} \cong \boxed{}$	7. Definition of congruent angles

Learn the Math

EXAMPLE 3 ▶ Prove the Linear Pairs Theorem.

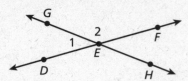

Given: ∠1 and ∠2 form a linear pair.   **Prove:** ∠1 and ∠2 are supplementary.

1. ∠1 and ∠2 form a linear pair.   1. Given

2. $\overleftrightarrow{ED}$ and $\overrightarrow{EF}$ are opposite rays.   2. Definition of linear pair

3. m∠DEF = 180°   3. Definition of straight angles

4. m∠1 + m∠2 = m∠DEF   4. Angle Addition Postulate

5. m∠1 + m∠2 = 180°   5. Transitive Property of Equality

6. ∠1 and ∠2 are supplementary.   6. Definition of supplementary angles

Do the Math

Prove the Linear Pairs Theorem.

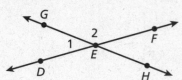

Given: ∠HEF and ∠2 form a linear pair.   **Prove:** ∠HEF and ∠2 are supplementary.

1. ∠HEF and ∠2 form a linear pair.   1. Given

2. $\overleftrightarrow{EH}$ and ray ☐ are opposite rays.   2. Definition of linear pair

3. m∠☐ = 180°   3. Definition of straight angles

4. m∠HEF + m∠☐ = m∠GEH   4. Subtraction Property of Equality

5. m∠HEF + m∠2 = 180°   5. Transitive Property of Equality

6. ∠HEF and ∠☐ are supplementary.   6. Definition of supplementary angles

Learn the Math

EXAMPLE 4 Prove the Vertical Angles Theorem.

Given: ∠1 and ∠2 are vertical angles.
Prove: ∠1 ≅ ∠2

1. ∠1 and ∠2 are vertical angles.	**1.** Given
2. ∠1 and ∠3 form a linear pair. ∠2 and ∠3 form a linear pair.	**2.** Definition of linear pair
3. ∠1 and ∠3 are supplementary. ∠2 and ∠3 are supplementary.	**3.** Linear Pairs Theorem

Notice that both ∠1 and ∠2 are supplementary to ∠3.

4. ∠1 ≅ ∠2	**4.** Congruent Supplements Theorem

Do the Math

Use the method in Example 4, or a method that uses the Angle Addition Postulate and the Transitive Property of Equality (as given in 2.4) to prove the Vertical Angles Theorem.

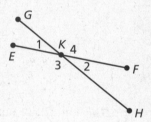

Given: ∠4 and ∠3 are vertical angles.   **Prove:** ∠4 ≅ ∠3

Name _____

LESSON 2.4
More Practice

ONLINE
Ed Video Tutorials and
Interactive Examples

Find the missing angle measure.

1. $m\angle A + m\angle B = 180°$, $m\angle B = 63°$; $m\angle A = \boxed{}°$

2. $\angle A$ and $\angle B$ are vertical angles. $m\angle B = 113°$; $m\angle A = \boxed{}°$

3. $\angle A$ and $\angle B$ are complementary angles. $m\angle A = 32°$; $m\angle B = \boxed{}°$

4. $\angle A$ and $\angle B$ form a linear pair. $m\angle A = 100°$; $m\angle B = \boxed{}°$

5. $\angle A \cong \angle B$, $\angle C$ is a complement of $\angle A$. $m\angle C = 25°$; $m\angle B = \boxed{}°$

6. $\angle A$ and $\angle B$ form a linear pair. $m\angle A = (5x + 3)°$; $m\angle B = (4x + 6)°$; $m\angle A = \boxed{}°$

Find the value of x.

7. $\angle A$ and $\angle B$ are vertical angles. $m\angle B = 60°$; $m\angle A = 3x°$; $x = \boxed{}$

8. $\angle A$ and $\angle B$ are vertical angles. $m\angle B = 31°$; $m\angle A = (6x - 5)°$; $x = \boxed{}$

9. $\angle A$ and $\angle B$ are vertical angles. $m\angle A = 4x°$; $m\angle B = (2x + 14)°$; $x = \boxed{}$

10. $\angle A$ and $\angle B$ are vertical angles. $m\angle A = 90°$; $m\angle B = 5x°$; $x = \boxed{}$

Use the rectangular figure to fill in the blanks in Problems 11–23.

11. $\angle 1$ and $\angle\boxed{}$, and $\angle 1$ and $\angle\boxed{}$ form linear pairs.

12. $\angle 1$ and $\angle\boxed{}$ are vertical angles.

13. $\angle 2$ and $\angle\boxed{}$ form a linear pair; $\angle 2$ and $\angle\boxed{}$ form a linear pair.

14. $\angle 1$ and $\angle\boxed{}$ are congruent angles.

15. $\angle 6$ and $\angle\boxed{}$ are complementary angles.

16. $\angle 2$ and $\angle\boxed{}$ are vertical angles.

17. $\angle 1 \cong \angle\boxed{}$

18. $\angle 1$ and $\angle\boxed{}$, and $\angle 1$ and $\angle\boxed{}$ are supplementary.

19. $m\angle 5 + m\angle\boxed{} = 90°$

20. $m\angle 1 = 40°$, $m\angle 4 = \boxed{}°$

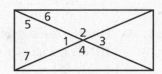

21. $m\angle 1 = 40°$, $m\angle 3 = \boxed{}°$

22. $m\angle 6 = 20°$, $m\angle 5 = \boxed{}°$

23. $m\angle 1 = 40°$, $m\angle 5 = 70°$, $m\angle 7 = \boxed{}°$

24. Open Ended What is the difference between a pair of complementary angles and a pair of supplementary angles? Can a pair of angles be both complementary and supplementary at the same time? Explain.

_____

_____

_____

25. Math on the Spot

A. Gene is making a flag with angles of two different colors that form a right angle. Find the measure of the complement of the acute angle whose measure is given.

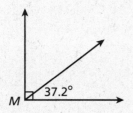

_____

B. Find the measure of the supplement of the obtuse angle whose measure is given.
   HINT: The answer will be in terms of x.

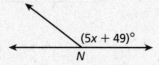

_____

26. $\angle A$ and $\angle B$ are vertical angles. $m\angle A = (6 + 3x)°$. $m\angle B = (5x - 2)°$.
Find the value of x.

Ⓐ 22

Ⓑ 18

Ⓒ 8

Ⓓ 4

Step It Out

Learn the Math

EXAMPLE 1 ▶ In Boston, Massachusetts, the Museum of Fine Arts is located on Huntington Avenue. The map shows the area near the museum. Louis Prang Street is parallel to Museum Road with Huntington Avenue crossing the streets.

Find the measures of ∠1 and ∠2. Justify your steps.

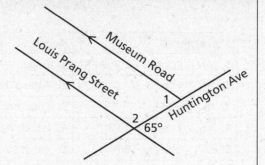

∠1 and the angle labeled 65° are alternate interior angles.   Definition of alternate interior angles.

m∠1 = 65°   Alternate Interior Angles Theorem

∠1 and ∠2 are consecutive interior angles.   Definition of consecutive interior angles.

m∠1 + m∠2 = 180°   Consecutive Interior Angles Theorem

65° + m∠2 = 180°   Substitution

65° − 65° + m∠2 = 180° − 65°   Subtraction Property of Equality

m∠2 = 115°   Simplify.

Do the Math

Two streets are parallel as they pass through Columbus Avenue. Find the measures of ∠1 and ∠2. Justify your steps.

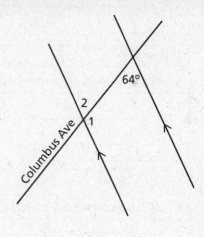

∠1 and the angle labeled 64° are consecutive interior angles.   _____

m∠1 + 64° = ☐°   _____

m∠1 + 64° − 64° = ☐° − 64°   _____

m∠1 = ☐°   _____

∠2 and the angle labeled 64° are alternate interior angles.   _____

m∠2 = ☐°   _____

Learn the Math

EXAMPLE 2 The barn door has two parallel boards with a diagonal board. If m∠3 = 65°, what is the angle measure of ∠2?

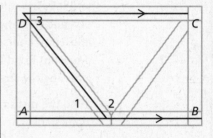

Statements	Reasons
1. $\overline{AB} \parallel \overline{CD}$ and m∠3 = 65°	1. Given
2. m∠1 = m∠3	2. Alternate Interior Angles Theorem
3. m∠1 = 65°	3. Substitution
4. m∠1 + m∠2 = 180°	4. Linear Pair Theorem
5. 65° + m∠2 = 180°	5. Substitution
6. m∠2 = 115°	6. Subtraction Property of Equality

Do the Math

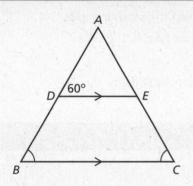

If $\overline{DE} \parallel \overline{BC}$, ∠B ≅ ∠C, and m∠ADE = 60°, prove that the sum of the measures of the interior angles of the trapezoid BDEC is 360°.

Statements	Reasons
1. $\overline{DE} \parallel \overline{BC}$, ∠B ≅ ∠C, and m∠ADE = 60°	1.
2. ∠ADE ≅ ∠B	2.
3. m∠B = 60°	3.
4. m∠B = m∠C	4.
5. m∠C = 60°	5.
6. ∠C is supplementary to ∠DEC.	6.
7. m∠DEC + m∠C = 180°	7.
8. m∠ADE + m∠BDE = 180°	8.
9. m∠BDE = 120°	9.
10. sum of the measures of the interior angles of BDEC = m∠BDE + (m∠DEC + m∠C) + m∠B	10.
11. sum of the measures of the interior angles of BDEC = 120° + 180° + 60° = 360°	11.

Name _____

LESSON 3.1
More Practice

ONLINE
Video Tutorials and
Interactive Examples

1. Name two pairs of alternate interior angles.

_____

2. What is the relationship between ∠2 and ∠8?

_____

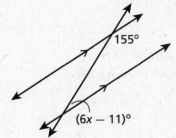

3. Which postulate or theorem justifies that ∠3 is supplementary to ∠6?

_____

4. Which postulate or theorem justifies that m∠4 is equal to m∠8?

_____

Find the value of x.

5.

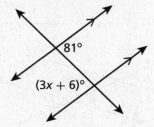

81°

(3x + 6)°

_____

6.

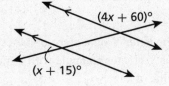

155°

(6x − 11)°

_____

7.

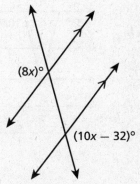

(8x)°

(10x − 32)°

_____

8.

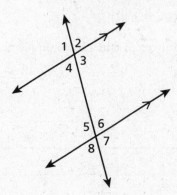

(4x + 60)°

(x + 15)°

_____

9. Construct Arguments Prove the Consecutive Interior Angles Theorem.

Given: $p \parallel q$

Prove: $\angle 1$ and $\angle 3$ are supplementary.

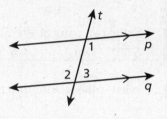

_____

_____

_____

_____

_____

_____

_____

10. Math on the Spot Given $n \parallel p$.
Find the measure of each angle.

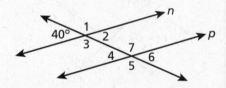

$m\angle 1 = \boxed{}$ $m\angle 2 = \boxed{}$

$m\angle 3 = \boxed{}$ $m\angle 4 = \boxed{}$

$m\angle 5 = \boxed{}$ $m\angle 6 = \boxed{}$ $m\angle 7 = \boxed{}$

11. Kevin draws the letter V on a piece of paper that has parallel lines. The letter V creates an angle with a measurement of $x°$. What is the value of x?

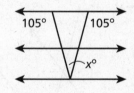

_____

_____

12. Use Structure Given $\ell \parallel m$ and $a \parallel b$. What are the values of x, y, and z?

Ⓐ $x = 105$, $y = 105$, and $z = 85$

Ⓑ $x = 95$, $y = 95$, and $z = 85$

Ⓒ $x = 85$, $y = 85$, and $z = 105$

Ⓓ $x = 85$, $y = 85$, and $z = 95$

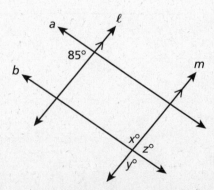

3.2

Step It Out

Learn the Math

EXAMPLE 1 Prove the Converse of the Corresponding Angles Postulate.

Given: $m\angle 2 = m\angle 6$

Prove: $\ell \parallel m$

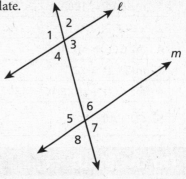

Statements	Reasons
$m\angle 2 = m\angle 6$	Given
$m\angle 2 = m\angle 4$	Vertical Angles Theorem
$m\angle 4 = m\angle 6$	Substitution
$\ell \parallel m$	Converse of Alternate Interior Angles Theorem

Do the Math

Use the diagram above from Learn the Math.

Given: $\angle 3$ and $\angle 6$ are supplementary.

Prove: $\ell \parallel m$

Statements	Reasons
$\angle 3$ and $\angle 6$ are supplementary.	
$m\angle 3 + m\angle 6 = \boxed{}^\circ$	Definition of supplementary angles
$m\angle 5 + m\angle 6 = \boxed{}^\circ$	Linear Pair Theorem
$m\angle 3 + \boxed{} = m\angle 5 + \boxed{}$	Substitution
$m\angle 3 + \boxed{} - \boxed{} = m\angle 5 + \boxed{} - \boxed{}$	Subtraction Property of Equality
$m\angle 3 = \boxed{}$	
$\ell \parallel \boxed{}$	Converse of Alternate Interior Angles Theorem

Learn the Math

EXAMPLE 2 Write a proof to prove that Malden Street is parallel to Clarendon Street.

Statements	Reasons
1. m∠BAC = 108°, m∠GCE = 72°	Given
2. ∠GCE ≅ ∠ACD	Vertical angles are congruent.
4. m∠GCE = m∠ACD	Definition of congruent angles
3. m∠ACD = 72°	Substitution
4. m∠ACD + m∠BAC = 180°	Substitution
5. $\overline{CD} \parallel \overline{AB}$	Converse of Consecutive Interior Angles Theorem

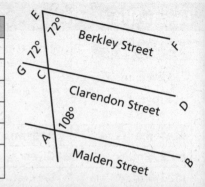

Do the Math

Use the diagram above from Learn the Math.

Learn the Math

EXAMPLE 3 Use the diagram to prove that $\overline{HJ} \parallel \overline{BE}$.

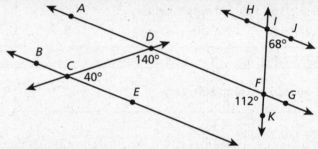

Statements	Reasons
1. m∠DCE = 40°; m∠CDF = 140°	Given
2. 140° + 40° = 180°	Addition
3. m∠CDF + m∠DCE = 180°	Substitution
4. ∠CDF is supplementary to ∠DCE.	Definition of supplementary angles
5. $\overline{DF} \parallel \overline{CE}$	Converse of Consecutive Interior Angles Theorem
6. m∠DFK = 112°	Given
7. m∠DFK + m∠GFK = 180°	Linear Pair Theorem
8. 112° + m∠GFK = 180°	Substitution
9. 112° − 112° + m∠GFK = 180° − 112°	Subtraction Property of Equality
10. m∠GFK = 68°	Simplify.
11. m∠FIJ = 68°	Given
12. m∠GFK = m∠FIJ	Transitive Property of Equality
13. $\overline{DF} \parallel \overline{HJ}$	Converse of Corresponding Angles Postulate
14. $\overline{HJ} \parallel \overline{CE}$	Transitive Property of Parallel Lines

Do the Math

Use the diagram above from Learn the Math. Prove $\overline{CD}$ is not parallel to $\overline{IK}$.

Name _____

Name the postulate or theorem that can be used to prove the lines parallel.

1. Given: $\angle 3 \cong \angle 5$ _____

2. Given: $\angle 4 \cong \angle 8$ _____

3. Given: $\angle 1 \cong \angle 7$ _____

4. Given: $\angle 1$ is supplementary to $\angle 8$. _____

5. Given: $\angle 3$ is supplementary to $\angle 6$. _____

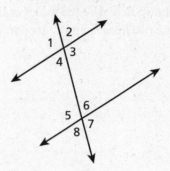

Determine if $s \parallel t$. State which postulate or theorem you would use to prove they are or are not parallel.

6.

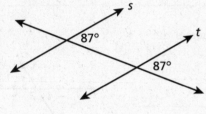

_____

_____

7.

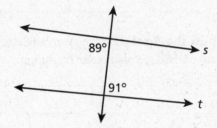

_____

_____

8.

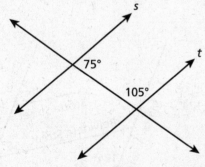

_____

_____

9.

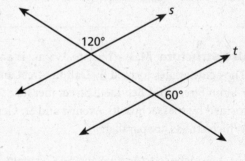

_____

_____

10. **Math on the Spot** A graphic designer is using quadrilaterals to make a design. Each quadrilateral is congruent to the one shown here. Use the values of the marked angles to show that the two lines ℓ_1 and ℓ_2 are parallel.

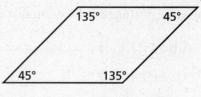

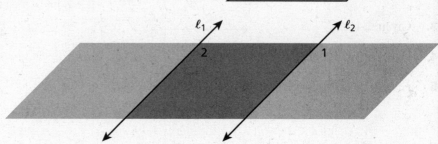

_____

_____

11. **Math on the Spot** Use the given angle relationship to decide whether the lines are parallel. Explain your reasoning.

A. If $\angle 2 \cong \angle 6$ _____

_____

_____

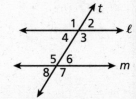

B. If $m\angle 4 = (2x - 12)°$, $m\angle 5 = (3x + 17)°$, and $x = 35$

_____

_____

_____

12. **Use Structure** Massachusetts Avenue is parallel to Dalton Street. The acute angles formed by Dalton Street and Scotia Street and Dalton Street and Belvidere Street measure 56°. The obtuse angle formed by Massachusetts Avenue and St. Germain Street measures 124°. Which streets are parallel?

(A) Massachusetts Avenue and St. Germain Street are parallel.

(B) Massachusetts Avenue and Scotia Street are parallel.

(C) St. Germain Street and Dalton Street are parallel.

(D) Belvidere Street, St. Germain Street, and Scotia Street are parallel.

Step It Out

Learn the Math

EXAMPLE 1 ▶ Draw the perpendicular bisector to $\overline{AB}$.

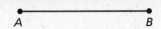

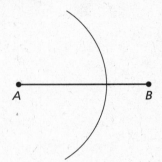

Place your compass on point A. Use a compass setting that is greater than half the length of $\overline{AB}$ and draw an arc.

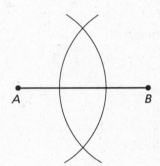

Leaving the compass open to the same setting, place the compass on point B. Draw another arc. It should intersect the other arc at two points.

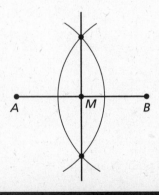

Use a straightedge to draw a segment connecting the points of intersection of the arcs. This segment intersects $\overline{AB}$ at point M, the midpoint of $\overline{AB}$.

Do the Math

Draw a perpendicular bisector to $\overline{MN}$.

Step 1	Place your compass on point M and draw an arc over the segment.
Step 2	Leaving the compass open to the same setting, place the compass on point N. Draw another arc.
Step 3	Use a straightedge to draw a segment connecting the two points where the arcs intersect.

Learn the Math

EXAMPLE 2 Draw a line that will bisect $\overline{MN}$ and pass through point P.

P
•

M   N

Place the compass on point P and open it to
point M.

Draw an arc with the compass that passes through the segment at point M
and point N.

Leaving the compass open to the same setting, place the compass on point M
and draw an arc under $\overline{MN}$.

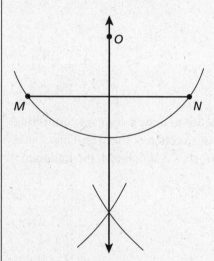

Leaving the compass open to the same setting, place the compass on point N and
draw another arc under $\overline{MN}$.

Use a straightedge to connect the point where the two arcs intersect with point P.

Do the Math

Draw a line that will bisect $\overline{AB}$ and pass through point C.

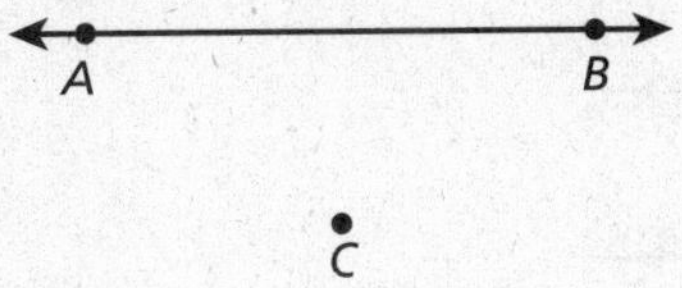

A •————————————• B

• C

Place the compass on point C and open it to point A.

Draw an arc with the compass that passes through the segment at point A and point B.

Leaving the compass open to the same setting, place the compass on point A and draw an arc above $\overline{AB}$.

Leaving the compass open to the same setting, place the compass on point B and draw another arc above $\overline{AB}$.

Use a straightedge to connect the point where the two arcs intersect with point C.

Learn the Math

EXAMPLE 3   Given: $\overline{DE} \parallel \overline{AB}$, $\overline{DE} \perp \overline{CF}$

$AF = 10$

$BF = 10$

$BC = 3x + 8$

$AC = 5x - 12$

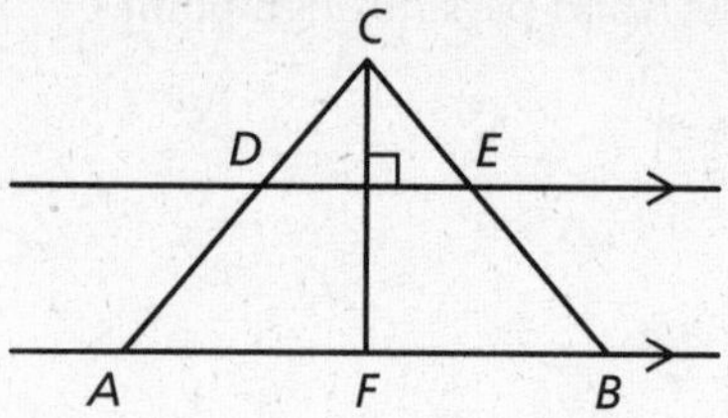

What is the length of $\overline{AC}$?

Solve for the value of x.

$\overline{AB} \perp \overline{CF}$	Perpendicular Transversal Theorem
$\overline{BC} \cong \overline{AC}$	Perpendicular Bisector Theorem
$BC = AC$	Definition of congruent line segments
$3x + 8 = 5x - 12$	Substitution
$3x + 8 - 8 = 5x - 12 - 8$	Subtraction Property of Equality
$3x = 5x - 20$	Simplify.
$3x - 5x = 5x - 20 - 5x$	Subtraction Property of Equality
$-2x = -20$	Simplify.
$\dfrac{-2x}{-2} = \dfrac{-20}{-2}$	Division Property of Equality
$x = 10$	Simplify.
$AC = 5(10) - 12$	Substitution
$AC = 38$	Simplify.

Do the Math

Using the same diagram and the following information, find the length of $\overline{BC}$.

$\overline{DE} \perp \overline{CF}$

$AF = 6$

$BF = 6$

$BC = 24 - x$

$AC = 9 + 2x$

Name

LESSON 3.3
More Practice

ONLINE
Ed Video Tutorials and
Interactive Examples

Solve for *x*.

1.
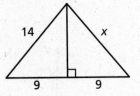

$x =$ _____

2.
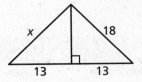

$x =$ _____

3.
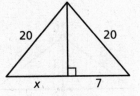

$x =$ _____

4.
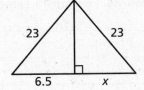

$x =$ _____

5.
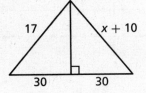

$x =$ _____

6.
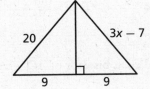

$x =$ _____

7. Math on the Spot Proving the Perpendicular Bisector Theorem Using Reflections

Given: Point P is on the perpendicular bisector m of $\overline{AB}$.

Prove: $\overline{PA} \cong \overline{PB}$

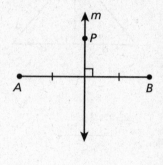

Statements	Reasons
Line m is the perpendicular bisector of $\overline{AB}$.	Given
The reflection of point P across line m is _____.	Definition of reflection
The reflection of point A across line m is _____.	Definition of reflection
$\overline{PA} \cong \overline{PB}$	

8. Construct Arguments Prove that $\overline{CD}$ is the perpendicular bisector of $\overline{AB}$.

_____

_____

_____

_____

_____

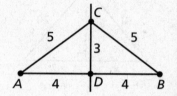

9. Use Structure Draw $\overline{AB}$ and construct its perpendicular bisector. Identify point C on the bisector. Measure the distance from point C to point A and from point C to point B. What theorem do your measurements justify? Explain your answer.

_____

_____

10. If $\overline{BD}$ is a perpendicular bisector of $\overline{AC}$, what is the height of $\triangle ABC$?

Ⓐ 6

Ⓑ 8

Ⓒ 10

Ⓓ 12.8

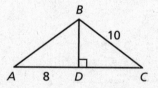

Step It Out

Learn the Math

EXAMPLE 1 ▸ Write an equation for a line parallel to $y = 2x - 7$ that passes through the point $(2, -1)$.

The parallel line has a slope of $m = 2$ and passes through $x = 2$ and $y = -1$.

Use the slope-intercept form and substitute the given information to solve for b.

$y = mx + b$

$-1 = (2)(2) + b$

$-1 = 4 + b$

$-5 = b$

Replace the values of m and b into the general slope-intercept form.

$y = mx + b$

$y = 2x + (-5)$

$y = 2x - 5$

Do the Math

Write an equation for a line parallel to $y = 0.75x + 3$ that passes through the point $(4, 1)$.

The parallel line has a slope of $m = \boxed{}$ and passes through $x = \boxed{}$ and $y = \boxed{}$.

Use the slope-intercept form and substitute the given information to solve for b.

$y = mx + b$

$\boxed{} = \left(\boxed{}\right)\left(\boxed{}\right) + b$

$\boxed{} = \boxed{} + b$

$\boxed{} = b$

Replace the values of m and b into the general slope-intercept form.

$y = mx + b = \boxed{}x + \boxed{}$

Learn the Math

EXAMPLE 2 ▸ Write an equation for a line parallel to $y = 4$ that passes through the point $(-3, 1)$.

The line $y = 4$ is a horizontal line, so a parallel line is also horizontal and passes through $(-3, 1)$. The equation is $y = 1$.

Do the Math

Write an equation for a line parallel to $x = -2$ that passes through the point $(4, -4)$.

The line $x = -2$ is a _____ line, so a parallel line is also _____ and passes through $(4, -4)$. The equation is $\boxed{} = \boxed{}$.

Learn the Math

EXAMPLE 3 A farmer is using grid paper to map a new pasture. The graph shows one side of a fence and a point where the farmer wants a parallel fence to start. Write an equation of the line that represents the new fence.

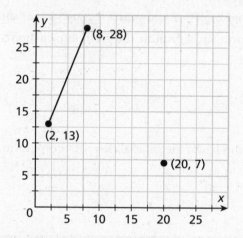

Find the slope of the given line. The coordinates are $(2, 13)$ and $(8, 28)$.

$$m = \frac{\text{rise}}{\text{run}} = \frac{28 - 13}{8 - 2} = \frac{15}{6} = \frac{5}{2}$$

Find the point the new line passes through.

$(20, 7)$

Find the y-intercept of the new line.

$$y = mx + b$$
$$7 = \left(\frac{5}{2}\right)(20) + b$$
$$7 = 50 + b$$
$$-43 = b$$

Write the equation of the new line.

$$y = mx + b = \frac{5}{2}x + (-43) = \frac{5}{2}x - 43$$

Do the Math

Irene is using a coordinate plane to design a logo for a business. She draws a line segment with endpoints at $(8, 2)$ and $(0, 4)$. She wants to draw a line segment that is parallel to this line segment that passes through the point $(-4, 12)$. Write an equation of the line that will contain the new line segment.

Name _____

Find the equation of the line parallel to the given line and passing through the given point.

1. $y = -3x + 2; (-2, -6)$

_____
_____
_____
_____
_____
_____

2. $y = \frac{1}{3}x - 4; (2, 1)$

_____
_____
_____
_____
_____
_____

3. $x = 4; (6, 2)$

_____
_____
_____
_____
_____
_____

4. $y = 3; (-2, 7)$

_____
_____
_____
_____
_____
_____

Find the equation for each line.

5. Line m passes through $(5, -3)$ and is parallel to a line that passes through $(1, -4)$ and $(9, -2)$.

_____
_____
_____
_____

6. Line h passes through $(2, 6)$ and is parallel to a line that passes through $(-3, 4)$ and $(1, 1)$.

_____
_____
_____
_____

7. **Open Ended** Write an equation of a line that is parallel to the line that passes through $(-4, -3)$ and $(2, -1)$. Find a point on the parallel line that is not the y-intercept. Explain the steps you used.

_____

_____

_____

8. **Math on the Spot** Write an equation in slope-intercept form for the line that passes through $(5, -6)$ and is parallel to the line described by $y = -x + 3$.

_____

_____

_____

9. **Critique Reasoning** Calvin states that it is not possible to find the equation of a line parallel to $y = 2$ and passing through the point $(5, -1)$ using the point-slope form because the equation of the line does not have an x-term. Explain the error in Calvin's reasoning. Then find the equation of the parallel line.

_____

_____

_____

10. Heather is using a coordinate plane to map the stars she sees one night. She marks one star on her map at $(-4, 3)$ and another at $(6, -9)$. She draws a line connecting these two points. She plots another star at $(2, 2)$. What is the equation of a line that passes through $(2, 2)$ and is parallel to the first line she drew? What is another point on the parallel line?

_____

_____

_____

11. On a map of a park, the start point of a path is located at the point $(7, 1)$ and the end point is $(3, 13)$. The path is a straight line from the start point to the end point. Another path in the park is parallel to the first path and starts at the point $(11, 11)$. What is the equation of the parallel path?

Ⓐ $y = 3x - 22$

Ⓑ $y = -\frac{1}{3}x + \frac{44}{3}$

Ⓒ $y = -3x - 22$

Ⓓ $y = -3x + 44$

Step It Out

Learn the Math

EXAMPLE 1 Write an equation for the line perpendicular to $\overleftrightarrow{CD}$ that passes through the point $(4, -2)$.

Identify two points on $\overleftrightarrow{CD}$: $(0, 7)$ and $(9, 10)$.

Find the slope of $\overleftrightarrow{CD}$.

$$m = \frac{10 - 7}{9 - 0} = \frac{3}{9} = \frac{1}{3}$$

Find the slope of the perpendicular line.

The slope of $\overleftrightarrow{CD}$ is $\frac{1}{3}$, so the slope of the perpendicular line is the opposite reciprocal -3.

Write the equation of the perpendicular line that passes through point $(4, -2)$.

$$y - y_1 = m(x - x_1)$$
$$y - (-2) = -3(x - 4)$$
$$y + 2 = -3x + 12$$
$$y = -3x + 10$$

Do the Math

Write the equation of the line that passes through $(-7, -5)$ and is perpendicular to the line that passes through $(4, 1)$ and $(7, 7)$.

Learn the Math

EXAMPLE 2 Write an equation for a line perpendicular to $y = 4$ that passes through the point $(-3, 1)$.

The line $y = 4$ is a horizontal line, so a perpendicular line is vertical and passes through $(-3, 1)$. The equation is $x = -3$.

Do the Math

Write an equation for a line perpendicular to $x = -2$ that passes through the point $(4, -4)$.

The line $x = -2$ is a _____ line, so a perpendicular line is _____ and passes through $(4, -4)$. The equation is

$\boxed{} = \boxed{}$.

Learn the Math

EXAMPLE 3 DeShawn likes to walk from his house to the library and to the park. DeShawn's house and library are on State Street, and the park is on Main Street, which is perpendicular to State Street. On a map, his house is located at $(1, 5)$ and the library is located at $(7, 14)$. The park is located at $(6, 1)$. Find the equation of the line that represents Main Street on the map.

Find the slope of the line that represents State Street.

$$m = \frac{\text{rise}}{\text{run}} = \frac{14 - 5}{7 - 1} = \frac{9}{6} = \frac{3}{2}$$

The slope of the perpendicular line is $m = -\frac{2}{3}$.

Find the y-intercept of the perpendicular line.

$$y = mx + b$$
$$1 = \left(-\frac{2}{3}\right)(6) + b$$
$$1 = -4 + b$$
$$5 = b$$

Write the equation of the new line.

$$y = mx + b = -\frac{2}{3}x + 5$$

Do the Math

Jillian draws a coordinate plane over a photograph that she took. The bottom of a building along the ground can be modeled by the equation $y = -0.2x + 2$. The side of the building is perpendicular to the bottom of the building and passes through the point $(6, 8)$. Write an equation of the line that represents the side of the building.

The slope of the perpendicular line is $m = \boxed{}$.

Use the point-slope form of the equation of a line.

$$y - y_1 = m(x - x_1)$$

$$y - \boxed{} = \boxed{}\left(x - \boxed{}\right)$$

$$y - \boxed{} = \boxed{} \, x \, \boxed{} \, \boxed{}$$

$$y = \boxed{} \, x \, \boxed{} \, \boxed{}$$

The equation is $y = \boxed{} \, x \, \boxed{} \, \boxed{}$.

Name _____

Find the equation of the line perpendicular to the given line and passing through the given point.

1. $y = -4x + 2; (-1, 4)$

2. $y = \frac{2}{3}x + 7; (-8, 2)$

3. $y = -3; (3, -7)$

4. $5x - 3y = 21; (5, 8)$

Find the equation of the line perpendicular to the given line and passes through the given point.

5. $\overleftrightarrow{AB}; (10, 15)$

6. $\overleftrightarrow{CD}; (-2, 1)$

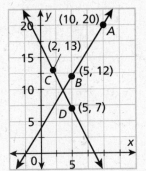

7. **Use Repeated Reasoning** Is it possible for segments along the lines $y = \frac{2}{5}x + 2$, $y = -2.5x + 2$, $y = \frac{2}{5}x - 2$, and $y = -2.5x - 3$ to form a rectangle? Justify your answer.

_____

_____

_____

8. **Math on the Spot** Write an equation in slope-intercept form for the line that passes through $(8, 5)$ and is perpendicular to the line described by $y = -4x + 7$.

_____

_____

_____

9. **Open Ended** Find the equation of a line that is perpendicular to the line $y = \frac{4}{3}x + 6$. Find a point on the perpendicular line that is not the y-intercept.

_____

_____

_____

10. Jessica is making a map of her school on a coordinate plane. Two hallways in the school are perpendicular to each other. The main hallway passes through the points $(-5, 9)$ and $(4, 6)$. The perpendicular hallway passes through the point $(-4, 3)$. Write equations for the lines that represent the main hallway and the perpendicular hallway.

_____

_____

_____

11. What is the equation of a line that is perpendicular to the line shown on the graph and passes through the point $(4, -6)$?

Ⓐ $y = \frac{3}{2}x + 12$

Ⓑ $y = -\frac{3}{2}x + 12$

Ⓒ $y = -\frac{3}{2}x$

Ⓓ $y = -\frac{2}{3}x$

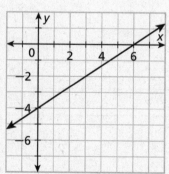

Step It Out

Learn the Math

EXAMPLE 1 Find the length of the segment of the line $y = -\frac{2}{3}x - 7$ from $x = -6$ to $x = 9$.

Find the coordinates of the endpoints of the segment by substituting the x-values into the equation.

When $x = -6$, $y = -\frac{2}{3}(-6) - 7 = 4 - 7 = -3$. The ordered pair is $(-6, -3)$.

When $x = 9$, $y = -\frac{2}{3}(9) - 7 = -6 - 7 = -13$. The ordered pair is $(9, -13)$.

Use the Distance Formula to find the distance between the two endpoints.

$$d = \sqrt{(x_2 - x_1)^2 + (y_2 - y_1)^2}$$
$$= \sqrt{\left(9 - (-6)\right)^2 + \left(-13 - (-3)\right)^2}$$
$$= \sqrt{15^2 + (-10)^2}$$
$$= \sqrt{225 + 100}$$
$$= \sqrt{325}$$
$$= 5\sqrt{13}$$

The length of the segment of the line $y = -\frac{2}{3}x - 7$ from $x = -6$ to $x = 9$ is $5\sqrt{13}$.

Do the Math

Find the length of the segment of the line $y = 2x + 1$ from $x = -2$ to $x = 5$.

When $x = -2$, $y = 2\left(\boxed{}\right) + 1 = \boxed{}$. The ordered pair is $\left(\boxed{}, \boxed{}\right)$.

When $x = 5$, $y = 2\left(\boxed{}\right) + 1 = \boxed{}$. The ordered pair is $\left(\boxed{}, \boxed{}\right)$.

$$d = \sqrt{(x_2 - x_1)^2 + (y_2 - y_1)^2}$$
$$= \sqrt{\left(\boxed{} - \boxed{}\right)^2 + \left(\boxed{} - \boxed{}\right)^2}$$
$$= \sqrt{\boxed{}}$$
$$= \boxed{}$$

The length of the segment of the line $y = 2x + 1$ from $x = -2$ to $x = 5$ is $\boxed{}$.

| EXAMPLE 2 | One side of the roof of a building can be represented by the equation $y = \frac{1}{3}x + 11$. The edge of the roof corresponds to $x = 0$ feet, and the peak of the roof corresponds to $x = 12$ feet. How long is the side of the roof? |

Determine the endpoints of the line segment described.

Edge: When $x = 0$, $y = \frac{1}{3}(0) + 11 = 11$. The ordered pair is $(0, 11)$.

Peak: When $x = 12$, $y = \frac{1}{3}(12) + 11 = 4 + 11 = 15$. The ordered pair is $(12, 15)$.

Use the Distance Formula to find the length.

$$d = \sqrt{(x_2 - x_1)^2 + (y_2 - y_1)^2}$$

$$= \sqrt{(12 - 0)^2 + (15 - 11)^2}$$

$$= \sqrt{12^2 + 4^2}$$

$$= \sqrt{144 + 16}$$

$$= \sqrt{160}$$

$$= 4\sqrt{10}$$

The length of the side of the roof is $4\sqrt{10}$ or about 12.65 feet.

Do the Math

One side of the roof of a different building can be represented by the equation $y = -\frac{1}{2}x + 27$. The peak of the roof corresponds to $x = 0$ feet, and the edge of the roof corresponds to $x = 14$ feet. How long is the side of the roof?

Peak: When $x = 0$, $y = -\frac{1}{2}\left(\boxed{}\right) + 27 = \boxed{}$. The ordered pair is $\left(\boxed{}, \boxed{}\right)$.

Edge: When $x = 14$, $y = -\frac{1}{2}\left(\boxed{}\right) + 27 = \boxed{}$. The ordered pair is $\left(\boxed{}, \boxed{}\right)$.

$$d = \sqrt{(x_2 - x_1)^2 + (y_2 - y_1)^2}$$

$$= \sqrt{\left(\boxed{} - \boxed{}\right)^2 + \left(\boxed{} - \boxed{}\right)^2}$$

$$= \sqrt{\boxed{}}$$

The length of the side of the roof is $\sqrt{\boxed{}}$ or about $\boxed{}$ feet.

Name _____

LESSON 4.3
More Practice

ONLINE
Video Tutorials and
Interactive Examples

Determine whether $\overline{AB}$ is congruent to $\overline{CD}$. Justify your answer.

1. $A(1, 5), B(6, 1); C(-2, 8), D(-6, 3)$

_____

_____

_____

_____

_____

_____

2. $A(3, -3), B(7, 4); C(0, 4), D(-7, 7)$

_____

_____

_____

_____

_____

_____

_____

3. $A(8, 2), B(3, 7); C(-3, 3), D(3, -1)$

_____

_____

_____

_____

_____

_____

4. $A(5, 3), B(8, -7); C(1, 4), D(11, 7)$

_____

_____

_____

_____

_____

_____

Find the length and the midpoint of the line segment between the given points.

5. $(-2, -1), (7, 3)$

_____

_____

_____

_____

_____

_____

6. $(2, -6), (4, 2)$

_____

_____

_____

_____

_____

_____

7. A triangle has vertices at $A(3, 5)$, $B(5, 0)$, and $C(8, 3)$. Is this triangle equilateral, isosceles, or scalene? Justify your answer.

_____

_____

_____

_____

8. **Critique Reasoning** Andre says that the midpoint of the line segment between $(-1, 8)$ and $(5, 6)$ is $(-3, 1)$. Erica states that Andre made an error in calculating the midpoint. What error did Andre make?

_____

_____

_____

9. **Open Ended** Write a real-world problem that can be solved using the Distance Formula. Then solve the problem and justify your results.

_____

_____

_____

_____

10. The main hill of a roller coaster can be modeled by a line segment on the equation $y = \frac{4}{7}x + \frac{65}{7}$, where x and y are in feet. The bottom of the main hill is at $x = 10$, and the top of the hill is at $x = 360$. What is the length of the track along the main hill of the roller coaster?

_____

_____

_____

_____

11. On a city map, two bus stops are located at the ordered pairs $(6, 8)$ and $(14, 20)$. The city is building a new bus stop that is located at the midpoint of a line segment connecting the existing bus stops. Find the coordinates of the new bus stop on the map.

Ⓐ $(4, 6)$

Ⓑ $(10, 14)$

Ⓒ $(8, 12)$

Ⓓ $(20, 28)$

Name _____

Step It Out

Learn the Math

EXAMPLE 1 Draw the preimage and image of the polygon with vertices $A(2, 3)$, $B(4, -1)$, $C(6, 1)$, and $D(3, 5)$ translated using the vector $\langle -4, 1 \rangle$.

Make a table to find the vertices of the image.

Preimage	$(x, y) \rightarrow (x - 4, y + 1)$	Image
$A(2, 3)$	$(2, 3) \rightarrow (2 - 4, 3 + 1)$	$A'(-2, 4)$
$B(4, -1)$	$(4, -1) \rightarrow (4 - 4, -1 + 1)$	$B'(0, 0)$
$C(6, 1)$	$(6, 1) \rightarrow (6 - 4, 1 + 1)$	$C'(2, 2)$
$D(3, 5)$	$(3, 5) \rightarrow (3 - 4, 5 + 1)$	$D'(-1, 6)$

Draw the preimage and image in a coordinate plane.

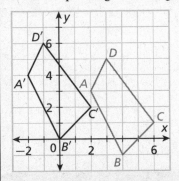

Do the Math

Draw the preimage and image of the polygon with vertices $X(-1, 4)$, $Y(2, 2)$, and $Z(0, -1)$ translated using the vector $\langle 2, -3 \rangle$.

Preimage	$(x, y) \rightarrow \left(x + \boxed{}, y - \boxed{}\right)$	Image
$X(-1, 4)$	$(-1, 4) \rightarrow \left(\boxed{} + \boxed{}, \boxed{} - \boxed{}\right)$	$\left(\boxed{}, \boxed{}\right)$
$Y(2, 2)$	$(2, 2) \rightarrow \left(\boxed{} + \boxed{}, \boxed{} - \boxed{}\right)$	$\left(\boxed{}, \boxed{}\right)$
$Z(0, -1)$	$(0, -1) \rightarrow \left(\boxed{} + \boxed{}, \boxed{} - \boxed{}\right)$	$\left(\boxed{}, \boxed{}\right)$

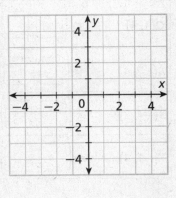

Learn the Math

EXAMPLE 2 ▸ Identify the vector that maps $ABCD$ to $A'B'C'D'$.

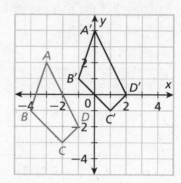

Make a table to find the difference between the vertices of the preimage and image.

Preimage	Image	Difference
$A(-3, 2)$	$A'(0, 4)$	$0 - (-3) = 3, 4 - 2 = 2$
$B(-4, -1)$	$B'(-1, 1)$	$-1 - (-4) = 3, 1 - (-1) = 2$
$C(-2, -3)$	$C'(1, -1)$	$1 - (-2) = 3, -1 - (-3) = 2$
$D(-1, -2)$	$D'(2, 0)$	$2 - (-1) = 3, 0 - (-2) = 2$

The vector that maps $ABCD$ to $A'B'C'D'$ is $\langle 3, 2 \rangle$.

Do the Math

Identify the vector that maps $QRST$ to $Q'R'S'T'$.

Preimage	Image	Difference
$Q(1, 1)$	$Q'\left(\Box, \Box\right)$	$\Box - 1 = \Box, \Box - 1 = \Box$
$R(-2, 1)$	$R'\left(\Box, \Box\right)$	$\Box - (-2) = \Box, \Box - 1 = \Box$
$S(-4, 2)$	$S'\left(\Box, \Box\right)$	$\Box - (-4) = \Box, \Box - 2 = \Box$
$T(-1, 4)$	$T'\left(\Box, \Box\right)$	$\Box - (-1) = \Box, \Box - 4 = \Box$

The vector that maps $QRST$ to $Q'R'S'T'$ is $\boxed{}$.

Name

LESSON 5.1
More Practice

ONLINE
Video Tutorials and
Interactive Examples

**Draw the figure with the given vertices. Then draw its
image after a translation by the given vector.**

1. $A(4, -2), B(1, -1), C(-3, 2)$;
vector $\langle -2, 5 \rangle$

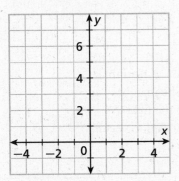

2. $A(-2, 4), B(2, 6), C(4, 0)$;
vector $\langle 3, -1 \rangle$

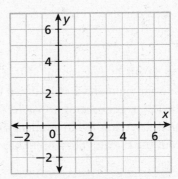

3. $A(1, 4), B(4, -3), C(-3, -2), D(-1, 3)$;
vector $\langle 2, -3 \rangle$

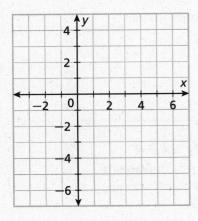

4. $A(4, 2), B(-2, 3), C(-2, 0),$
$D(1, -1)$; vector $\langle -4, 2 \rangle$

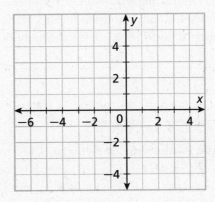

Give the component form of a vector that maps $\triangle JKL$ to $\triangle J'K'L'$.

5. $J(-5, 2), K(-1, -3), L(1, 5)$
$J'(-3, -1), K'(1, -6), L'(3, 2)$

_____

_____

_____

_____

_____

6. $J(3, 6), K(4, -1), L(6, 2)$
$J'(6, 7), K'(7, 0), L'(9, 3)$

_____

_____

_____

_____

7. **Open Ended** Draw a triangle on a coordinate plane that is completely in the first quadrant. Write a vector that will translate the triangle so that it is completely in the fourth quadrant. Draw the image on the same coordinate plane.

_____

_____

_____

8. **Math on the Spot** In a marching drill, it takes 7 steps to march 4 yards. A drummer starts 7 steps to the right and 7 steps down from the center of the field. She marches 14 steps to the left to her second position. Then she marches 21 steps up the field to her final position. What is the drummer's final position? What single translation vector moves her from the starting position to her final position?

_____

_____

_____

9. Randy leaves his house and walks 5 blocks north and then 2 blocks east to get to the library. Write a single translation vector that describes the change from his house to the library. If Randy's house is located at the point $(6, -3)$ on a map, and each unit represents 1 block, what is the location of the library on the map?

_____

_____

_____

10. **Critique Reasoning** Students are asked to find the coordinates of the image of $F(5, -2)$, $G(3, 4)$, and $H(-2, 3)$ after it is translated using the vector $\langle -3, 3 \rangle$. Ross says the coordinates are $F'(8, -5)$, $G'(6, 1)$, and $H'(1, 0)$. Samantha says the coordinates are $F'(2, 1)$, $G'(0, 7)$, and $H'(-5, 6)$. Who is correct? Explain your reasoning.

_____

_____

_____

11. Francis is building a rectangular pool in his backyard. He marks the location of one corner of the pool as 7 feet east and 12 feet south of the center of his yard. He gives his friend directions to mark the opposite corner of the pool 8 feet west and 8 feet north of the center of his yard. What is a vector that could translate the point Francis marked to the point his friend marked?

 Ⓐ $\langle -1, 4 \rangle$

 Ⓑ $\langle 4, -1 \rangle$

 Ⓒ $\langle 20, -15 \rangle$

 Ⓓ $\langle -15, 20 \rangle$

Step It Out

Learn the Math

> **EXAMPLE 1** Find the center of rotation and angle of rotation of the rotation that maps $\triangle ABC$ onto $\triangle A'B'C'$.

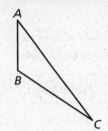

Draw a line segment between the two sets of corresponding points. Draw the perpendicular bisectors of the points. The point of intersection of the perpendicular bisectors is the center of rotation.

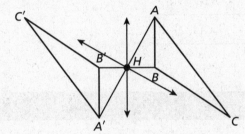

Connect two corresponding vertices to the center of rotation. Measure this angle. It is the angle of rotation.

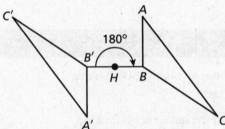

The angle of rotation is 180°.

Do the Math

Find the center of rotation and angle of rotation of the rotation that maps $\triangle XYZ$ onto $\triangle X'Y'Z'$.

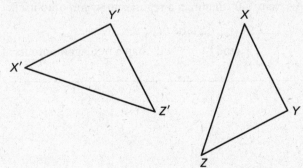

The angle of rotation is ☐°.

Learn the Math

EXAMPLE 2 ▸ Draw the preimage and image of the polygon with vertices $A(3, 3)$, $B(4, 1)$, $C(2, -1)$ and after a rotation counterclockwise 90°.

Make a table to find the vertices of the image. Draw the preimage and image in a coordinate plane.

Preimage	$(x, y) \rightarrow (-y, x)$	Image
$A(3, 3)$	$(3, 3) \rightarrow (-3, 3)$	$A'(-3, 3)$
$B(4, 1)$	$(4, 1) \rightarrow (-1, 4)$	$B'(-1, 4)$
$C(2, -1)$	$(2, -1) \rightarrow (1, 2)$	$C'(1, 2)$

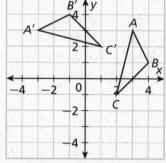

Do the Math

Draw the preimage and image of the polygon with vertices $A(-4, 7)$, $B(2, 3)$, $C(-1, -1)$, and $D(-5, 4)$ after a rotation counterclockwise 270°.

Learn the Math

EXAMPLE 3 ▸ Describe any rotations less than 360° that map the hexagon onto itself.

Divide 360° by 6, the number of sides in the hexagon, to find the rotations that will map the hexagon onto itself.

$$\frac{360°}{6} = 60°$$

Rotations of 60°, 120°, 180°, 240°, and 300° will map the hexagon onto itself.

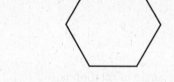

Do the Math

Describe any rotations less than 360° that map a regular pentagon onto itself.

Rotations of ⬜°, ⬜°, ⬜°, and ⬜° will map a pentagon onto itself.

Name _____

Draw the preimage and image of each polygon under the given rotation.

1. $A(-1, 4), B(3, 4), C(2, -1), D(0, 1)$

Counterclockwise 270°

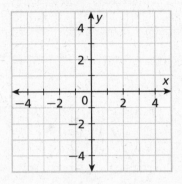

2. $A(-5, -6), B(-4, 1), C(1, -2), D(-2, -5)$

Counterclockwise 90°

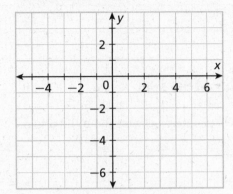

3. $A(0, 3), B(3, 5), C(1, -2), D(-1, 0)$

Counterclockwise 180°

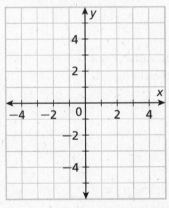

4. $A(2, 4), B(3, 1), C(3, 0), D(1, -2)$

Counterclockwise 90°

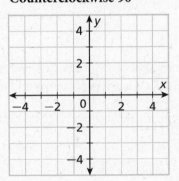

Describe any rotations less than or equal to 360° that map the polygon onto itself.

5. regular octagon

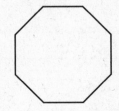

_____

_____

_____

6. equilateral triangle

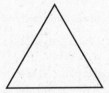

_____

_____

_____

7. **Use Repeated Reasoning** Given the preimage of a triangle with vertices at
$L(4, -6)$, $M(5, -1)$, and $N(7, -3)$, rotate the image counterclockwise 810°. What are
the coordinates of the vertices of the image?

_____

_____

_____

8. **Math on the Spot** Rotate $\triangle ABC$ with
vertices $A(-1, 1)$, $B(-4, 2)$, and $C(-2, 5)$
by 90° counterclockwise about the origin.

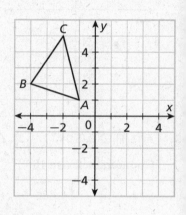

_____

_____

_____

_____

_____

9. **Reason** Cindy says that she has a regular polygon in her hands that rotates onto itself
when rotated 90°. What regular polygon does Cindy have? Explain your reasoning.

_____

_____

_____

10. **Reason** Andrea draws a figure in the first quadrant of a coordinate plane. She rotates
the figure counterclockwise. The x-coordinates of the image are the same as the
y-coordinates of the preimage. The y-coordinates of the image are the opposite of the
x-coordinates of the preimage. What is the smallest angle of rotation of the image?
Explain your reasoning.

_____

_____

_____

11. Hong is playing a board game and spins a spinner. Before spinning, the point of the
spinner is at $(-2, 6)$. After spinning, the point is at $(-6, -2)$. What is the angle of
rotation between the starting point and ending point of the spinner?

Ⓐ 90° counterclockwise

Ⓒ 270° counterclockwise

Ⓑ 180° counterclockwise

Ⓓ 360° counterclockwise

Step It Out

Learn the Math

EXAMPLE 1 $\triangle A'B'C'$ is the image of $\triangle ABC$ after a reflection. Draw the line of reflection.

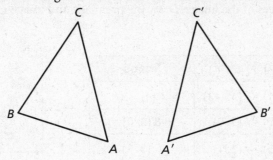

Draw line segments that connect the corresponding vertices. The line of reflection is the perpendicular bisector of these segments.

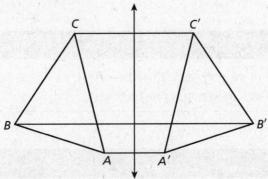

Do the Math

Draw the line of reflection.

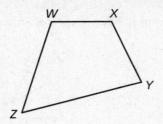

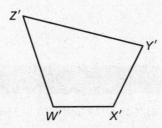

Learn the Math

EXAMPLE 2 ▶ Draw the preimage and image of the polygon with vertices $A(-2, 1)$, $B(0, 5)$, and $C(1, 3)$ after a reflection across the line $y = x$.

Make a table to find the vertices of the image. Draw the preimage and image in a coordinate plane.

Preimage	$(x, y) \rightarrow (y, x)$	Image
$A(-2, 1)$	$(-2, 1) \rightarrow (1, -2)$	$A'(1, -2)$
$B(0, 5)$	$(0, 5) \rightarrow (5, 0)$	$B'(5, 0)$
$C(1, 3)$	$(1, 3) \rightarrow (3, 1)$	$C'(3, 1)$

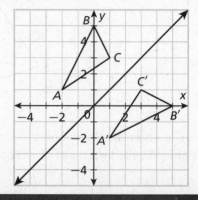

Do the Math

Draw the preimage and image of the polygon with vertices $J(-4, 4)$, $K(-2, 3)$, $L(-1, -1)$, and $M(-5, -3)$ after a reflection across the y-axis.

Learn the Math

EXAMPLE 3 ▶ Reflect a triangle with vertices at $R(-4, 2)$, $S(-3, 3)$, and $T(-2, 1)$ across the line $x = -1$. Then reflect its image across the x-axis.

The new points should be straight across and the same distance from the line of reflection.

Reflect RST across the line $x = -1$ to form $R'S'T'$.   Reflect $R'S'T'$ across the x-axis to form $R''S''T''$.

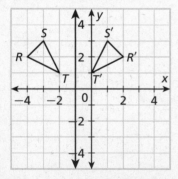   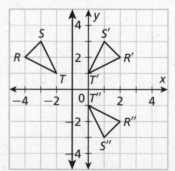

Do the Math

Reflect a triangle with vertices at $F(4, -4)$, $G(5, -2)$, and $H(1, -3)$ across the line $y = -1$. Then reflect its image across the y-axis.

In each diagram, $\triangle A'B'C'$ is the image of $\triangle ABC$ after a reflection.
Draw the line of reflection.

1.

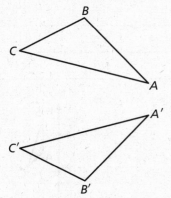

2.

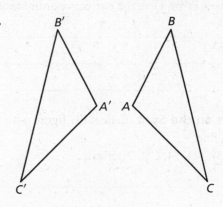

Find the coordinates of the vertices of the image of *ABCD* after each reflection.

3. $A(-1, 6), B(-5, 3), C(-4, -2), D(-1, 1)$
across the y-axis

_____

_____

_____

4. $A(3, 4), B(0, 2), C(-1, 3), D(2, 6)$
across the line $y = x$

_____

_____

_____

5. $A(-1, -5), B(-2, -3), C(4, -2), D(5, -4)$
across the line $y = -x$

_____

_____

_____

6. $A(1, 6), B(4, 5), C(2, 2), D(0, 2)$ across
the x-axis

_____

_____

_____

7. Reflect the triangle across the line
$x = 1$ and the x-axis.

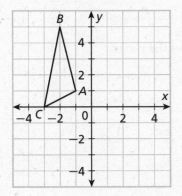

8. Reflect the triangle across the line
$y = -2$ and the y-axis.

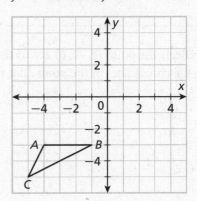

9. Critique Reasoning Connor reflects the triangle $A(4, 2)$, $B(5, 0)$, $C(3, -1)$ across the line $y = -x$ and says the image is $A'(-4, -2)$, $B'(-5, 0)$, $C'(-3, 1)$. Explain Connor's error. Give the correct coordinates for $\triangle A'B'C'$.

_____

_____

_____

10. Math on the Spot Reflect the figure with the given vertices across the given line.

$A(1, 3)$, $B(1, 5)$, $C(2, 2)$; x-axis.

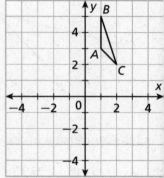

_____

_____

_____

_____

_____

11. Marco reflects the triangle $X(4, -5)$, $Y(4, -2)$, $Z(5, -4)$ across the line $x = 3$, and then reflects the image across the y-axis. What are the coordinates of the triangle after being reflected across the y-axis? How could these reflections be written as a single translation?

_____

_____

_____

12. Critique Reasoning Michael says that reflecting a point across the x-axis and then reflecting the point again across the y-axis is the same as rotating the point $180°$ counterclockwise. Is he correct? Explain your reasoning.

_____

_____

_____

13. Frankie reflects the point $P(-2, 6)$ across the line $y = -x$ and then across the y-axis. What are the coordinates of the point after the reflections?

Ⓐ $P''(-2, -6)$

Ⓑ $P''(2, -6)$

Ⓒ $P''(6, 2)$

Ⓓ $P''(-6, 2)$

Step It Out

Learn the Math

EXAMPLE 1 How many lines of symmetry does a regular octagon have? What is the angle of rotational symmetry for a regular octagon?

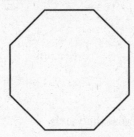

A regular octagon has 8 lines of symmetry.

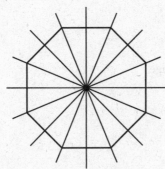

Divide 360° by the number of sides to find the angle of rotational symmetry for a regular octagon.

$$\frac{360°}{8} = 45°$$

The angle of rotational symmetry for a regular octagon is 45°.

Do the Math

How many lines of symmetry does a regular nonagon have? What is the angle of rotational symmetry for a regular nonagon?

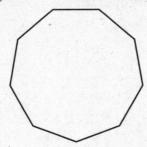

A regular nonagon has _____ lines of symmetry. The angle of

rotational symmetry is $\frac{360°}{\boxed{}} = \boxed{}°$.

Learn the Math

EXAMPLE 2　The *x*-axis and *y*-axis are lines of symmetry of an image. Use lines of symmetry to draw the entire image.

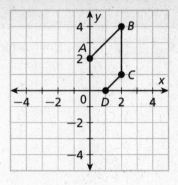

Reflect the part of the image shown across the *x*-axis.

$(x, y) \rightarrow (x, -y)$

$A(0, 2) \rightarrow G(0, -2)$

$B(2, 4) \rightarrow F(2, -4)$

$C(2, 1) \rightarrow E(2, -1)$

D is on the *x*-axis, so it does not change.

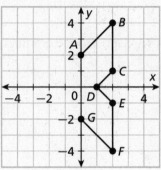

Reflect the new image across the *y*-axis.

$(x, y) \rightarrow (-x, y)$

$B(2, 4) \rightarrow B'(-2, 4)$

$C(2, 1) \rightarrow C'(-2, 1)$

$D(1, 0) \rightarrow D'(-1, 0)$

$E(2, -1) \rightarrow E'(-2, -1)$

$F(2, -4) \rightarrow F'(-2, -4)$

A and *G* are on the *y*-axis, so they do not change.

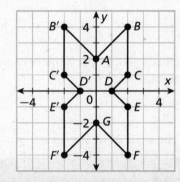

Do the Math

The *x*-axis and *y*-axis are lines of symmetry of an image. Use lines of symmetry to draw the entire image.

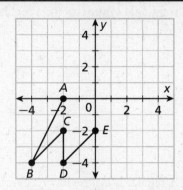

Name _____

LESSON 5.4
More Practice

ONLINE
⊙Ed Video Tutorials and
Interactive Examples

Determine if each figure has line symmetry. If so, draw all the lines of symmetry.

1.

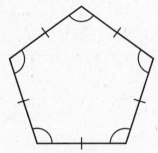

2.

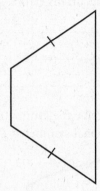

Determine if each figure has rotational symmetry. If so, describe the rotations up to and including 360° that map the figure onto itself.

3.

_____

4.

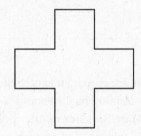

_____

The *x*-axis and *y*-axis are lines of symmetry of an image. Use the lines of symmetry to draw the entire image.

5.

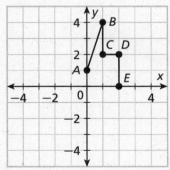

6.

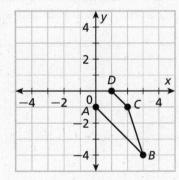

7. **Critique Reasoning** Kirk states that the angle of rotational symmetry for an equilateral triangle is 60° because the angles of a triangle measure 180°, and 180° divided by 3 equals 60°. Explain his error.

_____

_____

_____

8. **Math on the Spot** Describe the symmetry of each diatom. Draw any lines of symmetry. If there is rotational symmetry, give the angle.

A.

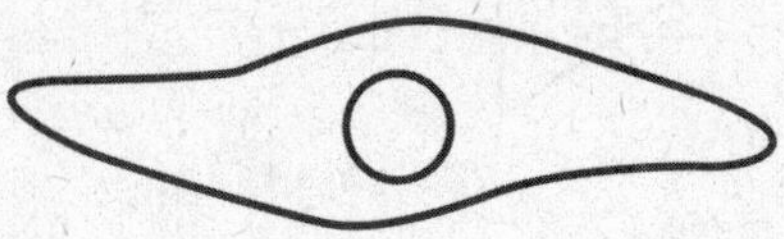

B.

_____   _____

9. Alexandra and Maris are playing a game where they guess how many sides the regular polygon the other is holding has. Alexandra says her regular polygon has exactly 12 lines of symmetry. Maris says her regular polygon has an angle of rotational symmetry of 24°. How many sides does each regular polygon have?

_____

_____

_____

10. Reggie states that a counterclockwise rotation of 216° will map a regular pentagon onto itself. Is Reggie correct? Explain your reasoning.

_____

_____

_____

11. How many lines of symmetry does the figure have?

Ⓐ 0

Ⓑ 1

Ⓒ 2

Ⓓ 4

Step It Out

Learn the Math

EXAMPLE 1 Triangle $A'B'C'$ is a dilation of triangle ABC. Find the scale factor k.

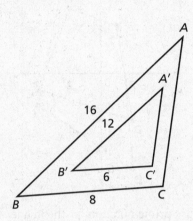

$k = \dfrac{A'B'}{AB}$ Create a ratio of the length of one side of the image to the length of the corresponding side of the pre-image.

$k = \dfrac{A'B'}{AB} = \dfrac{12}{16}$ Use the measurements given in the figure to replace the name of each segment length.

$k = \dfrac{A'B'}{AB} = \dfrac{12}{16} = \dfrac{3}{4}$ Simplify the fraction to find the scale factor.

$k = \dfrac{B'C'}{BC} = \dfrac{6}{8} = \dfrac{3}{4}$ Check your answer by comparing another pair of corresponding sides.

$k = \dfrac{3}{4}$ The ratio between the length of the image to the length of the preimage for any pair of corresponding sides is $\frac{3}{4}$, which is the scale factor k.

The value of k is less than 1, which means the preimage has been reduced to create the image. When the value of k is greater than 1, the preimage is enlarged to create the image.

Do the Math

Figure $P'Q'R'S'$ is a dilation of Figure $PQRS$. Predict whether $0 < k < 1$ or $k > 1$, and explain your prediction. Then find the scale factor and check your answer.

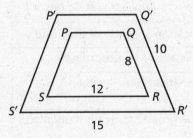

The value of k will be _____, because _____
_____.

Write a ratio between a side length of the image to the corresponding side length of the preimage.

$k = \dfrac{\square}{\square} = \dfrac{\square}{\square} = \dfrac{\square}{\square}$

Check your answer using another pair of corresponding sides.

$k = \dfrac{\square}{\square} = \dfrac{\square}{\square} = \dfrac{\square}{\square}$

Learn the Math

EXAMPLE 2 Draw a vertical stretch with a factor of 2 of quadrilateral $ABCD$ with vertices $A(-1, 3)$, $B(2, 4)$, $C(4, -1)$, and $D(-2, -3)$ centered at the origin.

Write a coordinate rule for the transformation, and create a table to organize the coordinates. Rule: $(x, y) \rightarrow (x, 2y)$

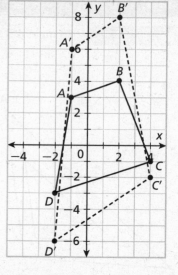

Preimage	Image
$A(-1, 3)$	$A'(-1, 6)$
$B(2, 4)$	$B'(2, 8)$
$C(4, -1)$	$C'(4, -2)$
$D(-2, -3)$	$D'(-2, -6)$

Plot and connect the points to draw the vertical stretch, remembering to use prime notation for the image.

Do the Math

Draw a horizontal stretch with a factor of $\frac{2}{3}$ of quadrilateral $EFGH$ with vertices $E(-3, 3)$, $F(-9, -1)$, $G(-3, -1)$, and $H(3, 3)$ centered at the origin.

Learn the Math

EXAMPLE 3 Using the coordinate points, predict and explain what kind of transformation will happen in each case.

Transformation	Prediction
$(x, y) \rightarrow (kx, ky)$	Dilation, because each coordinate is multiplied by scale factor k
$(x, y) \rightarrow (-y, x)$	90° rotation, by examining the location and sign of the x and y
$(x, y) \rightarrow (x + c, y)$	Translation, because a constant c is added to a coordinate
$(x, y) \rightarrow (x, ky)$, where $0 < k < 1$	Vertical compression, because a positive value less than 1 is multiplied by the y-coordinate
$(x, y) \rightarrow (kx, y)$, where $k > 1$	Horizontal stretch, because a value greater than 1 is multiplied by the x-coordinate

Do the Math

Using each given rule, predict the transformation as either a translation, rotation, dilation, a vertical stretch or compression, or a horizontal stretch or compression.

Transformation	Prediction
$(x, y) \rightarrow (x, y + 3)$	
$(x, y) \rightarrow (2x, y)$	
$(x, y) \rightarrow (-y, -x)$	

Name _____

Identify the type of transformation that would result from
the given coordinate rule.

1. $(x, y) \rightarrow (6x, y)$

2. $(x, y) \rightarrow (4x, 4y)$

_____

3. $(x, y) \rightarrow \left(x + \frac{1}{2}, y - 7\right)$

4. $(x, y) \rightarrow \left(\frac{1}{5}x, y\right)$

_____

5. $(x, y) \rightarrow (x, 3y)$

6. $(x, y) \rightarrow (9x, 9y)$

_____

Use the rule to transform the quadrilateral with vertices $A(2, 4)$, $B(9, 4)$, $C(12, -2)$, and $D(-3, -4)$.
Graph and label the image and the preimage.

7. $(x, y) \rightarrow 2(x, y)$

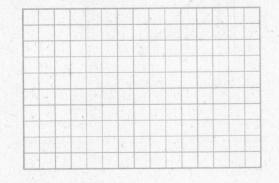

8. $(x, y) \rightarrow \left(x, \frac{1}{2}y\right)$

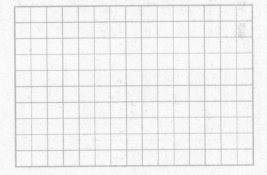

9. **Use Structure** Lewis is building a train layout and wants to build a model of the train station in his city. He wants it to be exactly to scale to match his engine. The engine measures 8 inches long and is the model of a train that is 80 feet long. If the station in his city is 30 feet by 60 feet by 40 feet, what are the dimensions of his model of the train station?

_____

_____

_____

10. In the transformation graphed, the solid-lined figure is the preimage and the dashed-line figure is the image.

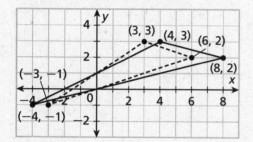

What rule would result in the transformation shown? _____

11. **Math on the Spot** Tell whether the transformation is a dilation.

A.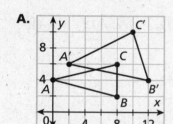

B.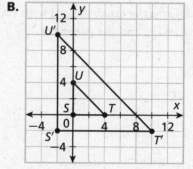

_____   _____

_____   _____

12. Which transformation represents a dilation centered at the origin?

Ⓐ $(x, y) \rightarrow (x, 3y)$

Ⓑ $(x, y) \rightarrow (0.25x, y)$

Ⓒ $(x, y) \rightarrow (2x, -4y)$

Ⓓ $(x, y) \rightarrow (0.75x, 0.75y)$

Step It Out

Learn the Math

EXAMPLE 1 Find a sequence of rigid motions that maps the original figure to the final image for the transformation. Give coordinate notation for the transformations you use.

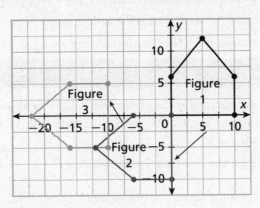

Use a table to compare the points between the figures.

Figure 1	(10, 6)	(0, 6)	(5, 12)	(10, 0)	(0, 0)
Figure 2	(−6, −10)	(−6, 0)	(−12, −5)	(0, −10)	(0, 0)
Figure 3	(−16, −5)	(−16, 5)	(−22, 0)	(−10, −5)	(−10, 5)

$(x, y) \rightarrow (−y, −x)$ Create a rule that transforms Figure 1 onto Figure 2.

$(x, y) \rightarrow (x − 10, y + 5)$ Create a rule that transforms Figure 2 onto Figure 3.

Do the Math

Find a sequence of rigid motions that maps the original figure to the final image for the transfer.

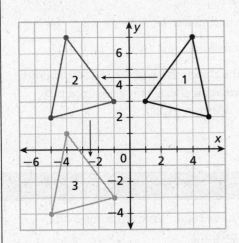

Create a table to compare the points between the figures.

$(x, y) \rightarrow \left(−\boxed{}, y\right)$ Write a rule that transforms Figure 1 onto Figure 2.

$(x, y) \rightarrow \left(x, y − \boxed{}\right)$ Write a rule that transforms Figure 2 onto Figure 3.

Learn the Math

EXAMPLE 2 A figure is transformed by a dilation centered at the origin with a scale factor of 3 and then a translation of 2 units to the left and 5 units up. Write a function that represents the composition of the transformations.

Write a rule in coordinate notation for the first transformation: $(x, y) \rightarrow (3x, 3y)$

Write a rule in coordinate notation for the second transformation: $(x, y) \rightarrow (x - 2, y + 5)$

Combine the rules to write the composition of the transformations: $(x, y) \rightarrow (3x - 2, 3y + 5)$

Do the Math

A figure is transformed by a dilation centered at the origin with a scale factor of 2, reflected across the x-axis, and translated 4 units left. Write a function that represents the composition of the transformations.

Write a rule in coordinate notation for the first transformation: $(x, y) \rightarrow \left(\boxed{}x, \boxed{}y \right)$

Write a rule in coordinate notation for the second transformation: $(x, y) \rightarrow \left(x, \boxed{}y \right)$

Write a rule in coordinate notation for the third transformation: $(x, y) \rightarrow \left(x - \boxed{}, y \right)$

Write the composition of the transformations: $(x, y) \rightarrow \left(2x - \boxed{}, \boxed{}y \right)$

Learn the Math

EXAMPLE 3 Write the composition of the functions used in the glide reflection to map A to B and C to D.

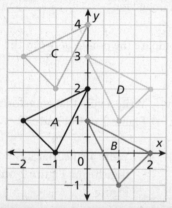

The glide reflection is a reflection of A across the y-axis and a translation 1 unit down.

Write a rule for the first transformation: $(x, y) \rightarrow (-x, y)$

Write a rule for the second transformation: $(x, y) \rightarrow (x, y - 1)$

Combine the rules to write the composition of the transformations. Notice because each transformation affects only one coordinate, the order of transformations does not matter.

$(x, y) \rightarrow (-x, y - 1)$

Do the Math

A figure is transformed by a glide reflection about the x-axis and 5 units right. Write a rule for each transformation in the glide reflection and the composition of the functions.

Name _____

Find a sequence of rigid motions that maps one figure to the other.

1. $ABCD$: $(0, 4), (3, 6), (3, 1), (6, 3)$ to $EFGH$: $(-9, 12), (0, 18), (0, 3), (9, 9)$

_____

Apply the composition of transformation to triangle ABC with coordinates $A(-2, 8)$, $B(2, 4)$, and $C(-2, 6)$. Write the coordinates of the image.

2. $(x, y) \rightarrow \left(-\dfrac{1}{2}x + 3, -\dfrac{1}{2}y + 3\right)$

_____

3. $(x, y) \rightarrow (3x - 5, 3y + 4)$

_____

Write a sequence of transformations to map Figure 1 to Figure 2. Then write a sequence of transformations to map Figure 2 to Figure 1.

4.

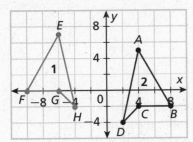

5.

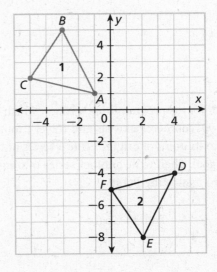

_____   _____

_____   _____

Write a composition of the sequence of transformations in the same order they are given.

6. ABC is dilated by a factor of 5, where the center of dilation is the origin, and rotated counterclockwise 90° about the origin.

_____

7. XYZ is rotated clockwise 180° about the origin, reflected over the x-axis, and translated 5 units up.

_____

8. **Math on the Spot** Draw the result of the composition of rigid motions.

   A. Reflect △ABC across line ℓ and then translate it along $\vec{v}$.

   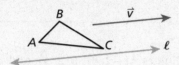

   B. △JKL has vertices $J(3, 2)$, $K(0, 1)$, and $L(3, -2)$. Rotate △JKL 90° counterclockwise about the origin and then reflect it across the x-axis.

   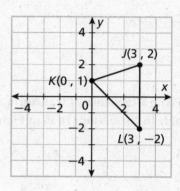

9. **STEM** Joey is programming a robot, which is facing right, to travel forward 2 feet, pivot 90° counterclockwise, and travel 1 foot up to reach its goal. The robot must travel back to its point of origin. Write a series of transformations to describe the robot's path to its goal. Then write another series of transformations to describe the robot's path back to its starting point.

   Path to Goal   Path Back to Starting Point

   _____   _____

   _____   _____

   _____   _____

10. **Use Structure** Figure $S'T'U'$ has been transformed with function $(x, y) \rightarrow \left(\frac{2}{3}(x + 5), \frac{2}{3}(y - 7)\right)$. What transformation will map it to the preimage STU?

    Ⓐ $(x, y) \rightarrow \left(-\frac{2}{3}(x - 5), -\frac{2}{3}(y + 7)\right)$

    Ⓑ $(x, y) \rightarrow \left(\frac{3}{2}(x - 5), \frac{3}{2}(y + 7)\right)$

    Ⓒ $(x, y) \rightarrow \left(-\frac{3}{2}(x + 5), -\frac{3}{2}(y - 7)\right)$

    Ⓓ $(x, y) \rightarrow \left(\frac{2}{3}(x - 5), \frac{2}{3}(y + 7)\right)$

Step It Out

Learn the Math

EXAMPLE 1 Determine whether the two triangles are congruent. If they are, write a congruence statement.

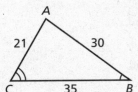 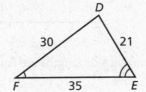

The markings on the figure show the following corresponding parts are congruent:

Sides: $\overline{AB} \cong \overline{DF}$, $\overline{AC} \cong \overline{DE}$, $\overline{BC} \cong \overline{FE}$

Angles: $\angle B \cong \angle F$, $\angle C \cong \angle E$

By the Third Angles Theorem, $\angle A \cong \angle D$.

All pairs of corresponding sides and angles are congruent, so $\triangle ABC \cong \triangle DFE$.

Do the Math

Determine whether the two triangles are congruent. If they are, write a congruence statement.

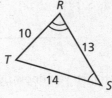 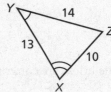

Pairs of Corresponding Parts

Sides: _____

Angles: _____

$\triangle \boxed{} \cong \triangle \boxed{}$

Learn the Math

EXAMPLE 2 Find the measures of $\angle J$ and $\angle M$ in the triangles.

$\angle J \cong \angle M$ by the Third Angles Theorem.
Set the measures of the angles equal.

$m\angle J = m\angle M$

$5x + 2 = 7x - 30$

$2 = 2x - 30$

$32 = 2x$

$16 = x$

Find the measures of the angles. $m\angle J = (5x + 2)^\circ = \left(5(16) + 2\right)^\circ = 82^\circ$.

So, $m\angle J = 82^\circ$ and $m\angle M = 82^\circ$.

Do the Math

Find the measures of $\angle C$ and $\angle F$ in the triangles.

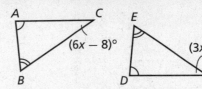

Learn the Math

EXAMPLE 3 A brick wall is made using bricks that are congruent. The dimensions of the sides of two bricks are given in inches. Find the length and width of the bricks.

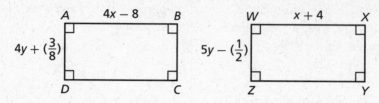

The bricks are congruent, so you know that the corresponding side lengths are equal.

$AB = WX$

$4x - 8 = x + 4$

$3x - 8 = 4$

$3x = 12$

$x = 4$

$AD = WZ$

$4y + \dfrac{3}{8} = 5y - \dfrac{1}{2}$

$\dfrac{3}{8} = y - \dfrac{1}{2}$

$\dfrac{7}{8} = y$

Substitute the values of x and y to find the length and width of the bricks.

$AB = 4x - 8 = 4(4) - 8 = 16 - 8 = 8$

$AD = 4y + \dfrac{3}{8} = 4\left(\dfrac{7}{8}\right) + \dfrac{3}{8} = \dfrac{28}{8} + \dfrac{3}{8} = \dfrac{31}{8} = 3\dfrac{7}{8}$

The sides of the bricks are 8 inches long and $3\dfrac{7}{8}$ inches wide.

Do the Math

The sides of two identical door stops are triangles. Find the length and the height of the door stops in inches.

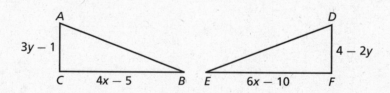

Name _____

LESSON 7.1
More Practice

🔵**Ed** **ONLINE**
Video Tutorials and
Interactive Examples

Tell whether the triangles are congruent. Explain your reasoning.

1.

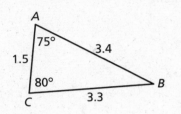

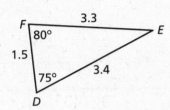

2.

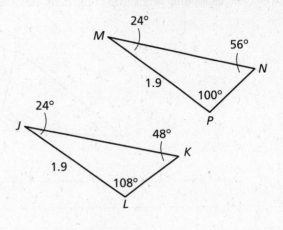

_____
_____

_____
_____

Describe a sequence of transformations that proves the figures are congruent.

3.

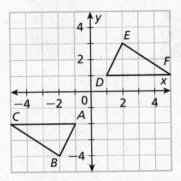

4.

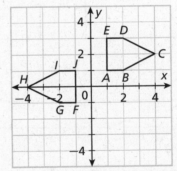

_____

_____

Find the value of the variables that results in congruent triangles.

5.

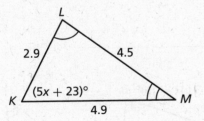

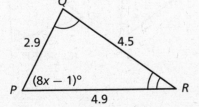

6.

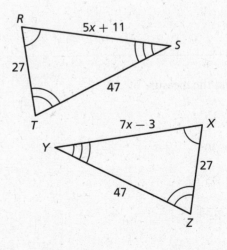

_____

_____

7. **Critique Reasoning** Mike believes the two triangles are congruent because the corresponding angles are congruent. Is Mike correct? Explain your reasoning.

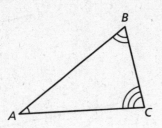 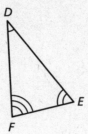

_____

_____

8. **Math on the Spot** Decide whether the figures in the pair are congruent. If not, explain.

A.

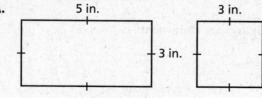

5 in.

3 in.

3 in.

B.

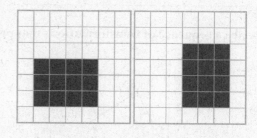

_____   _____

_____   _____

9. A company uses two pentagons as their corporate logo. What transformations can you use to show that the pentagons are congruent?

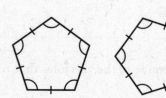

_____

10. Find the measure of ∠B.

Ⓐ 15°

Ⓑ 30°

Ⓒ 75°

Ⓓ 135°

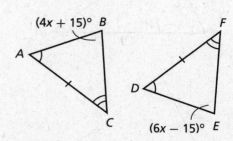

$(4x + 15)°$ B

A

D

C

$(6x - 15)°$ E

F

Step It Out

Learn the Math

EXAMPLE 1   Given that △FGH ≅ △PQR, find the measures of ∠R and ∠Q and the lengths of $\overline{FG}$ and $\overline{PR}$.

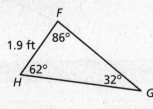
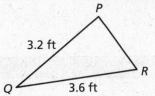

Because △FGH ≅ △PQR, ∠R ≅ ∠H and ∠Q ≅ ∠G.

m∠R = 62°

m∠Q = 32°

Also, because △FGH ≅ △PQR, $\overline{FG}$ ≅ $\overline{PQ}$ and $\overline{PR}$ ≅ $\overline{FH}$.

FG = 3.2 ft

PR = 1.9 ft

Do the Math

Given that △ABC ≅ △XYZ, find the measures of ∠A and ∠Z and the lengths of $\overline{AB}$ and $\overline{XZ}$.

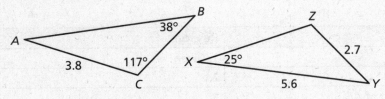

Because △ABC ≅ △XYZ, ∠A ≅ ∠☐ and ∠Z ≅ ∠☐.

m∠A = ☐

m∠Z = ☐

Also, because △ABC ≅ △XYZ, $\overline{AB}$ ≅ ☐ and $\overline{XZ}$ ≅ ☐.

AB = ☐

XZ = ☐

Learn the Math

EXAMPLE 2 Write a two-column proof.

Given: $\triangle ABC \cong \triangle ADC$
Prove: $\overline{AC}$ bisects $\angle DAB$

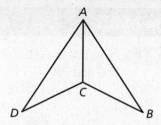

Statements	Reasons
1. $\triangle ABC \cong \triangle ADC$	1. Given
2. $\angle DAC \cong \angle BAC$	2. Corresponding parts of congruent figures are congruent.
3. $\overline{AC}$ bisects $\angle DAB$.	3. Definition of angle bisector

Do the Math

Write a two-column proof.

Given: $\triangle ABC \cong \triangle CDF$

Prove: C is the midpoint of $\overline{AF}$

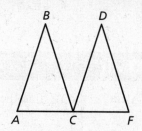

Statements	Reasons
1.	1. Given
2.	2.
3. C is the midpoint of $\overline{AF}$.	3.

Name

LESSON 7.2
More Practice

ONLINE
Video Tutorials and
Interactive Examples

Tell whether the figures are congruent. Explain your reasoning.

1.

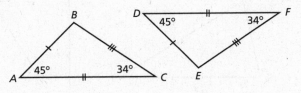

2.

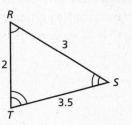

_____

_____

_____

In each diagram, △ABC ≅ △DEF. Find the indicated value.

3. m∠E

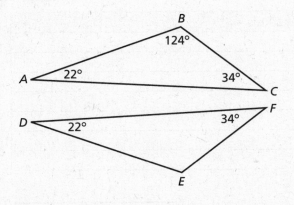

4. DE

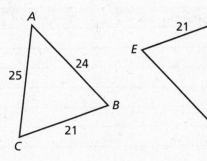

_____

_____

In each diagram, △ABC ≅ △DEF. Find the value of the variable.

5.

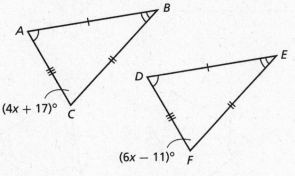

6.

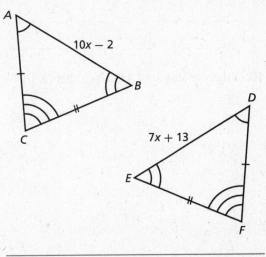

_____

_____

7. Critique Reasoning Doris is given two congruent triangles. She says that it is not possible to prove that the perimeters are equal because perimeter is not a "corresponding part." Is Doris correct? Explain your reasoning.

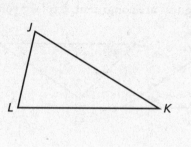

_____

_____

8. Math on the Spot Write a two-column proof.

Given: $\overline{AD} \perp \overline{DC}$, $\overline{BC} \perp \overline{DC}$, $\angle DAC \cong \angle CBD$, $\overline{AD} \cong \overline{BC}$, $\overline{BD} \cong \overline{AC}$

Prove: $\triangle ACD \cong \triangle BDC$

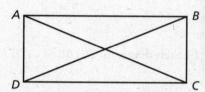

Statements	Reasons

9. Reason Do you have enough information to show that $\triangle KLM \cong \triangle NLM$? If so, explain why they are congruent. If not, what information do you need?

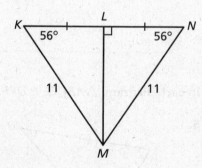

_____

_____

10. Find the length of $\overline{AB}$, given that $\triangle ABC \cong \triangle DEF$.

Ⓐ 3

Ⓑ 6

Ⓒ 22

Ⓓ 43

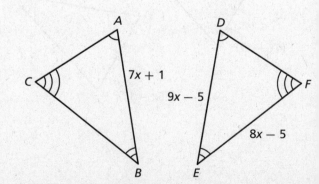

Step It Out

Learn the Math

EXAMPLE 1 In the diagram, $ABCD \cong WXYZ$. Find a sequence of rigid motions that maps one figure onto the other.

Make a table of the coordinates to look for a pattern.

$A(-2, 3)$	$W(1, 0)$
$B(-2, -1)$	$X(1, -4)$
$C(-5, -1)$	$Y(4, -4)$
$D(-4, 2)$	$Z(3, -1)$

Notice that the x-coordinates in $ABCD$ are negative and the x-coordinates in $WXYZ$ are positive. $ABCD$ is reflected across the y-axis. The coordinates of the image of $ABCD$ after being reflected across the y-axis are $A'(2, 3)$, $B'(2, -1)$, $C'(5, -1)$, and $D'(4, 2)$.

Find the difference between the coordinates of $WXYZ$ and $A'B'C'D'$.

$x: 2 - 1 = 1$, $y: 3 - 0 = 3$

The sequence of rigid motions is a reflection across the y-axis, followed by a translation.

Reflection: $(x, y) \rightarrow (-x, y)$; Translation: $(x, y) \rightarrow (x - 1, y - 3)$

Do the Math

In the diagram, $FGHJ \cong PQRS$. Find a sequence of rigid motions that maps one figure onto the other.

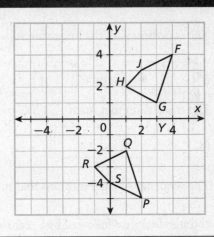

Learn the Math

EXAMPLE 2 In the diagram, $\triangle JLK \cong \triangle RST$. Find a sequence of rigid motions that maps $\triangle JLK$ to $\triangle RST$.

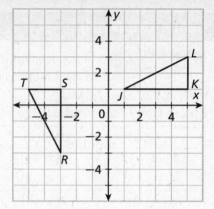

From the diagram, you can see a rotation of 90° counterclockwise is needed to map $\triangle JLK$ to $\triangle RST$. When you rotate $\triangle JLK$ 90° counterclockwise, the coordinates of the image are $J'(-1, 1)$, $K'(-1, 5)$, and $L'(-3, 5)$.

$\triangle J'K'L'$ must be translated to map to $\triangle RST$. Subtract the coordinates of the corresponding points to find the translation.

$J'(-1, 1) \rightarrow R(-3, -3)$

$x: -3 - (-1) = -2$, $y: -3 - 1 = -4$

$\triangle J'K'L'$ is translated 2 units to the left and 4 units down to map to $\triangle RST$.

The sequence of rigid motions that maps $\triangle JLK$ to $\triangle RST$ is a rotation 90° counterclockwise followed by a translation 2 units to the left and 4 units down.

Do the Math

In the diagram, $\triangle ABC \cong \triangle DEF$. Find a sequence of rigid motions that maps $\triangle ABC$ to $\triangle DEF$.

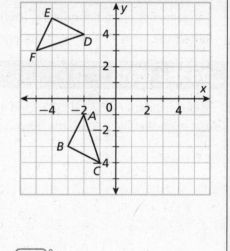

A rotation of ☐° counterclockwise is needed to map $\triangle ABC$ to $\triangle DEF$.

The coordinates of the image are $A'\left(\boxed{}, \boxed{}\right)$,

$B'\left(\boxed{}, \boxed{}\right)$, and $C'\left(\boxed{}, \boxed{}\right)$.

The translation that maps $\triangle A'B'C'$ to $\triangle DEF$ is

$(x, y) \rightarrow \left(\boxed{}, \boxed{}\right)$.

The sequence of rigid motions that maps $\triangle ABC$ to $\triangle DEF$ is a rotation ☐°

counterclockwise followed by a translation ☐ unit(s) to the ____ and

☐ unit(s) ____.

Name

LESSON 7.3
More Practice

ONLINE
🙂 Ed Video Tutorials and
Interactive Examples

Write a sequence of rigid motions that maps one figure onto the other using coordinate notation.

1. $ABCD \cong JKLM$

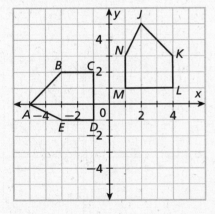

2. $\triangle FGH \cong \triangle JKL$

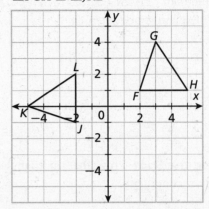

3. $ABCDE \cong JKLMN$

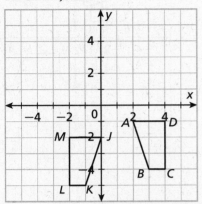

4. $\triangle ABC \cong \triangle DEF$

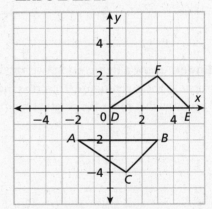

Use the definition of congruence to decide whether the two figures are congruent. Explain your answer using coordinate notation for any transformations you use.

5.

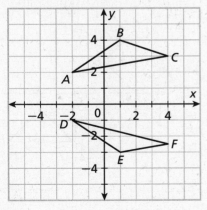

6.

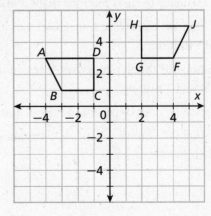

7. **Critique Reasoning** Brian states that you can map
ABCD to *FGHJ* by rotating 180°. Leo states that you
can map *ABCD* to *FGHJ* by reflecting across the
x-axis and then reflecting across the *y*-axis. Who is
correct? Explain your reasoning.

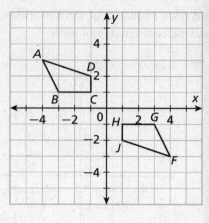

_____

_____

8. **Math on the Spot** Prove that the triangles with the given
vertices are congruent.

$A(2, 5), B(6, 2), C(2, 2)$

$P(-6, -4), Q(-2, -1), R(-6, -1)$

_____

_____

9. **Open Ended** Draw a figure using two rigid motions that
is congruent to the given figure. Describe the sequence
of rigid motions that maps the original figure onto your figure.

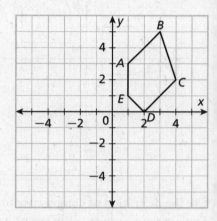

_____

_____

10. Which sequence of rigid motions maps △*ABC* to △*DEF*.

Ⓐ rotation 90° clockwise, translation 4 units right
and 1 unit up

Ⓑ rotation 90° counterclockwise, translation 4 units
right and 1 unit up

Ⓒ rotation 90° clockwise, translation 4 units down

Ⓓ rotation 90° counterclockwise, translation 4 units
down

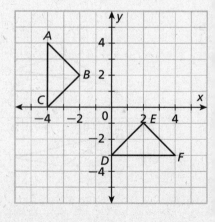

Name _____

Step It Out

Learn the Math

EXAMPLE 1 ▶ Darcy cut a piece of wood as shown. She drew a line from A to C that bisects $\angle A$ and $\angle C$. Can she use this information to conclude that the sides AB and AD are the same length?

From the given information, you know that $\overline{AC}$ bisects $\angle A$ and $\angle C$. Write a proof.

Given: $\overline{AC}$ bisects $\angle A$, $\overline{AC}$ bisects $\angle C$

Prove: $\overline{AB} \cong \overline{AD}$

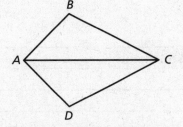

Statements	Reasons
1. $\overline{AC}$ bisects $\angle A$, $\overline{AC}$ bisects $\angle C$	1. Given
2. $\angle BAC \cong \angle DAC$, $\angle BCA \cong \angle DCA$	2. Definition of angle bisector
3. $\overline{AC} \cong \overline{AC}$	3. Reflexive Property of Congruence
4. $\triangle ABC \cong \triangle ADC$	4. ASA Triangle Congruence Theorem
5. $\overline{AB} \cong \overline{AD}$	5. Corresponding parts of congruent figures are congruent.
6. $AB = AD$	6. Definition of congruent segments

Sides AB and AD are the same length.

Do the Math

A. Use the given information to show that $\overline{AE} \cong \overline{DE}$.

Given: $\overline{BE} \cong \overline{CE}$, $\angle ABE \cong \angle DCE$

Prove: $\overline{AE} \cong \overline{DE}$

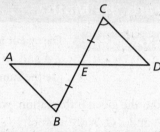

Statements	Reasons

B. Write a proof that shows $\triangle GHK \cong \triangle JKH$.

Given: $\overline{GH} \parallel \overline{KJ}$, $\angle GKH \cong \angle KHJ$

Prove: $\triangle GHK \cong \triangle JKH$

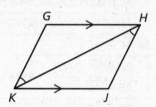

Statements	Reasons

Name

LESSON 8.1
More Practice

ONLINE
@Ed Video Tutorials and
Interactive Examples

Determine if the triangles are congruent. Explain your reasoning.

1.

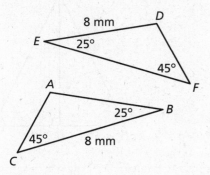

8 mm

D

E 25°

45°

F

A

25° B

45° 8 mm

C

_____

_____

2.

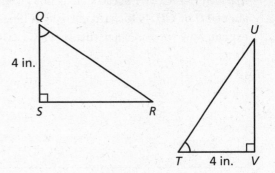

Q

4 in.

S R

U

T 4 in. V

_____

_____

3.

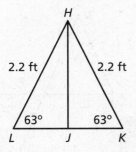

H

2.2 ft 2.2 ft

63° 63°

L J K

_____

_____

4.

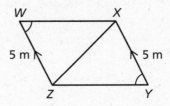

W X

5 m 5 m

Z Y

_____

_____

5. Write a two-column proof.

Given: $\overline{AC}$ bisects $\angle BAD$, $\angle BCA \cong \angle DCA$

Prove: $BC = DC$

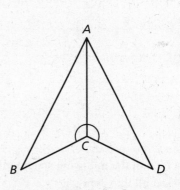

A

C

B D

Statements	Reasons
1.	1.
2.	2.
3.	3.
4.	4.
5.	5.
6.	6.
7.	7.

6. **Critique Reasoning** Richard states that he cannot show that △JFH ≅ △JGH because he is not given any information about $\overline{FH}$ or $\overline{GH}$. Is Richard correct? If he is not correct, explain how you can show that △JFH ≅ △JGH.

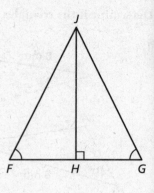

_____

_____

7. **Math on the Spot** Manda wants to know the distance between her front door and her neighbor's. She located points P, Q, and R. How can she find MN?

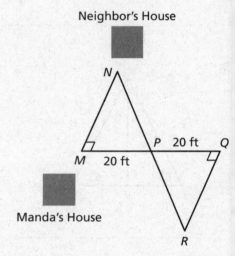

Neighbor's House

Manda's House

_____

_____

8. Explain how you can show that $\overline{KL} \cong \overline{HJ}$.

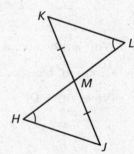

_____

_____

_____

9. Which of the following statements are true in the figure? Select all that apply.

Ⓐ $\overline{YZ}$ bisects ∠WZX

Ⓑ $\overline{XY} \cong \overline{YZ}$

Ⓒ △XYZ ≅ △WYZ

Ⓓ $\overline{XZ} \cong \overline{WZ}$

Ⓔ ∠XYZ ≅ ∠WZY

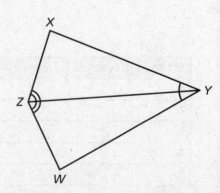

Name _____

Step It Out

Learn the Math

EXAMPLE 1 ▶ The diagram shows the legs of a tray table. The legs of the table, $\overline{AB}$ and $\overline{CD}$, bisect each other. Prove that the distance between B and C is the same as the length of $\overline{AD}$.

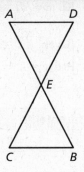

You can create a two-column proof to shown that the distance between B and C is the same as the length of $\overline{AD}$.

Given: $\overline{AB}$ bisects $\overline{CD}$

Prove: $BC = AD$

Statements	Reasons
1. $\overline{AB}$ bisects $\overline{CD}$	1. Given
2. $\overline{AE} \cong \overline{BE}$; $\overline{CE} \cong \overline{DE}$	2. Definition of bisected segments
3. $\angle AED \cong \angle BEC$	3. Vertical Angle Theorem
4. $\triangle AED \cong \triangle BEC$	4. SAS Triangle Congruence Theorem
5. $\overline{BC} \cong \overline{AD}$	5. CPCTC
6. $BC = AD$	6. Definition of congruent segments

Do the Math

A. A pattern on a carpet is shown in the diagram. $\overline{FG}$ and $\overline{FJ}$ are the same length, and $\overline{FH}$ bisects $\angle GFJ$.

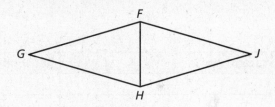

Write a two-column proof that shows $\angle FGH$ and $\angle FJH$ are congruent.

Given: $FG = FJ$, $\overline{FH}$ bisects $\angle GFJ$

Prove: $\angle FGH \cong \angle FJH$

Statements	Reasons

Do the Math

B. Use the fact that $\overline{KN} \cong \overline{MN}$ and that $\overline{NL}$ bisects $\angle KNM$ to prove that KL and ML are the same length.

Given: $\overline{KN} \cong \overline{MN}$, $\overline{NL}$ bisects $\angle KNM$

Prove: $KL = ML$

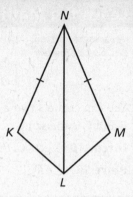

Statements	Reasons

C. Use the given information to show that $\overline{AB} \cong \overline{CD}$.

Given: $\overline{BE} \cong \overline{CE}$, $\overline{AE} \cong \overline{DE}$

Prove: $\overline{AB} \cong \overline{CD}$

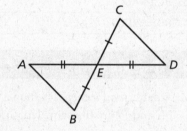

Statements	Reasons

Determine if the triangles are congruent. Explain your reasoning.

1.

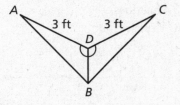

2.

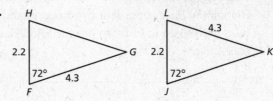

_____
_____
_____

_____
_____
_____

3.

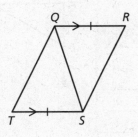

4.

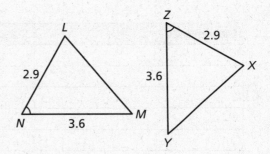

_____
_____
_____

_____
_____
_____

Find the value of the variable that results in congruent triangles. Explain.

5.

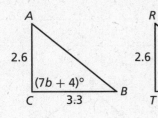

6.

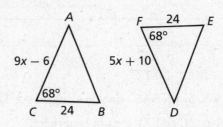

_____
_____
_____

_____
_____
_____

7. **Critique Reasoning** Julio states that he can use the SAS Triangle Congruence Theorem to prove that two right triangles are congruent. He constructs two right triangles to have congruent hypotenuses and one set of congruent legs. What does Julio need to do in order to use the SAS Triangle Congruence Theorem? Explain your reasoning

_____

_____

_____

8. **Math on the Spot** Prove the triangles are congruent.

   Given: $\ell \parallel m$, $\overline{AB} \cong \overline{CD}$

   Prove: $\triangle ADB \cong \triangle ADC$

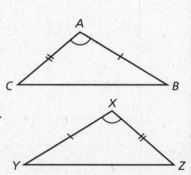

Statements	Reasons

9. **Reason** Four sidewalks form two right triangles. Sidewalk A and Sidewalk B intersect at a right angle. Sidewalk B extends 500 feet on either side of the intersection with Sidewalk A. Sidewalk C and Sidewalk D start at the ends of Sidewalk B and intersect Sidewalk A at the same point. Do you have enough information to prove that the two right triangles are congruent? Explain your reasoning.

_____

_____

_____

10. Is $\triangle ABC \cong \triangle XYZ$?

   (A) Yes, by the SAS Triangle Congruence Theorem they are congruent.

   (B) No, $\overline{AC}$ and $\overline{XY}$ are not congruent.

   (C) No, $\overline{AB}$ and $\overline{XZ}$ are not congruent.

   (D) No, you need to know the measure of another angle in each triangle.

Step It Out

Learn the Math

EXAMPLE 1 Two triangular tiles are a part of a mosaic. The lengths of the sides of the tiles are given. For what value of x can you use the SSS Triangle Congruence Theorem to prove the triangles are congruent? What is the length of the third side?

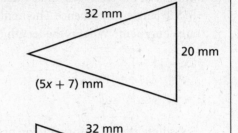

The two triangles have two corresponding sides that have the same length. In order to be congruent using the SSS Triangle Congruence Theorem, the third sides must have the same length.

Set the side lengths equal to each other and solve.

$5x + 7 = 8x - 8$

$\quad\ \ 7 = 3x - 8$

$\quad 15 = 3x$

$\quad\ \ 5 = x$

Substitute the value for x in one of the expressions for the side length.

$5x + 7 = 5(5) + 7$

$\qquad\ \ = 25 + 7$

$\qquad\ \ = 32$

or

$8x - 8 = 8(5) - 8$

$\qquad\ \ = 40 - 8$

$\qquad\ \ = 32$

The lengths of the sides are 32 millimeters each.

Do the Math

A. A table has two support braces that attach to the legs and the bottom of the table. For what value of x can you use the SSS Triangle Congruence Theorem to prove the triangles are congruent? What is the length of the third side?

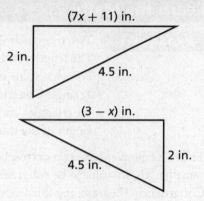

(7x + 11) in.

2 in.

4.5 in.

(3 − x) in.

4.5 in.

2 in.

$7x + 11 = \boxed{}$

$x = \boxed{}$

Substitute the value for x in one of the expressions for the side length.

$7x + 11 = 7\left(\boxed{}\right) + 11$

$= \boxed{}$

$= \boxed{}$

The length of the side is $\boxed{}$ inches.

B. Justin bought two bookends that have triangular ends. What values of the variables allow you to use the SSS Triangle Congruence Theorem to prove the two triangles are congruent? The sides using the same variables are corresponding. What are the lengths of the sides?

8.2 in. (3x − 13) in. (x + 1) in. 8.2 in.

4y in. (10y − 3) in.

Solve.

$3x - 13 = \boxed{}$ and $4y = \boxed{}$

$x = \boxed{}$ $y = \boxed{}$

Substitute to find the side lengths.

$3x - 13 =$ and $4y =$

$3\left(\boxed{}\right) - 13 = \boxed{}$ $4\left(\boxed{}\right) = \boxed{}$

The lengths of the sides are $\boxed{}$ inches and $\boxed{}$ inches.

Determine which triangle congruence theorem can be used to show that the triangles are congruent. Explain your reasoning.

1.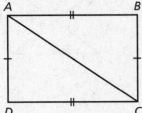

2.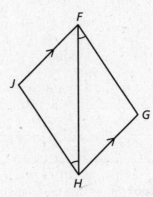

_____

_____

_____

3.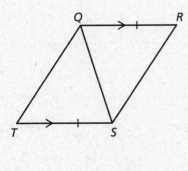

4.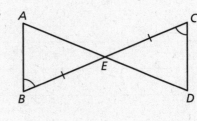

_____

_____

_____

Find the values of x and y for which $\triangle ABC$ and $\triangle XYZ$ are congruent.

5. ABC: side lengths of $6, 8, 7x - 12$
XYZ: side lengths of $6, 4y, 3x$

6. ABC: side lengths of $4x + 3, 5, 8y - 1$
XYZ: side lengths of $6x - 1, 5, y + 6$

_____

_____

_____

7. Critique Reasoning Mark states that he does not have enough information to prove that $\triangle ABC \cong \triangle BAD$. Is he correct? Explain your reasoning.

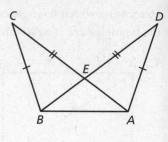

_____

_____

_____

8. Math on the Spot Show that the triangles are congruent for the given value of the variable.

Claim: $\triangle UVW \cong \triangle YXZ$ when $x = 5$

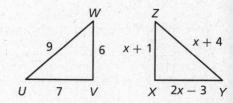

_____

_____

_____

9. Two earrings are shaped like triangles. For what values of x and y can you use the SSS Triangle Congruence Theorem to prove the triangles are congruent?

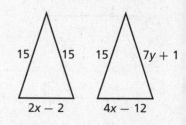

_____

_____

_____

10. Which triangle congruence theorem can you use to prove $\triangle HJL \cong \triangle KJL$?

Ⓐ SAS

Ⓑ SSS

Ⓒ ASA

Ⓓ The triangles are not congruent.

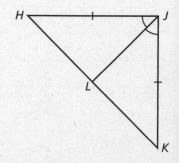

Step It Out

Learn the Math

EXAMPLE 1 Write a proof that shows $\overline{WX} \cong \overline{YX}$ to prove the HL Triangle Congruence Theorem.

Given: $\angle VWX$ and $\angle ZYX$ are right angles, $\overline{VW} \cong \overline{ZY}$, and X is the midpoint of $\overline{VZ}$.

Prove: $\overline{WX} \cong \overline{YX}$

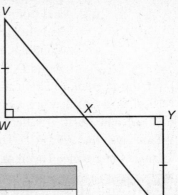

Statements	Reasons
1. $\overline{VW} \cong \overline{ZY}$, X is the midpoint of $\overline{VZ}$, $\angle VWX$ and $\angle ZYX$ are right angles.	1. Given
2. $\overline{VX} \cong \overline{ZX}$	2. Definition of midpoint of a line segment
3. $VW = ZY$ and $VX = ZX$	3. Definition of congruence
4. $\triangle VWX$ and $\triangle ZYX$ are right triangles.	4. Definition of right triangles
5. $WX^2 = VX^2 - VW^2$; $YX^2 = ZX^2 - ZY^2$	5. Pythagorean Theorem
6. $VX^2 - VW^2 = ZX^2 - ZY^2$	6. Substitution
7. $WX^2 = YX^2$	7. Substitution
8. $WX = YX$	8. Take the square root of both sides.
9. $\overline{WX} \cong \overline{YX}$	9. Definition of congruence

Then by the SSS Triangle Congruence Theorem, $\triangle VWX \cong \triangle ZYX$. So, if the hypotenuse and leg of both triangles are congruent to each other, the triangles are congruent by the HL Triangle Congruence Theorem is proven.

Do the Math

Write a proof that shows $\triangle LMP \cong \triangle NMP$ using the HL Triangle Congruence Theorem.

Given: $\overline{MP} \perp \overline{LN}$, $\overline{MN} \cong \overline{ML}$

Prove: $\triangle LMP \cong \triangle NMP$

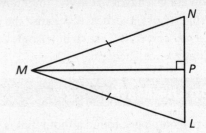

Statements	Reasons

Learn the Math

EXAMPLE 2 ▶ Four buildings on a college campus are located at points *A*, *B*, *C*, and *D*. There is a road from *A* to *B* and from *C* to *D*. These roads are the same length and are parallel. A fountain is located at point E, along the sidewalks that connect *B* and *C* and *A* and *D*. Show that △*ABE* ≅ △*DCE*.

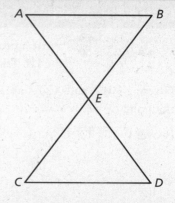

From the diagram, you know that ∠*AEB* and ∠*CED* are vertical angles, so they are congruent. $\overline{AB}$ is parallel to $\overline{CD}$, so ∠*EAB* and ∠*EDC* are alternate interior angles and are congruent. We are given that $\overline{AB} \cong \overline{CD}$. The triangles are congruent by the AAS Triangle Congruence Theorem.

Do the Math

Jackie cuts a piece of fabric as shown to be part of a quilt she is making. There are a pair of parallel sides and a pair of congruent angles as shown. Show that △*ABC* ≅ △*CDA*.

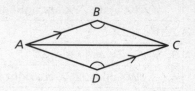

Learn the Math

EXAMPLE 3 ▶ Another part of the campus has buildings *F*, *G*, *H*, and *J*, with sidewalks connecting the buildings as shown. The distance from *F* to *H* is the same as the distance from *G* to *J*. The sidewalk from *F* to *G* and the sidewalk from *J* to *H* are both perpendicular to the sidewalk from *G* to *H*. Show that △*FGH* ≅ △*JHG*.

You are given that $\overline{FH} \cong \overline{JG}$. You know that $\overline{GH}$ is congruent to itself by the Reflexive Property of Congruence. Because the given segments are perpendicular, you know that △*FGH* and △*JHG* are right triangles. The triangles are congruent by the HL Triangle Congruence Theorem.

Do the Math

A paleontologist found a tooth that is shaped like an isosceles triangle. The paleontologist marked the length of the tooth with a line perpendicular to the base of the tooth. Show that the two triangles created by the perpendicular line are congruent.

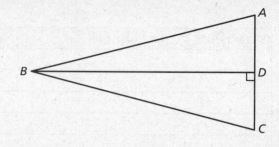

Name

LESSON 8.4
More Practice

ONLINE
⊙Ed Video Tutorials and
Interactive Examples

Determine which triangle congruence criteria should be used to
prove the two triangles are congruent.

1.

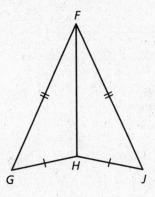

2.

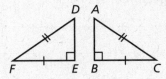

_____

_____

3.

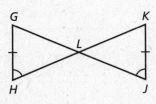

4.

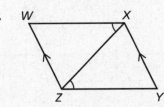

_____

_____

5.

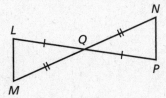

6.

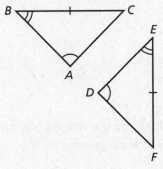

_____

_____

7. Open Ended Sketch two equilateral triangles that share a side. Mark the triangles in a way that they can be proven to be congruent using the HL Triangle Congruence Theorem. Explain your reasoning.

_____

_____

8. Math on the Spot Determine if you can use the HL Triangle Congruence Theorem to prove that the triangles are congruent. If not, tell what else you need to know.

A.

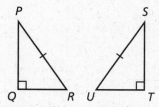

B.

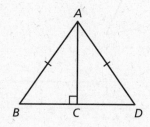

_____   _____

_____   _____

_____   _____

9. Reason Helen is designing a corporate logo. She knows that $\overline{AB} \cong \overline{CD}$ and that $\angle ABF$ and $\angle CDF$ are right angles. Can she prove that $\triangle ABC \cong \triangle CDA$? Explain your reasoning.

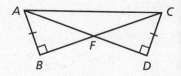

10. Determine which triangle congruence criteria should be used to prove the two triangles are congruent.

Ⓐ ASA

Ⓑ HL

Ⓒ AAS

Ⓓ SAS

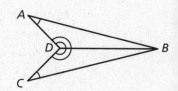

Step It Out

Learn the Math

EXAMPLE 1 The Corollary to the Triangle Sum Theorem states that the two acute angles in a right triangle are complementary.

Given: $\triangle DEF$ is a right triangle; $\angle E$ is a right angle.

Prove: $\angle D$ and $\angle F$ are complementary angles.

Statements	Reasons
1. $\triangle DEF$ is a right triangle; $\angle E$ is a right angle	1. Given
2. $m\angle E = 90°$	2. Definition of right angle
3. $m\angle D + m\angle E + m\angle F = 180°$	3. Triangle Sum Theorem
4. $m\angle D + 90° + m\angle F = 180°$	4. Substitution Property
5. $m\angle D + m\angle F = 90°$	5. Subtraction Property of Equality
6. $\angle D$ and $\angle F$ are complementary angles	6. Definition of Complementary Angles

Do the Math

Given: $\angle A$ and $\angle B$ are complementary angles.

Prove: $\triangle ABC$ is a right triangle.

Statements	Reasons
1.	1.
2.	2.
3.	3.
4.	4.
5.	5.
6.	6.
7.	7.

Learn the Math

EXAMPLE 2 One triangular face of the Great Pyramid of Giza has base angles that measure 51.5°. Find the measure of the vertex angle.

Use the Triangle Sum Theorem.

$51.5° + 51.5° + x° = 180°$

$103° + x° = 180°$

$x = 77$

The vertex angle of the triangular face is 77 degrees.

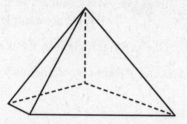

Do the Math

A. Find the value of the unknown angle measure.

Use the Triangle Sum Theorem.

$\boxed{} + \boxed{} + \boxed{} = \boxed{}$

$\boxed{} + x° = \boxed{}$

$x = \boxed{}$

The missing angle of the triangle is $\boxed{}$.

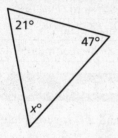

B. In an isosceles triangle, the vertex angle is 34°. What is the measure of the two congruent base angles?

Let x be the measure of one of the base angles.

Use the Triangle Sum Theorem.

$\boxed{} + x° + x° = \boxed{}$

$\boxed{} + 2x° = \boxed{}$

$2x° = \boxed{}$

$x = \boxed{}$

Each of the base angles is $\boxed{}$.

Name _____

LESSON 9.1
More Practice

ONLINE
Ed | Video Tutorials and
Interactive Examples

Find the value of x for each triangle below.

1.

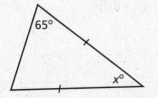

65°

$x°$

_____

_____

2.

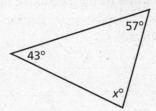

57°

43°

$x°$

_____

_____

3.

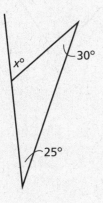

$x°$

30°

25°

_____

_____

4.

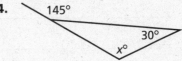

145°

30°

$x°$

_____

_____

5.

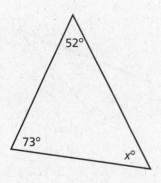

52°

73°

$x°$

_____

_____

6.

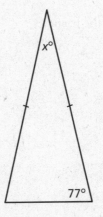

$x°$

77°

_____

_____

7. **Open Ended** Draw a triangle with two known angle measures. Use the Triangle Sum Theorem to calculate the measure of the third angle. Then, use the same angle measures to draw a second triangle. Explain whether or not the second triangle will be congruent to the first.

_____

_____

_____

_____

8. **Math on the Spot** Solve for x in the triangle. Explain your reasoning.

_____

_____

_____

_____

9. **Critical Thinking** A triangle has two angles that measure 37° and 25°. Lewis states that the measure of the exterior angle of the unknown angle is 62°, while Andrew states that the measure of the exterior angle is 75°. Who is correct? Explain your reasoning.

_____

_____

_____

10. What is the value of x in the triangle?

Ⓐ 25°

Ⓑ 52°

Ⓒ 111°

Ⓓ 125°

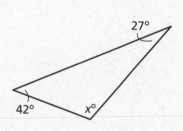

Name _____

Step It Out

Learn the Math

> **EXAMPLE 1** An amusement park is being built and the tilt-a-whirl is to be placed at point A with the log ride at point B and a haunted house at point C. Where should a Ferris wheel be placed to be equidistant from the other three attractions?

Find the perpendicular bisector of $\overline{AB}$.

Midpoint of $\overline{AB}$: $\left(\dfrac{0+4}{2}, \dfrac{0+6}{2}\right) = (2, 3)$ Slope of $\overline{AB}$: $\dfrac{6-0}{0-4} = -\dfrac{3}{2}$

Perpendicular Bisector of $\overline{AB}$: $y = \dfrac{2}{3}x + \dfrac{5}{3}$

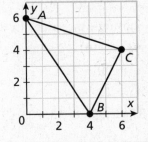

Find the perpendicular bisector of $\overline{BC}$.

Midpoint of $\overline{BC}$: $\left(\dfrac{4+6}{2}, \dfrac{0+4}{2}\right) = (5, 2)$ Slope of $\overline{BC}$: $\dfrac{4-0}{6-4} = \dfrac{4}{2} = 2$

Perpendicular Bisector of $\overline{BC}$: $y = -\dfrac{1}{2}x + \dfrac{9}{2}$

Find the intersection between the two perpendicular bisectors.

$\dfrac{2}{3}x + \dfrac{5}{3} = -\dfrac{1}{2}x + \dfrac{9}{2}$ $y = \dfrac{2}{3}\left(\dfrac{17}{7}\right) + \dfrac{5}{3} = \dfrac{34}{21} + \dfrac{5}{3} = \dfrac{69}{21}$

$4x + 10 = -3x + 27$ The Ferris Wheel should be placed at the circumcenter

$7x = 17$ of the other three attractions at $\left(\dfrac{17}{7}, \dfrac{69}{21}\right)$.

$x = \dfrac{17}{7}$

Do the Math

Find the circumcenter of $\triangle DEF$;

$D(0, 5)$, $E(4, 4)$, and $F(3, 1)$.

Midpoint of $\overline{DE} = \left(\boxed{}, \boxed{}\right)$ Slope of $\overline{DE} = \boxed{}$

Perpendicular Bisector of $\overline{DE}$: $y = \boxed{}\, x - \boxed{}$

Midpoint of $\overline{FE} = \left(\boxed{}, \boxed{}\right)$ Slope of $\overline{FE} = \boxed{}$

Perpendicular Bisector of $\overline{FE}$: $y = \boxed{}\, x + \boxed{}$

Solve for the intersection point.

$\boxed{}\, x - \boxed{} = \boxed{}\, x + \boxed{}$

$\boxed{} = \boxed{}$

$\boxed{} = \boxed{}$

$x = \boxed{}$

$y = \boxed{} = \boxed{}$

The circumcenter of $\triangle DEF$ is

$\left(\boxed{}, \boxed{}\right)$.

Learn the Math

EXAMPLE 2 The circumcenter of $\triangle RST$ is A. Find the length of $\overline{AS}$.

Solve for x.

$2x + 3 = 3x - 7$

$\quad -x = -10$

$\quad\ x = 10$

Substitute the value of x into the expression for AS.

$AS = 3(10) - 7$

$\quad = 30 - 7$

$AS = 23$

The length of $\overline{AS}$ is 23.

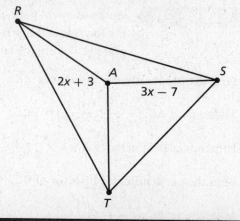

Do the Math

The circumcenter of $\triangle LMN$ is B. Find the length of $\overline{BL}$.

Solve for x.

$$\boxed{} = \boxed{}$$

$$2x = \boxed{}$$

$$x = \boxed{}$$

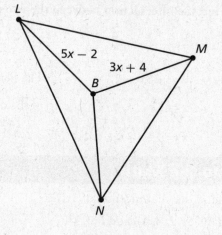

Substitute the value of x into the expression for BL.

$BL = 5\left(\boxed{}\right) - 2$

$\quad = \boxed{} - 2$

$BL = \boxed{}$

The length of $\overline{BL}$ is $\boxed{}$.

Name

LESSON 9.2
More Practice

ONLINE
Video Tutorials and
Interactive Examples

Find the circumcenter of each triangle.

1.

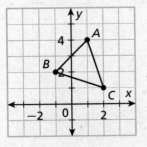

_____
_____
_____
_____

2.

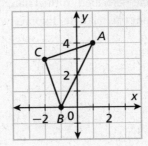

_____
_____
_____
_____

3.

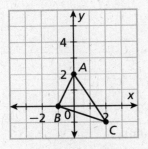

_____
_____
_____
_____

4.

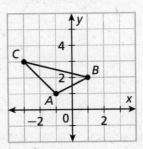

_____
_____
_____
_____

5. $\triangle ABC$; $A(-3, 2)$, $B(-2, 5)$, $C(1, -2)$

_____
_____
_____

6. $\triangle DEF$; $D(5, 2)$, $E(-1, 3)$, $F(0, -4)$

_____
_____
_____

7. Open Ended Draw an obtuse triangle. Describe whether the circumcenter will be the center of a circle inscribed in the triangle, or if it will be the center of a circle circumscribed about the triangle. Explain your reasoning.

_____

_____

_____

_____

8. Math on the Spot Find the circumcenter of a triangle with points $A(-5, 3)$, $B(-1, 3)$, and $C(-5, -5)$. Explain your reasoning.

_____

_____

_____

_____

9. Critical Thinking Why do you only need two perpendicular bisectors to find the circumcenter of a triangle? How can the third perpendicular bisector be used to check your answer?

_____

_____

_____

_____

10. The circumcenter of $\triangle DEF$ is Q. Find the value of x.

Ⓐ 2

Ⓑ 3

Ⓒ 4

Ⓓ 5

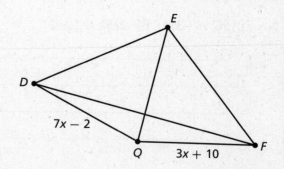

Step It Out

Learn the Math

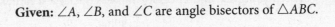

EXAMPLE 1 ▶

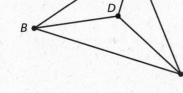

Given: ∠A, ∠B, and ∠C are angle bisectors of △ABC.

Prove: Point D is equidistant from each side of △ABC.

Construct perpendicular segments from point D to the sides of △ABC.

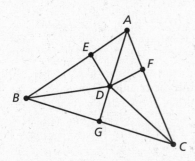

Since ∠DBG ≅ ∠DBE, $\overline{BD}$ ≅ $\overline{BD}$, and ∠BED ≅ ∠BGD, then △BED ≅ △BGD by AAS Triangle Congruence Theorem. Therefore, $\overline{ED}$ ≅ $\overline{DG}$. Through similar logic and the Transitive Property of Equality, $\overline{ED}$ ≅ $\overline{DG}$ ≅ $\overline{DF}$.

Do the Math

Given: Circle D is inscribed in △ABC. The center of the circle is point D.

Prove: $\overline{AD}$, $\overline{BD}$, and $\overline{CD}$ bisect their respective angles.

Since the circle is inscribed in △ABC, each side of △ABC is _____ to the circle. Given that point D is the center of the circle, this means the perpendicular distance between point D and each of $\overline{AB}$, $\overline{BC}$, and $\overline{CA}$ is the _____. This also means that point D is _____ from the sides of △ABC. Thus, for ∠B, △BED ≅ △BDG by the _____ Theorem since $\overline{ED}$ ≅ $\overline{DG}$, $\overline{BD}$ ≅ $\overline{BD}$, and ∠BED and _____ are right angles. Thus, ∠EBD ≅ ∠DBG and $\overline{BD}$ bisects its angle. The same argument applies for the other angles.

Learn the Math

EXAMPLE 2 A circular path will be paved within a triangular playground. The path will be between a slide, a swing set, and a seesaw. What is the largest radius of a circle that can be placed?

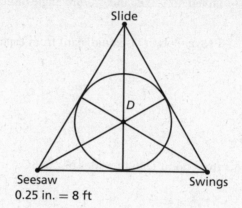

Slide

D

Seesaw   Swings
0.25 in. = 8 ft

1. Construct the angle bisector of each angle.

2. Find the incenter of the triangle and construct a circle inscribed within the triangle.

3. Use a ruler to measure the radius. The radius is 0.5 inches.

4. Use the scale to determine the radius of the largest possible circle

$$\frac{0.25 \text{ in.}}{8 \text{ ft}} = \frac{0.5 \text{ in.}}{x \text{ ft}}, x = 16 \text{ ft. So, the largest radius for the path is 16 feet.}$$

Do the Math

A farmer is using a map to decide where to place a rotating sprinkler to irrigate a triangular field, designated as $\triangle DEF$ on the map. The sprinkler head will be placed at a point equidistant from each side of $\triangle DEF$ so that the water will reach each side when sprayed. On the map, this distance is 0.75 inches. The scale of the map is 0.25 in.: 24 ft.

What is the largest area that the sprinkler can irrigate without irrigating outside the field?

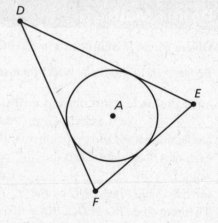

Name _____

Step It Out

Learn the Math

EXAMPLE 3 ▸ Point *A* is the incenter of △*DEF*. If ∠*DFE* = 108° and ∠*FEA* = 21°, find m∠*FDA*.

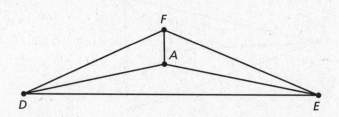

Statements	Reasons
1. m∠DFE + m∠FED + m∠FDE = 180°	1. Triangle Sum Theorem
2. m∠DFE + 2(m∠FEA) + 2(m∠FDA) = 180°	2. Since *A* is the incenter, it lies on the angle bisectors of ∠FED and ∠FDE, so ∠FED = 2(m∠FEA) and ∠FDE = 2(m∠FDA).
3. 108° + 2(21°) + 2(m∠FDA) = 180°	3. Substitution
4. 108° + 42° + 2(m∠FDA) = 180°	4. Addition
5. 150° + 2(m∠FDA) = 180°	5. Simplify
6. 2(m∠FDA) = 30°	6. Subtraction
7. m∠FDA = 15°	7. Division

Do the Math

Point T is the incenter of $\triangle LMN$. If $\angle LMN = 74°$ and $\angle MLT = 11°$, find m$\angle MNT$.

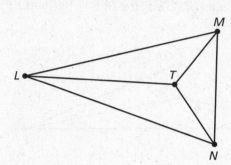

Statements	Reasons
1. m$\angle LMN$ + m$\angle MNL$ + m$\angle NLM$ = ⬚°	**1.** Triangle Sum Theorem
2. m$\angle LMN$ + 2(m$\angle MNT$) + ⬚ = 180°	**2.** Since T is the incenter, it lies on the _____ of $\angle MNL$ and $\angle NLM$, so m$\angle MNL$ = 2(m$\angle MNT$) and $\angle NLM$ = 2 (m$\angle MLT$).
3. 74° + 2(m$\angle MNT$) + 2(⬚) = 180°	**3.** Substitution
4. 74° + 22° + 2(m$\angle MNT$) = 180°	**4.** Commutative Property of Addition
5. ⬚° + 2(m$\angle MNT$) = 180°	**5.** Simplify.
6. 2(m$\angle MNT$) = 84°	**6.** Subtraction Property of Equality
7. m$\angle MNT$ = ⬚°	**7.** Division Property of Equality

Name _____

LESSON 9.3
More Practice

ONLINE
Video Tutorials and
Interactive Examples

1. $\overline{CE}$ bisects $\angle C$. Find x.

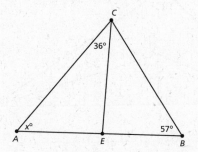

2. $\overline{BD}$ bisects $\angle ABC$. Find x

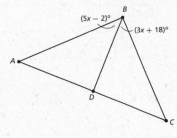

3. $\overline{CD}$ bisects $\angle C$. Find x.

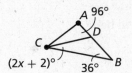

4. $\overline{AD}$ bisects $\angle CAB$. Find x

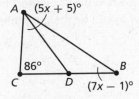

5. If P is the incenter of $\triangle FGH$ and $PW = 5$, what is the length of $\overline{PV}$?

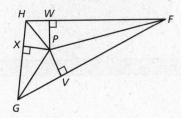

6. Construct the angle bisectors and incenter of the triangle below.

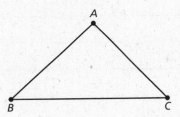

7. If P is the incenter of $\triangle FGH$ and $m\angle GPV = 65°$ and $m\angle GHF = 96°$, what is $m\angle PFV$?

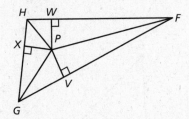

8. If the area of the circle with center A is 121π square feet, what is the length of $\overline{BA}$?

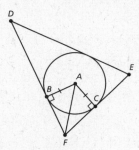

9. **Math on the Spot** Find the angle measures in the triangle, given that point Q is the incenter of △FGH.

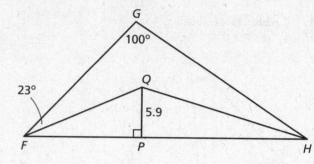

_____

_____

_____

_____

_____

_____

_____

10. **Use Structure** An architect is designing a circular window to be installed in the gable of a house. The metal window frame will be 1 foot wide and will be bordered by the roof above and a wood beam below. The distance from the center of the window to the roof is 3 feet. What will be the circumference of the circular glass pane that will be needed?

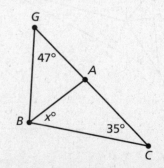

_____

_____

_____

_____

_____

_____

_____

$\overline{CD}$ and $\overline{BD}$ are angle bisectors of △*CAB*.
Find each measure.

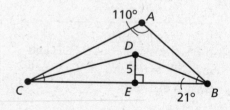

11. distance from *D* to $\overline{AB}$

12. m∠*DCA*

13. m∠*EDB*

14. $\overline{AB}$ bisects ∠*GBC*. Solve for *x*.
    - Ⓐ 41
    - Ⓑ 49
    - Ⓒ 82
    - Ⓓ 98

Step It Out

Learn the Math

EXAMPLE 1 ▸ A two-tier holiday tray is being designed with a larger triangular base and a smaller triangular upper level. Each level is shown in the diagram. Describe the location of the center of gravity for each level, given that $AE = CD = 12$ in. and $TV = SW = 18$ in.

Point M is the centroid of $\triangle ABC$.

$$AM = \frac{2}{3}AE$$
$$= \frac{2}{3}(12)$$
$$= 8 \text{ in.}$$

Point N is the centroid of $\triangle STU$.

$$TN = \frac{2}{3}TV$$
$$= \frac{2}{3}(18)$$
$$= 12 \text{ in.}$$

Tray:

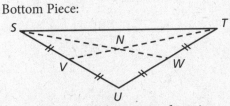

Top Piece:

Bottom Piece:

So, the center of gravity of the top piece is 8 inches from A and C, and the center of gravity of the bottom piece is 12 inches from S and T.

Do the Math

A triangular metal plate is being welded onto the upper surface of the spherical head of a robot statue to make it look like a hat. The triangular plate will be attached only at the center of gravity. The plate is shown. Describe the location of the welding point, given that $BN = AM = 45$ inches.

Point $\boxed{}$ is the centroid of $\triangle ABC$.

$$BW = \frac{\boxed{}}{\boxed{}}BN$$

$$= \frac{\boxed{}}{\boxed{}}\left(\boxed{}\right)$$

$$= \boxed{} \text{ inches}$$

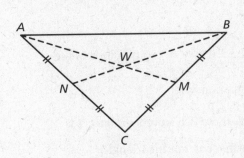

So, the welding point for the triangular hat piece is $\boxed{}$ inches from A and B.

Learn the Math

EXAMPLE 2 Locate the orthocenter of △ABC.

The orthocenter is the point at which the altitudes of the triangle meet. The side opposite C is horizontal, so the altitude will be vertical. The altitude is a segment on the vertical line that passes through $(3, 5)$.

The slope of line $\overline{BC}$ is -2 so the slope of the altitude through point A is $\frac{1}{2}$.

The point where these two altitudes intersect is $(3, 4)$, which is the orthocenter of the triangle.

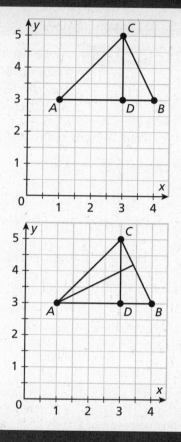

Do the Math

Find the orthocenter of △KLM. where $K(1, 1)$, $L(1, 5)$, and $M(5, 1)$ are the coordinates of the triangle.

The orthocenter is the point at which the altitudes of the triangle meet. The side opposite M is vertical, so the altitude will be horizontal. The altitude is a segment on the horizontal line that passes through

[ ].

The slope of line $\overline{LM}$ is [ ] so the slope of the

altitude through point K is [ ].

The point where these two altitudes intersect is

[ ], the orthocenter of the triangle.

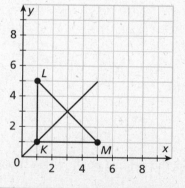

Name _____

In each △*ABC*, points *K*, *L*, and *M* are the midpoints of the sides opposite vertices *A*, *B*, and *C*, respectively. Determine the distance from the given vertex to the centroid.

1. $AK = 27$ cm; vertex *A*

_____

_____

_____

_____

2. $CM = 108$ in.; vertex *C*

_____

_____

_____

_____

In each construction below, the point of intersection within the triangle represents the centroid of the triangle. Determine the value of *x*.

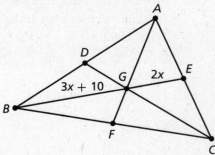

3.

_____

_____

_____

_____

4.

_____

_____

_____

_____

Determine the orthocenter of each triangle with the given vertices.

5. $(0, 0)$, $(0, 5)$, and $(6, 0)$

_____

_____

_____

_____

6. $(4, 5)$, $(4, 2)$, and $(-2, 2)$

_____

_____

_____

_____

7. **Open Ended** Give an example of a situation where knowing the location of the centroid is essential in the design and construction industry. Explain your answer.

_____

_____

_____

8. **Math on the Spot** Determine the orthocenter for $\triangle OPQ$ where the vertices are given by $O(0, 0)$, $P(4, 8)$, and $Q(6, 0)$.

    _____

    _____

    _____

    _____

    _____

9. **Critique Reasoning** While attempting to solve the problem shown at the right, Eugene wrote the following explanation:

    > The orthocenter exists where the three altitudes intersect in a triangle, and the centroid is the location of the point of intersection of the three medians of a triangle. Since there is no triangle where the medians and the altitudes are the same set of lines, a triangle cannot have an orthocenter that is in the exact same location as the centroid.

    Can a triangle have an orthocenter that is at the exact same location as the centroid?

    Explain the error in Eugene's reasoning.

    _____

    _____

    _____

    _____

10. Maya wants to be able to take a series of four triangles and place them in a mobile design where all four triangles are attached at one point and are balanced so that they stay horizontal. Which statement best describes where she should attach each triangle?

    (A) where the medians intersect

    (B) where the altitudes intersect

    (C) where perpendicular bisectors intersect

    (D) at any vertex

Step It Out

Learn the Math

EXAMPLE 1 ▶ $\triangle ABC$ represents a steel bracket that is used to hold two pieces of wood together. The bracket needs greater support in the middle. Use the Midpoint Formula to find the coordinates of the new support beam, $\overline{DE}$. Use slopes to show that $\overline{DE}$ is parallel to $\overline{AB}$, and the distance formula to calculate the length of $\overline{DE}$ and $\overline{AB}$.

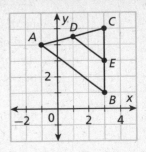

Midpoint of $\overline{AC}$ and $\overline{CB}$ $\qquad D\left(\dfrac{-1+3}{2}, \dfrac{4+5}{2}\right) = \left(1, \dfrac{9}{2}\right)$

$$E\left(\dfrac{3+3}{2}, \dfrac{1+5}{2}\right) = (3, 3)$$

Slopes Slope of $\overline{DE}$: $\dfrac{4.5-3}{1-3} = \dfrac{1.5}{-2} = -.75$ $\qquad$ Slope of $\overline{AB}$: $\dfrac{4-1}{-1-3} = -\dfrac{3}{4} = -.75$

Distance Formula

$$AB = \sqrt{(-1-3)^2 + (4-1)^2} = \sqrt{16+9} = 5 \qquad DE = \sqrt{(1-3)^2 + (4.5-3)^2} = \sqrt{4+2.25} = 2.5$$

$$AB = 2DE \qquad \text{or} \qquad DE = \dfrac{1}{2}AB$$

The new support beam is located at $D\left(1, \dfrac{9}{2}\right)$ and $E(3, 3)$, with a length of 2.5 units, half the length of $\overline{AB}$. $\overline{DE}$ is parallel to $\overline{AB}$.

Do the Math

A shirt company wants to insert their slogan into the middle of $\triangle ABC$, parallel to side $\overline{AB}$. Given that $A(1, 2)$, $B(4, 5)$ and $C(5, 2)$, calculate the coordinates of the slogan, $\overline{DE}$, and length of the slogan DE.

Midpoint of $\overline{AC}$ and $\overline{CB}$:

$$\overline{AC}: D\left(\dfrac{\boxed{}}{2}, \dfrac{\boxed{}}{2}\right) = \left(\boxed{}, \boxed{}\right) \qquad\qquad \overline{CB}: E\left(\dfrac{\boxed{}}{2}, \dfrac{\boxed{}}{2}\right) = \left(\boxed{}, \boxed{}\right)$$

Distance Formula

$$AB = \sqrt{\left(\boxed{}\right)^2 + \left(\boxed{}\right)^2} = \sqrt{\boxed{}} = \boxed{}$$

$$DE = \dfrac{1}{2}AB = \dfrac{1}{2}\left(\boxed{}\right)$$

$$DE = \boxed{}$$

Learn the Math

EXAMPLE 2 A backyard game involves tossing bean bags onto a triangular game mat. The interior triangle is made up of the midsegments of all sides of $\triangle XYZ$, and the goal of the game is to toss as many of your bags into the interior triangle as possible. For what value of x is the length of $\overline{MN}$ half the length of $\overline{ZY}$? What are the lengths of the three sides of the interior triangle?

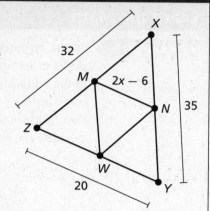

$MN = \frac{1}{2}ZY$ Midsegment Theorem

$2x - 6 = \left(\frac{1}{2}\right)(20)$ Substitution

$2x - 6 = 10$ Simplify

$2x = 16$ Addition Property of Equality

$x = 8$ Division Property of Equality

$MN = 10$

$MW = \frac{1}{2}XY$ $NW = \frac{1}{2}XZ$

$MW = \frac{1}{2}(35) = 12.5$ $NW = \frac{1}{2}(32) = 16$

The lengths of the sides of the interior triangle are 10, 12.5, and 16 units.

Do the Math

A dart game has an equilateral triangle with detachable midsegments for a target so you can create different game boards. What is the value of x for the game board labeled $\triangle XYZ$? What is the length of $\overline{MN}$?

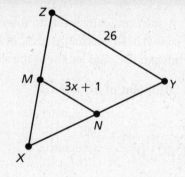

$MN = \frac{1}{2}ZY$

$\boxed{} = \left(\frac{1}{2}\right)\left(\boxed{}\right)$

$\boxed{} = \boxed{}$

$x = \boxed{}$

$MN = 3\left(\boxed{}\right) + 1 = \boxed{}$

Name

LESSON 9.5
More Practice

ONLINE
Ed
Video Tutorials and
Interactive Examples

For Problems 1–4, each triangle has a midsegment. Find the value of the variable for each triangle. Show your work.

1.

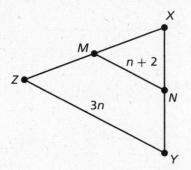

2.

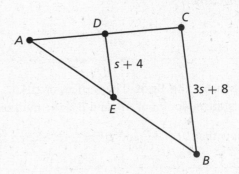

_____

_____

_____

_____

3.

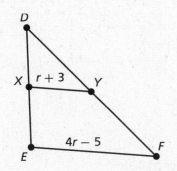

4.

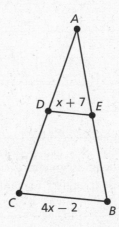

_____

_____

_____

_____

5. $\triangle ABC$ has midsegment $\overline{MN}$ parallel to $\overline{BC}$. If $MN = 4x - 5$ and $BC = 46$, what is x?

_____

_____

_____

6. $\triangle DEF$ has midsegment $\overline{XY}$ parallel to $\overline{DE}$. If $XY = 2x + 5$ and $DE = 86$, what is x?

_____

_____

_____

7. **Open Ended** Draw and label $\triangle ABC$ with two congruent midsegments that are larger than the third midsegment. Explain the process you used to ensure midsegment congruency.

_____

_____

8. **Math on the Spot** The vertices of $\triangle ABC$ are $A(-5, 3)$, $B(3, -1)$, and $C(-3, -3)$. D is the midpoint of $\overline{AB}$, and E is the midpoint of $\overline{BC}$.

Show that $\overline{DE} \parallel \overline{AC}$ and $DE = \frac{1}{2}AC$. Sketch $\overline{DE}$.

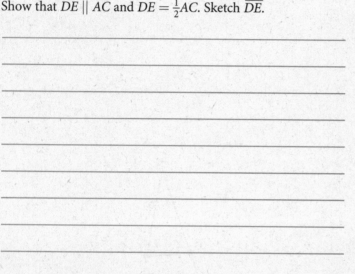

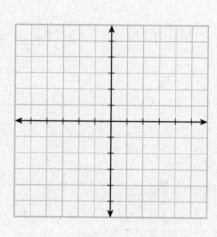

9. **Critical Thinking** The midsegments divide a triangle into four smaller triangles. What is true about these triangles? Explain.

_____

_____

10. For $\triangle ABC$, $\overline{WN} \parallel \overline{CA}$ and $\overline{WN}$ bisects $\overline{AB}$ and $\overline{BC}$. What is an appropriate name for $\overline{WN}$?

Ⓐ perpendicular bisector

Ⓑ angle bisector

Ⓒ midpoint

Ⓓ midsegment

Step It Out

Learn the Math

EXAMPLE 1 List the sides and angles of the triangle in order from smallest to largest for each triangle.

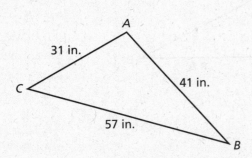

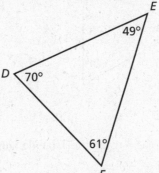

The longest side is always opposite the largest angle, and the shortest side is opposite the smallest angle.

For △ABC:

Sides in order from smallest to largest: $\overline{AC}$, $\overline{AB}$, $\overline{BC}$

Angles in order from smallest to largest: ∠B, ∠C, ∠A

For △DEF:

Angles in order from smallest to largest: ∠E, ∠F, ∠D

Sides in order from smallest to largest: $\overline{DF}$, $\overline{DE}$, $\overline{EF}$

Do the Math

List the sides and angles of the triangle in order from smallest to largest.

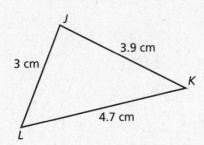

The longest side is always opposite the largest angle,

and the shortest side is opposite the smallest angle.

Sides in order from smallest to largest: ☐ , ☐ , ☐

Angles in order from smallest to largest: ∠☐ , ∠☐ , ∠☐

Learn the Math

EXAMPLE 2 List the sides and angles in order from smallest to largest for each triangle.

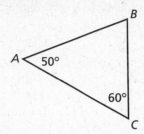
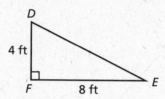

For △ABC:

Find the measure of ∠B using the Triangle Sum Theorem.

m∠B = 180° − 50° − 60° = 70°

Angles in order from smallest to largest: ∠A, ∠C, ∠B

Sides in order from smallest to largest: $\overline{BC}$, $\overline{AB}$, $\overline{AC}$

For △DEF:

From the Pythagorean Theorem, you know that the length of the hypotenuse of a right triangle is greater than the length of the legs of the triangle.

Sides in order from smallest to largest: $\overline{DF}$, $\overline{EF}$, $\overline{DE}$

Angles in order from smallest to largest: ∠E, ∠D, ∠F

Do the Math

List the sides and angles in order from smallest to largest.

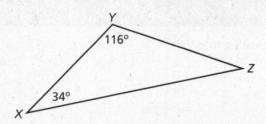

m∠Z = ☐° − ☐° − ☐° = ☐°

Angles in order from smallest to largest: ∠☐, ∠☐, ∠☐

Sides in order from smallest to largest: ☐, ☐, ☐

Determine whether a triangle can be formed with the given side lengths. Explain.

1. 5 in., 7 in., 12 in.

_____

_____

_____

2. 8 ft, 10 ft, 16 ft

_____

_____

_____

Use the two given side lengths of a triangle to describe the possible values for *x*, which represents the third side length.

3. 5, 14

_____

_____

_____

4. 23, 35

_____

_____

_____

5. 17, 20

_____

_____

_____

6. 47, 54

_____

_____

_____

List the sides and angles in order from smallest to largest.

7.

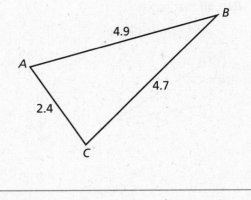

_____

_____

_____

8.

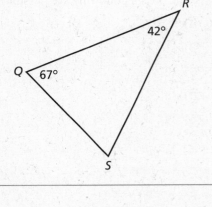

_____

_____

_____

9. **Math on the Spot** The lengths of two sides of a triangle are 5 inches and 9 inches. Find the possible lengths for the third side.

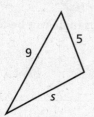

_____

_____

_____

10. **Critique Reasoning** Betty says that she does not have enough information to list the sides and angles in order from smallest to largest because she does not know all three side lengths or all three angle measures. Is she correct? Explain your reasoning. If there is enough information, list the sides and angles in order from smallest to largest.

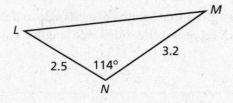

_____

_____

_____

11. **Reason** Three cities form a triangle on a map. The distance from Edgeberg to Harmwood is 127 miles. The distance from Edgeberg to Cedar Heights is 103 miles. Is it possible for the distance from Harmwood to Cedar Heights to be 25 miles? Explain your reasoning.

_____

_____

_____

12. Which of the following are possible lengths of side $\overline{AB}$? Select all that apply.

Ⓐ 9

Ⓑ 11

Ⓒ 12

Ⓓ 38

Ⓔ 39

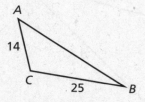

Name

Step It Out

Learn the Math	Do the Math

EXAMPLE 1 Compare *BC* and *DC* using the information in the diagram.

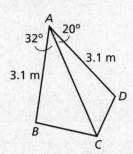

Compare the sides and angles in △*ABC* and △*ADC*.

m∠*BAC* > m∠*DAC*, $\overline{AB} \cong \overline{AD}$, $\overline{AC} \cong \overline{AC}$

By the Hinge Theorem, *BC* > *DC*.

Compare m∠*BAC* and m∠*DAC* using the information in the diagram.

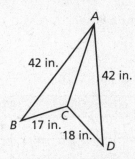

$\overline{AB}$ ☐ $\overline{AD}$, $\overline{AC}$ ☐ $\overline{AC}$, *BC* ☐ *DC*

By the Converse of the Hinge Theorem,

m∠*BAC* ☐ m∠*DAC*.

Learn the Math	Do the Math

EXAMPLE 2 Find the range of possible values for *x*.

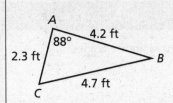 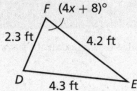

The Converse of the Hinge Theorem can be used to conclude that m∠*DFE* < m∠*CAB*.

$$4x + 8 < 88$$
$$4x < 80$$
$$x < 20$$

Find all positive values for m∠*DFE*.

$$4x + 8 > 0$$
$$4x > -8$$
$$x > -2$$

The range of values for *x* is $-2 < x < 20$.

Find the range of possible values for *x*.

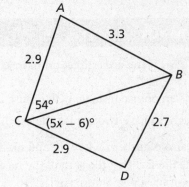

Learn the Math

EXAMPLE 3 Prove that m∠ACB > m∠CBD using the Converse of the Hinge Theorem.

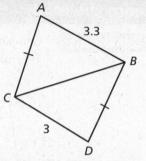

Given: $\overline{AC} \cong \overline{BD}$

Prove: m∠ACB > m∠CBD

Statements	Reasons
1. $\overline{AC} \cong \overline{BD}$	1. Given
2. $\overline{BC} \cong \overline{BC}$	2. Reflexive Property of Congruence
3. $AB > CD$	3. Given
4. m∠ACB > m∠CBD	4. Converse of the Hinge Theorem

Do the Math

Prove that m∠ACB > m∠XZY using the Converse of the Hinge Theorem.

Given: $AC = XZ$, $BC = YZ$
Prove: m∠ACB > m∠XZY

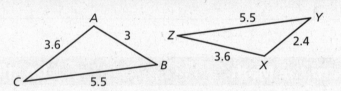

Learn the Math

EXAMPLE 4 Write an indirect proof to show that a triangle cannot have two obtuse angles.

Given: △ABC is an obtuse triangle with obtuse ∠A.

Prove: △ABC cannot have two obtuse angles.

Suppose ∠B is also obtuse. m∠A > 90° and m∠B > 90°, so m∠A + m∠B > 180°.
This contradicts the fact that the sum of the measures of the angles of a triangle is 180°.
So, △ABC cannot have two obtuse angles.

Do the Math

Write an indirect proof to show that supplementary angles cannot both be acute angles.

Given: ∠1 and ∠2 are supplementary angles.
Prove: ∠1 and ∠2 cannot both be acute angles.

Name _____

LESSON 10.2
More Practice

ONLINE
Ed Video Tutorials and
Interactive Examples

Compare the given measures.

1. *AB* and *DE*

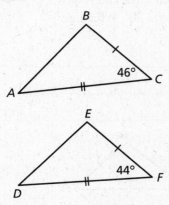

2. *AB* and *BD*

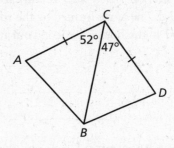

3. m∠*WXY* and m∠*ZYX*

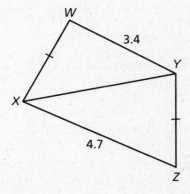

4. m∠*LNM* and m∠*QSR*

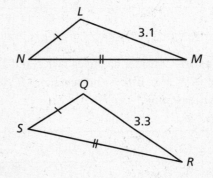

Describe the restrictions on the value of the variable.

5.

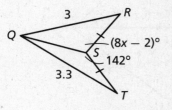

6.

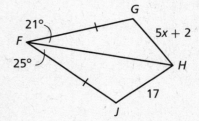

7. **Model with Mathematics** Two cars leave the same house. The first car travels east 1.5 miles and then turns and travels 2.5 miles. The angle formed by the roads traveled by the first car is 55°. The second car travels 1.5 miles west and then turns and travels 2.5 miles. The angle formed by the roads traveled by the second car is 50°. Which car is closer to the house? Explain your reasoning.

_____

_____

_____

8. **Critique Reasoning** Laura says that she can use the Converse of the Hinge Theorem to prove that m∠ADC > m∠ABC because CD > AB. Explain the error that Laura made. What is the conclusion she can make using the Converse of the Hinge Theorem?

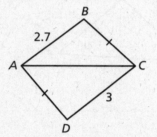

_____

_____

_____

9. **Reason** Consider triangles △JKL and △MKL. The triangles have a common side $\overline{KL}$ and $\overline{JK} \cong \overline{MK}$. If $\overline{JL}$ is shorter than $\overline{ML}$, how are ∠JKL and ∠MKL related? Explain your reasoning.

_____

_____

_____

10. Which of the following values of x are possible in the figure? Select all that apply.

Ⓐ $x = 1$

Ⓑ $x = 2$

Ⓒ $x = 3$

Ⓓ $x = 9$

Ⓔ $x = 10$

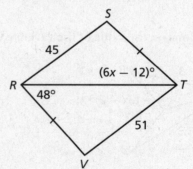

Step It Out

Learn the Math

EXAMPLE 1

Rebecca is creating a picture out of beach glass. She finds a piece that is shaped like a parallelogram. The diagram shows the dimensions of the piece of beach glass. What are the lengths of side $\overline{AB}$ and side $\overline{BC}$?

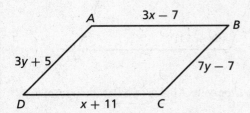

From the Opposite Sides of a Parallelogram Theorem, you know that $\overline{AB} \cong \overline{CD}$ and $\overline{AD} \cong \overline{BC}$.

Find the values of x and y.

$\overline{AB} \cong \overline{CD}$	$\overline{AD} \cong \overline{BC}$
$AB = CD$	$AD = BC$
$3x - 7 = x + 11$	$3y + 5 = 7y - 7$
$2x - 7 = 11$	$5 = 4y - 7$
$2x = 18$	$12 = 4y$
$x = 9$	$3 = y$

Substitute the value of x to find AB.

$AB = 3(9) - 7 = 27 - 7 = 20$

Substitute the value of y to find BC.

$BC = 7(3) - 7 = 21 - 7 = 14$

A blanket has a pattern of black and white parallelograms. The dimension of one of the parallelograms is shown. What is the measure of $\angle Z$?

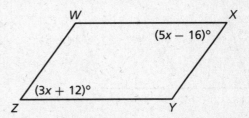

From the Opposite Angles of a Parallelogram Theorem, you know that $\angle X \cong \angle Z$.

Find the value of x.

$$\angle X \cong \angle Z$$
$$m\angle X = m\angle Z$$
$$5x - 16 = 3x + 12$$
$$2x - 16 = 12$$
$$2x = 28$$
$$x = 14$$

Substitute the value of x to find $m\angle Z$.

$$m\angle Z = \left(3(14) + 12\right)^\circ = (42 + 12)^\circ = 54^\circ$$

Do the Math

A. Rebecca found another piece of beach glass that is shaped like a parallelogram with the dimensions shown. What are the lengths of sides $\overline{KL}$ and $\overline{LM}$?

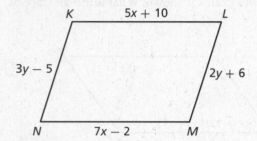

From the Opposite Sides of a Parallelogram Theorem, you know that $\overline{MN} \cong \boxed{}$ and $\overline{KN} \cong \boxed{}$.

Find the values of x and y.

$\overline{MN} \cong \boxed{}$

$MN = \boxed{}$

$7x - 2 = \boxed{}$

$\boxed{} x - 2 = \boxed{}$

$\boxed{} x = \boxed{}$

$x = \boxed{}$

$\overline{KN} \cong \boxed{}$

$KN = \boxed{}$

$3y - 5 = \boxed{}$

$y - 5 = \boxed{}$

$y = \boxed{}$

Substitute the value of x to find KL.

$KL = 5 \left(\boxed{} \right) + 10 = \boxed{} + 10 = \boxed{}$

Substitute the value of y to find LM.

$LM = 2 \left(\boxed{} \right) + 6 = \boxed{} + 6 = \boxed{}$

B. Marvin is solving a puzzle with geometric shapes. One of the pieces is shaped like a parallelogram. The dimensions of the parallelogram are shown. What is the measure of $\angle J$?

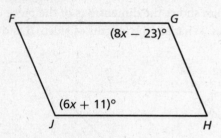

From the Opposite Angles of a Parallelogram Theorem, you know that $\angle \boxed{} \cong \angle J$.

Find the value of x.

$\angle \boxed{} \cong \angle J$

$m\angle \boxed{} = m\angle J$

$\boxed{} = 6x + 11$

$\boxed{} x - \boxed{} = 11$

$\boxed{} x = \boxed{}$

$x = \boxed{}$

Substitute the value of x to find $m\angle J$.

$m\angle J = \left(6 \left(\boxed{} \right) + 11 \right)^{\circ} = \left(\boxed{} + 11 \right)^{\circ}$

$= \boxed{}^{\circ}$

ABCD is a parallelogram. $AB = 4.3$, $BC = 2.3$, $AE = 1.4$, $m\angle ADC = 116°$.
Find each measure.

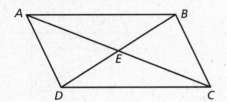

1. CE

_____

2. CD

_____

3. $m\angle ABC$

_____

4. AD

_____

QRST **is a parallelogram. Find each measure.**

5. ST

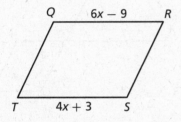

_____
_____

6. QT

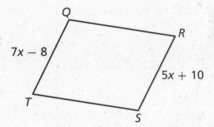

_____
_____

7. $m\angle R$

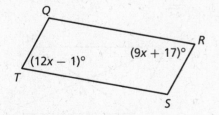

_____
_____

8. TR

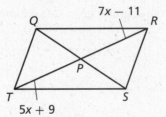

_____
_____

9. Math on the Spot Three vertices of a parallelogram are
$A(-3, 3)$, $B(-4, 0)$, and $C(2, -4)$. Find the coordinates
of vertex D.

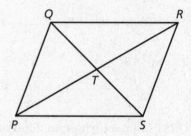

_____

_____

_____

10. Critique Reasoning *PQRS* is a parallelogram. Floyd states that he
knows that $\overline{PT} \cong \overline{QT}$ by the Diagonals of a Parallelogram Theorem.
Is Floyd correct? Explain your reasoning.

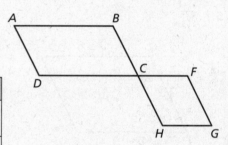

_____

_____

_____

11. Reason Write a two-column-proof.

Given: *ABCD* and *CFGH* are parallelograms.
Prove: $\angle A \cong \angle G$.

Statements	Reasons

12. *LMNP* is a parallelogram. $LN = 24$ centimeters. What is the length of $\overline{NK}$?

Ⓐ 12 inches

Ⓑ 24 inches

Ⓒ 36 inches

Ⓓ 48 inches

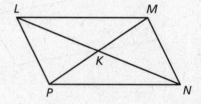

Step It Out

Learn the Math

EXAMPLE 1 Write a two-column proof to prove that *ABCD* is a parallelogram.

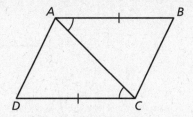

Given: $\overline{AB} \cong \overline{DC}$, $\angle ACD \cong \angle CAB$

Prove: *ABCD* is a parallelogram.

Statements	Reasons
1. $\overline{AB} \cong \overline{DC}$, $\angle ACD \cong \angle CAB$	1. Given
2. $\overline{AC} \cong \overline{AC}$	2. Reflexive Property of Congruence
3. $\triangle DCA \cong \triangle BAC$	3. SAS Triangle Congruence Theorem
4. $\overline{AD} \cong \overline{BC}$	4. CPCTC
5. *ABCD* is a parallelogram.	5. Converse of the Opposite Sides of a Parallelogram Theorem

Do the Math

Write a two-column proof to prove that the same figure *ABCD* is a parallelogram. Use a theorem other than the Converse of the Opposite Sides of a Parallelogram Theorem.

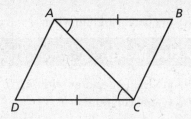

Given: $\overline{AB} \cong \overline{DC}$, $\angle ACD \cong \angle CAB$

Prove: *ABCD* is a parallelogram.

Statements	Reasons

Learn the Math

EXAMPLE 2 A tabletop can be modeled by *PQRS*. For what values of *x* and *y* is *PQRS* a parallelogram?

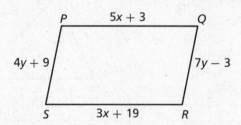

For *PQRS* to be a parallelogram, $\overline{PQ} \cong \overline{SR}$ and $\overline{PS} \cong \overline{QR}$.

Find the values of *x* and *y*.

$\overline{PQ} \cong \overline{SR}$ $\overline{PS} \cong \overline{QR}$

$PQ = SR$ $PS = QR$

$5x + 3 = 3x + 19$ $4y + 9 = 7y - 3$

$2x + 3 = 19$ $9 = 3y - 3$

$2x = 16$ $12 = 3y$

$x = 8$ $4 = y$

PQRS is a parallelogram when $x = 8$ and $y = 4$.

Do the Math

Wally modeled a window with *FGHJ*. For what values of *x* and *y* is *FGHJ* a parallelogram?

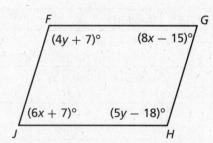

Name _____

LESSON 11.2
More Practice

ONLINE
Video Tutorials and
Interactive Examples

Determine whether the quadrilateral is a parallelogram. Justify your answer.

1.

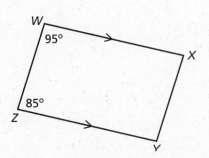

2.

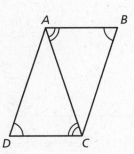

_____

_____

3.

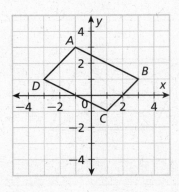

4.

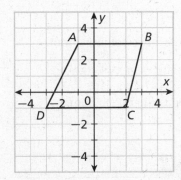

_____

_____

Find the values of the variables that make *JKLM* a parallelogram.

5.

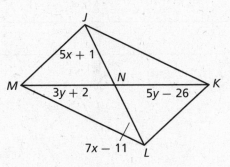

6.

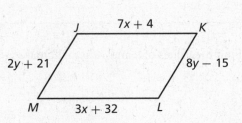

_____

_____

7. **Math on the Spot** Show that $ABCD$ is a parallelogram for $x = 5$ and $y = 2$.

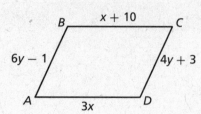

_____

_____

8. **Construct Arguments** Explain why a quadrilateral with vertices $W(6, 5)$, $X(7, 2)$, $Y(9, 3)$, and $Z(8, 6)$ is a parallelogram.

_____

_____

9. **Reason** Write a two column-proof.

   Given: $\overline{LK} \cong \overline{NK}$, $\angle PLK \cong \angle MNK$

   Prove: $LMNP$ is a parallelogram.

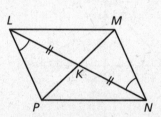

Statements	Reasons

10. Find the values of x and y that will make $ABCD$ a parallelogram.

   (A) $x = 15, y = 16$

   (B) $x = 2, y = 8$

   (C) $x = 2, y = 16$

   (D) $x = 15, y = 8$

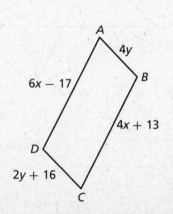

Step It Out

Learn the Math

EXAMPLE 1 The coordinate grid shows rhombus *ABCD*. Verify that the diagonals are perpendicular.

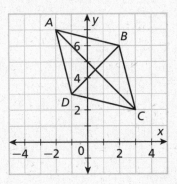

To verify the diagonals are perpendicular, find the slope of each diagonal.

slope of $\overline{AC} = \dfrac{7-2}{-2-3} = \dfrac{5}{-5} = -1$

slope of $\overline{BD} = \dfrac{6-3}{2-(-1)} = \dfrac{3}{3} = 1$

The slopes of the diagonals are opposite reciprocals of each other, so the diagonals are perpendicular.

Do the Math

The coordinate grid shows rhombus *FGHJ*. Verify that the diagonals are perpendicular.

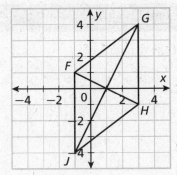

153

Learn the Math

EXAMPLE 2 ▶ A television screen is represented by rectangle *ABCD*. The length of $\overline{AC}$ is $2x + 19$ inches. The length of $\overline{BD}$ is $5x - 20$ inches. What is the length of each diagonal of the television? What is the length of $\overline{BC}$?

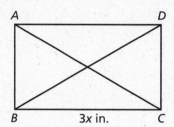

ABCD is a rectangle, so the diagonals are equal to each other.

$$AC = BD$$
$$2x + 19 = 5x - 20$$
$$19 = 3x - 20$$
$$39 = 3x$$
$$13 = x$$

Substitute in the expression for *AC* to find the length of the diagonals.

$$AC = 2(13) + 19 = 26 + 19 = 45$$

The length of a diagonal is 45 inches.

Substitute in the expression for *BC* to find the length.

$$BC = 3(13) = 39$$

The length of $\overline{BC}$ is 39 inches.

Do the Math

FGHJ represents a different television. What is the length of the diagonal of the television? The measurements are in inches.

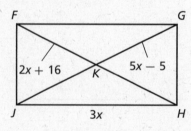

Name _____

LESSON 11.3
More Practice

ONLINE
Video Tutorials and
Interactive Examples

Each parallelogram is a rectangle. Find the length of the diagonals.

1. $WY = 6x + 1, XZ = 9x - 26$

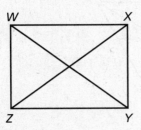

2. $QS = 8x - 11, RT = 4x + 21$

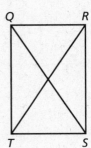

_____   _____

Each parallelogram is a rhombus. Find the side length.

3. CD

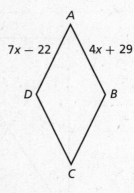

4. FJ

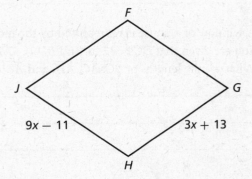

_____   _____

Each parallelogram is a rhombus. Find the angle measure.

5. $m\angle PGH = (8x + 3)°$

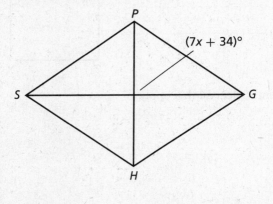

6. $m\angle MNK = (13x + 1)°$

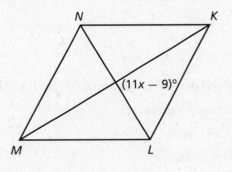

_____   _____

7. Math on the Spot *ABCD* is a rhombus. Find each measure.

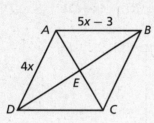

DC

$5x - 3$

$4x$

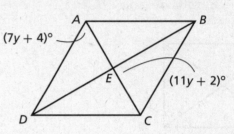

m∠*ADB*

$(7y + 4)°$

$(11y + 2)°$

_____

_____

8. Critique Reasoning Lena states that if a parallelogram has all right angles, then it cannot ever be a rhombus. Is she correct? Explain your reasoning.

_____

_____

_____

9. A window of a house is represented by the model. You are given that *DC* = 32 in. and *BD* = 57.7 in. What are the lengths of $\overline{BC}$, $\overline{AC}$, $\overline{AD}$, and $\overline{AB}$?

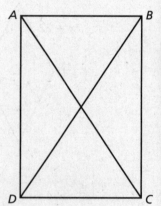

_____

_____

_____

10. Reason Are you given enough information to conclude that *WXYZ* is a square? Explain.

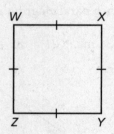

_____

_____

11. For which types of quadrilaterals are the diagonals congruent? Select all that apply.

Ⓐ parallelogram

Ⓑ rectangle

Ⓒ rhombus

Ⓓ square

Ⓔ trapezoid

Step It Out

Learn the Math

EXAMPLE 1 Prove that if the diagonals of a parallelogram are congruent, then the parallelogram is a rectangle.

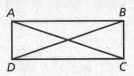

Given: ABCD is a parallelogram; $\overline{AC} \cong \overline{BD}$
Prove: ABCD is a rectangle.

Statements	Reasons
1. ABCD is a parallelogram; $\overline{AC} \cong \overline{BD}$	1. Given
2. $\overline{AB} \cong \overline{CD}$	2. Opposite Sides of a Parallelogram Theorem
3. $\overline{AD} \cong \overline{AD}$	3. Reflexive Property of Congruence
4. $\triangle ABD \cong \triangle DCA$	4. SSS Triangle Congruence Theorem
5. $\angle BAD \cong \angle CDA$	5. CPCTC
6. $m\angle BAD = m\angle CDA$	6. Definition of Congruent Angles
7. $m\angle BAD + m\angle CDA = 180°$	7. Consecutive Interior Angles Theorem
8. $m\angle BAD + m\angle BAD = 180°$	8. Substitution
9. $2m\angle BAD = 180°$	9. Simplify
10. $m\angle BAD = 90°$	10. Division Property of Equality

Do the Math

Complete the proof to show that each angle in ABCD is a right angle.

Learn the Math

EXAMPLE 2 Write a paragraph proof to prove that if one pair of consecutive sides of a parallelogram are congruent, then the parallelogram is a rhombus.

Given: PQRS is a parallelogram; $\overline{PQ} \cong \overline{PS}$
Prove: PQRS is a rhombus.

PQRS is a parallelogram, so by the Opposite Sides of a Parallelogram Theorem, $\overline{PQ} \cong \overline{RS}$ and $\overline{PS} \cong \overline{QR}$. $\overline{PQ} \cong \overline{PS}$, so by the Transitive Property of Congruence, $\overline{PQ} \cong \overline{QR}$. All four sides of the parallelogram are congruent, so PQRS is a rhombus by definition.

Do the Math

Prove that if one pair of consecutive sides of a parallelogram are congruent, then the parallelogram is a rhombus using an indirect proof.

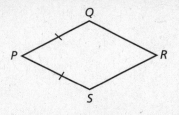

Learn the Math

EXAMPLE 3 Use the given information to determine whether the conclusion about *ABCD* is valid.

Given: $\overline{AB} \cong \overline{CD}$, $\overline{AB} \parallel \overline{CD}$, $\overline{AC} \cong \overline{BD}$

Conclusion: *ABCD* is a rectangle.

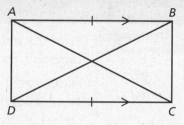

$\overline{AB} \cong \overline{CD}$ and $\overline{AB} \parallel \overline{CD}$. One pair of opposite sides are congruent and parallel, so *ABCD* is a parallelogram.

$\overline{AC} \cong \overline{BD}$. The diagonals of the parallelogram are congruent, so *ABCD* is a rectangle.

Do the Math

Use the given information to determine whether the conclusion about *WXYZ* is valid.

Given: $\overline{WX} \parallel \overline{YZ}$, $\overline{WZ} \parallel \overline{XY}$, $\overline{XY} \cong \overline{YZ}$

Conclusion: *WXYZ* is a rhombus.

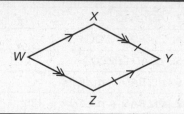

Learn the Math

EXAMPLE 4 Determine whether parallelogram *PQRS* is a rectangle, rhombus, or square.

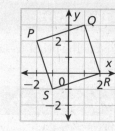

Determine if *PQRS* is a rectangle.

$PR = \sqrt{(-2-2)^2 + (2-0)^2} = \sqrt{16+4} = \sqrt{20}$

$QS = \sqrt{\left(1-(-1)\right)^2 + \left(3-(-1)\right)^2} = \sqrt{4+16} = \sqrt{20}$

$PR = QS$, so *PQRS* is a rectangle.

Determine if *PQRS* is a rhombus.

slope of $\overline{PR} = \dfrac{2-0}{-2-2} = -\dfrac{1}{2}$; slope of $\overline{QS} = \dfrac{3-(-1)}{1-(-1)} = 2$

$\overline{PR} \perp \overline{QS}$, so *PQRS* is a rhombus. *PQRS* is a rectangle and a rhombus, so *PQRS* is a square.

Do the Math

Determine whether parallelogram *KLMN*, with vertices $K(-2, 4)$, $L(4, 2)$, $M(3, -1)$, and $N(-3, 1)$ is a rectangle, rhombus, or square.

Name _____

Each quadrilateral is a parallelogram. Determine if you have enough
information to determine if each parallelogram is a rhombus.
Explain your reasoning.

1.

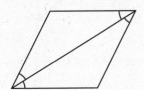

2.

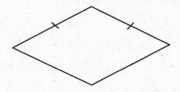

_____   _____

_____   _____

_____   _____

Determine whether the parallelogram is a rectangle, rhombus, or square. List all names that apply.

3.

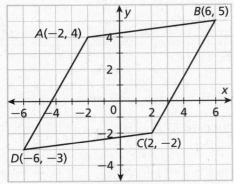

4.

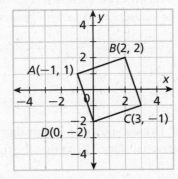

_____   _____

Find the value of *x* that makes each parallelogram the given type.

5. rectangle

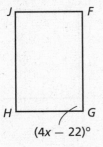

$(4x - 22)°$

6. rhombus

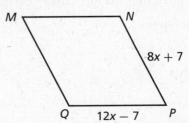

$8x + 7$

$12x - 7$

_____   _____

7. **Math on the Spot** Determine if the conclusion is valid. If not, tell what additional information is needed to make it valid.

A. Given: $\overline{PQ} \cong \overline{RS}$, $\overline{PS} \cong \overline{QR}$, $\overline{PQ} \perp \overline{QR}$, and $\overline{PR} \perp \overline{QS}$
Conclusion: PQRS is a square.

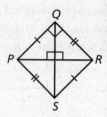

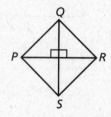

B. Given: $\overline{PR} \perp \overline{QS}$
Conclusion: PQRS is a rhombus.

8. **Critique Reasoning** Michelle maps her property on a coordinate plane. She knows the property is shaped like a parallelogram. The vertices of the property on her map are $A(1, -6)$, $B(2, 8)$, $C(12, 8)$, and $D(11, -6)$. She states that her property is also a rectangle. Is she correct? Explain your reasoning.

9. **Open Ended** Draw a square on a coordinate plane that does not have vertical or horizontal sides. Verify that the figure you drew is a square.

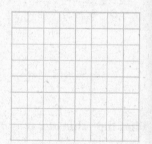

10. Using the given information, classify the quadrilateral. Select all that apply.

Ⓐ parallelogram
Ⓑ rectangle
Ⓒ rhombus
Ⓓ square
Ⓔ trapezoid

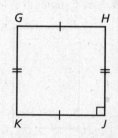

Step It Out

Learn the Math

EXAMPLE 1 Prove that if a quadrilateral is a kite, then its diagonals are perpendicular.

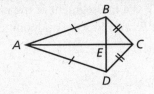

Given: $\overline{AB} \cong \overline{AD}$ and $\overline{BC} \cong \overline{DC}$

Prove: $\overline{AC} \perp \overline{BD}$

Statements	Reasons
1. $\overline{AB} \cong \overline{AD}$ and $\overline{BC} \cong \overline{DC}$	1. Given
2. $\overline{AC} \cong \overline{AC}$	2. Reflexive Property of Congruence
3. $\triangle ABC \cong \triangle ADC$	3. SSS Triangle Congruence Theorem
4. $\angle BCA \cong \angle DCA$	4. CPCTC
5. $\overline{CE} \cong \overline{CE}$	5. Reflexive Property of Congruence
6. $\triangle BCE \cong \triangle DCE$	6. SAS Triangle Congruence
7. $\angle BEC \cong \angle DEC$	7. CPCTC
8. $m\angle BEC = m\angle DEC$	8. Definition of Congruent Angles
9. $m\angle BEC + m\angle DEC = 180°$	9. Linear Pair Theorem
10. $m\angle BEC + m\angle BEC = 180°$	10. Substitution
11. $2m\angle BEC = 180°$	11. Simplify
12. $m\angle BEC = 90°$	12. Division Property of Equality
13. $\overline{AC} \perp \overline{BD}$	13. Definition of Perpendicular Lines

Do the Math

Prove that if a quadrilateral is a kite, then at least one pair of opposite angles are congruent by an indirect proof.

Learn the Math

EXAMPLE 2 Find the length of $\overline{BC}$.

$\overline{AB} \parallel \overline{CD}$ and $\angle C \cong \angle D$, so $ABCD$ is an isosceles trapezoid, and $\overline{AD} \cong \overline{BC}$.

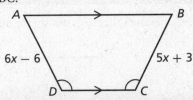

$6x - 6 = 5x + 3$

$x - 6 = 3$

$x = 9$

$BC = 5(9) + 3 = 48$

Do the Math

Find the measure of $\angle J$.

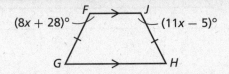

Learn the Math

EXAMPLE 3 Find *SR*.

$\overline{TV}$ is a midsegment of trapezoid *PQRS* because *T* is the midpoint of $\overline{PS}$ and *V* is the midpoint of $\overline{QR}$.

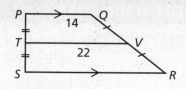

$$TV = \frac{PQ + SR}{2}$$

$$22 = \frac{14 + SR}{2}$$

$$44 = 14 + SR$$

$$30 = SR$$

Do the Math

Find *CD*.

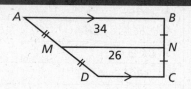

Learn the Math

EXAMPLE 4 Describe any reflection symmetry and rotational symmetry in *WXYZ*.

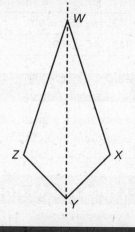

WXYZ has reflection symmetry across a vertical line through *W* and *Y*.

WXYZ does not have any rotational symmetry. There is no angle by which *WXYZ* can be rotated so that it can be mapped on to itself.

Do the Math

Describe any reflection symmetry and rotational symmetry in *KLMN*.

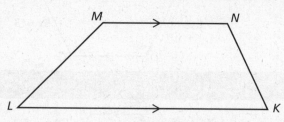

Find the given measure.

1. m∠B

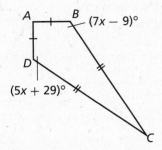

2. JH

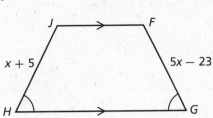

3. PQ

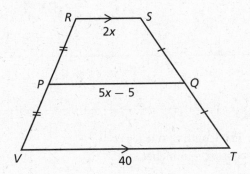

4. m∠EFD

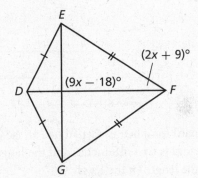

Does the figure have rotational symmetry or reflection symmetry? If so, then describe the symmetry.

5.

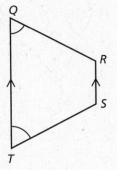

6.

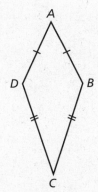

7. Math on the Spot Alicia is using a pattern to make a kite and she must cover the outer edges with a cloth binding. There are 2 feet of binding in one package. What is the total amount of binding needed to cover the edges of the kite? How many packages of binding must Alicia buy?

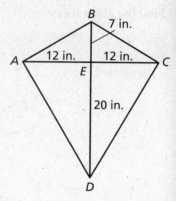

_____

_____

_____

8. Critique Reasoning Brooke states that from the diagram, she knows that the measure of ∠A is 68°. Does Brooke have enough information to make this conclusion? Explain your reasoning.

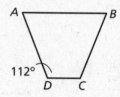

_____

_____

_____

9. A headboard for a bed is shaped like an isosceles trapezoid. The length of one leg of the trapezoid is $6x + 18$ inches and the length of the other leg is $8x + 6$ inches. What is the length of the legs?

_____

_____

10. Find m∠X.

Ⓐ 45°

Ⓑ 54°

Ⓒ 72°

Ⓓ 144°

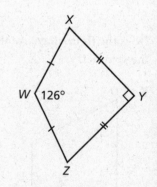

Step It Out

Learn the Math

> **EXAMPLE 1**

Andrew draws a quadrilateral, *ABCD*, then uses a projector to enlarge his drawing to trace it, forming similar quadrilateral *FGHJ*. What are the lengths of $\overline{GH}$ and $\overline{HJ}$?

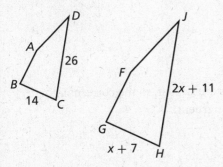

The quadrilaterals are similar, so the corresponding sides are proportional.

$$\frac{GH}{BC} = \frac{HJ}{CD}$$

$$\frac{x+7}{14} = \frac{2x+11}{26}$$

$$14(2x + 11) = 26(x + 7)$$

$$28x + 154 = 26x + 182$$

$$2x + 154 = 182$$

$$2x = 28$$

$$x = 14$$

$$GH = 14 + 7 = 21$$

$$HJ = 2(14) + 11 = 39$$

QRST and *WXYZ* are similar parallelograms. Find the measure of ∠*W*.

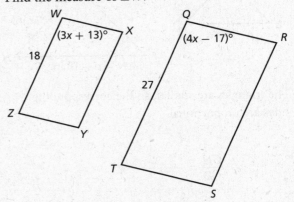

The parallelograms are similar, so the corresponding angles are congruent.

$$\angle W \cong \angle Q$$

$$m\angle W = m\angle Q$$

$$3x + 13 = 4x - 17$$

$$13 = x - 17$$

$$30 = x$$

$$m\angle W = \left(3(30) + 13\right)° = 103°$$

Do the Math

A. The two flags are folded into triangles. The triangles are similar. Find the lengths of $\overline{FH}$ and $\overline{GH}$.

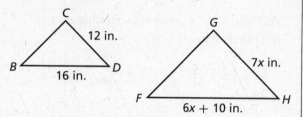

The triangles are similar, so the corresponding sides are proportional.

$$\frac{GH}{CD} = \frac{\boxed{}}{\boxed{}}$$

$$\frac{7x}{12} = \frac{\boxed{}}{\boxed{}}$$

$$12\left(\boxed{}\right) = \boxed{}(7x)$$

$$\boxed{}x + \boxed{} = \boxed{}x$$

$$\boxed{} = \boxed{}x$$

$$\boxed{} = x$$

$$FH = 6\left(\boxed{}\right) + 10 = \boxed{} \text{ in.}$$

$$GH = 7\left(\boxed{}\right) = \boxed{} \text{ in.}$$

B. $\triangle ABC$ and $\triangle LMN$ are similar triangles. Find the measure of $\angle M$.

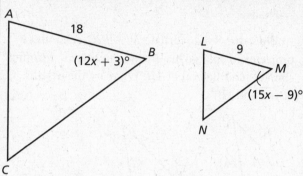

The triangles are similar, so the corresponding angles are congruent.

$$\angle B \cong \angle \boxed{}$$

$$m\angle B = m\angle \boxed{}$$

$$12x + 3 = \boxed{}$$

$$3 = \boxed{}x - 9$$

$$\boxed{} = \boxed{}x$$

$$\boxed{} = x$$

$$m\angle M = \left(15\left(\boxed{}\right) - 9\right)^\circ = \boxed{}^\circ$$

Name

LESSON 12.1
More Practice

ONLINE
Video Tutorials and
Interactive Examples

Determine whether each pair of figures is similar using similarity transformations. Explain your reasoning.

1. *ABCD* to *FGHJ*

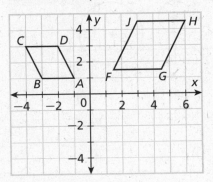

2. △*DEF* to △*KLM*

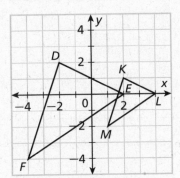

_____

_____

_____

_____

Figure *JKLM* is similar to figure *WXYZ*. Find the given length.

3. *WZ*

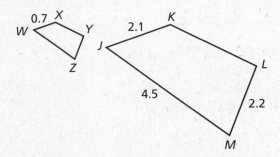

4. *JM*

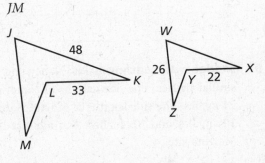

_____

_____

Determine whether each sequence of transformations produces a pair of similar figures. Explain your reasoning.

5. First: $(x, y) \rightarrow (3x, 3y)$

Second: $(x, y) \rightarrow (x - 4, y + 3)$

_____

_____

6. First: $(x, y) \rightarrow (-x, y)$

Second: $(x, y) \rightarrow \left(x, \frac{1}{2}y\right)$

_____

_____

7. Math on the Spot Prove that circle A with center $(0, 2)$ and radius 1 is similar to circle B with center $(4, 1)$ and radius 2.

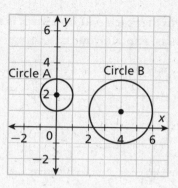

_____

_____

_____

8. Reason Two stores are shaped like rectangles. Store A is 125 feet long and 80 feet wide. Store B is 100 feet long and 60 feet wide. Do the stores form similar rectangles? Explain your reasoning. If they do not form similar rectangles, change one dimension so the rectangles are similar.

_____

_____

_____

9. Model with Mathematics Nancy and Martin are making kites. The kites are similar figures. The side lengths of Nancy's kite are 16 inches, 16 inches, 24 inches, and 24 inches. The side lengths of Martin's kite are $(5x + 5)$ inches, $(5x + 5)$ inches, $10x$ inches, and $10x$ inches. Assume that $10x > 5x + 5$. Find the perimeter of Martin's kite.

_____

_____

_____

10. Triangle ABC is similar to triangle PQR. Find BC.

- (A) 30.25
- (B) 32
- (C) 36
- (D) 64

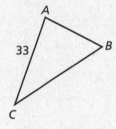

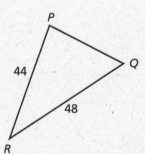

Step It Out

Learn the Math

EXAMPLE 1   The legs of a tray table are represented by $\overline{DE}$ and $\overline{FG}$. The top of the table is parallel to the ground. Find the distance between the bottom of the legs, *FE*.

$\overline{DG} \parallel \overline{FE}$, so $\angle DGH \cong \angle EFH$ by the Alternate Interior Angles Theorem. $\angle FHE \cong \angle GHD$ by the Vertical Angles Theorem. $\triangle FHE \sim \triangle GHD$ by the AA Triangle Similarity Theorem. Now we can find *FE*.

$$\frac{FE}{12} = \frac{24}{16}$$
$$16(FE) = 288$$
$$FE = 18$$

The distance between the bottom of the legs is 18 inches.

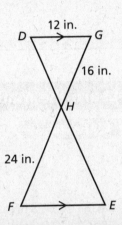

Do the Math

Find the value of *x*.

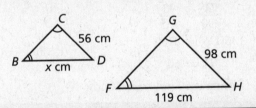

Learn the Math

EXAMPLE 2   Find the value of *x*.

Determine if the corresponding sides are proportional.

$$\frac{RS}{JK} = \frac{13.5}{18} = \frac{3}{4} \qquad \frac{RT}{JL} = \frac{15}{20} = \frac{3}{4}$$

The corresponding angles, $\angle R$ and $\angle J$ are congruent. The triangles are similar by the SAS Triangle Similarity Theorem.

$$\frac{x}{26} = \frac{15}{20}$$
$$20x = 390$$
$$x = 19.5$$

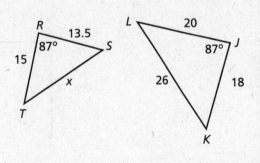

Do the Math

Find the value of x.

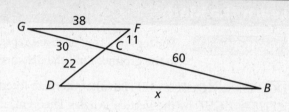

Learn the Math

EXAMPLE 3   Donna is standing on one side of a river across from her friend Sandy. She wants to determine how far she is from Sandy. Donna measures distances on her side of the river and will use these distances to find how far she is from Sandy. Let D be Donna's location and S be Sandy's location.

$\angle ACB \cong \angle DCS$ because they are vertical angles.
$\angle BAC \cong \angle SDC$ because they are right angles. So,
$\triangle ABC \sim \triangle DSC$ by the AA Triangle Similarity Theorem.

Find DS.

$$\frac{DS}{90} = \frac{90}{135}$$
$$135(DS) = 8100$$
$$DS = 60$$

Donna is 60 feet from Sandy.

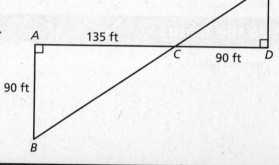

Do the Math

At a different location along the river, Francis stands across the river from Diego. He uses the same method as above to find his distance from Diego. How far is Francis from Diego?

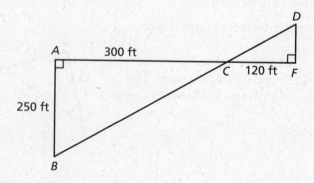

Determine whether each pair of triangles is similar. Justify your reasoning.

1. △ABC and △DEF

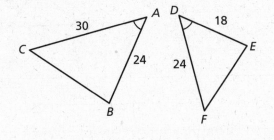

_____

_____

2. △JMN and △JKL

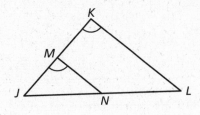

_____

_____

3. △ABC and △XYZ

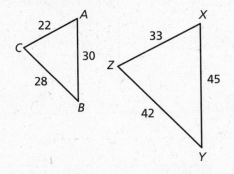

_____

_____

4. △PQR and △TSR

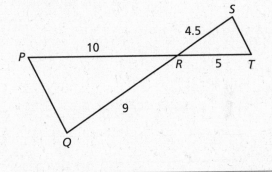

_____

_____

Determine whether each pair of triangles is similar. If possible, find the value of x. Justify your answers.

5.

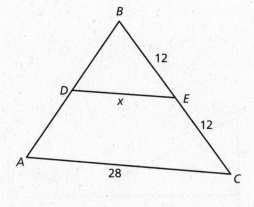

_____

_____

6.

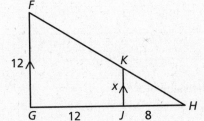

_____

_____

7. **Math on the Spot** Explain why $\triangle PQR \sim \triangle TSR$, and then find SR.

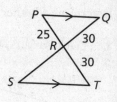

_____

_____

_____

8. **Critique Reasoning** James states that he can show that $\triangle ABC$ is similar to $\triangle EDC$. Kirk says that there is not enough information to show that the triangles are similar. Who is correct? Explain your reasoning.

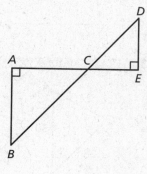

_____

_____

_____

9. **Model with Mathematics** Two trees are on opposite sides of a ravine at D and E. Sara marks the position at E, turns 90°, and walks to point C and marks the point and continues to A. She marks the point, turns 90°, and walks to point B, which is in line with points C and D. What is the distance between the two trees?

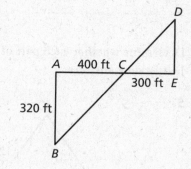

_____

_____

_____

10. Find the value of x.

Ⓐ 6.7

Ⓑ 13.4

Ⓒ 20.1

Ⓓ 26.8

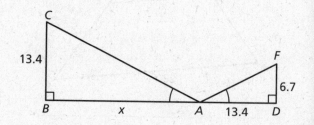

Step It Out

Learn the Math

EXAMPLE 1 ▶ In an auditorium, two aisles meet in front of the stage at point B. Each row of seats is parallel to each other. What is the distance from point F to point B?

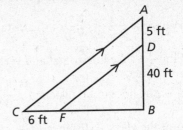

$\overline{AC} \parallel \overline{DF}$, so by the Triangle Proportionality Theorem, $\dfrac{BD}{AD} = \dfrac{BF}{CF}$.

Find BF.

$\dfrac{40}{5} = \dfrac{BF}{6} \rightarrow 240 = 5(BF) \rightarrow 48 = BF$

The distance from point F to point B is 48 feet.

Do the Math

In the same auditorium, find the distance from point G to point D.

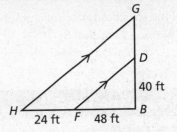

Learn the Math

EXAMPLE 2 ▶ Verify that $\overline{YZ} \parallel \overline{VW}$.

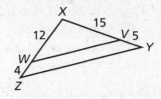

To use the Converse of the Triangle Proportionality Theorem to show that $\overline{YZ} \parallel \overline{VW}$, the proportion $\dfrac{XW}{WZ} = \dfrac{XV}{VY}$ must be true.

$\dfrac{XW}{WZ} \overset{?}{=} \dfrac{XV}{VY}$

$\dfrac{12}{4} \overset{?}{=} \dfrac{15}{5}$

$3 = 3$ The proportion is true, so $\overline{YZ} \parallel \overline{VW}$.

Do the Math

Determine if $\overline{KL} \parallel \overline{MN}$.

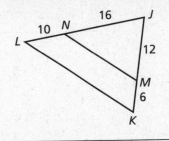

Learn the Math

EXAMPLE 3 Find the coordinates of a point P that divides $\overline{AB}$ into a ratio of 1 to 2 from $A(-2, 7)$ to $B(10, -2)$.

Point P is $\dfrac{1}{2+1} = \dfrac{1}{3}$ of the distance from A to B.

Find $\dfrac{1}{3}$ of the horizontal and vertical distance from A to B.

$\dfrac{1}{3}$ of the horizontal distance $= \dfrac{1}{3}\big(10 - (-2)\big) = 4$

$\dfrac{1}{3}$ of the vertical distance $= \dfrac{1}{3}(-2 - 7) = -3$

Point P is 4 units horizontally and 3 units vertically from point A.

$P(x, y) = (-2 + 4, 7 - 3) = (2, 4)$

Do the Math

Find the coordinates of a point that divides $\overline{AB}$ into a ratio of 1 to 4 from $A(-6, -7)$ to $B(4, 8)$.

Learn the Math

EXAMPLE 4 Construct a point P that partitions a segment into a ratio of 2 to 1 from A to B.

Draw $\overline{AC}$. Place your compass on A and draw an arc through $\overline{AC}$. Label the point D. Move to D and draw an arc of the same length and label it E. Move to E and draw an arc of the same length and label it F. You draw a total of 3 arcs because the ratio is 2 to 1. Draw a line to connect F and B. Construct an angle congruent to $\angle AFB$ with E as the vertex and an angle with D as the vertex. This process creates 3 parallel segments.

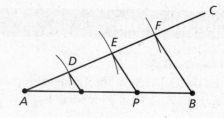

This construction divides $\overline{AB}$ into 3 equal parts. Place point P at the location that divides in the ratio that is 2 parts to 1 part.

Do the Math

Construct a point P that partitions a segment into a ratio of 3 to 1 from X to Y.

X Y

Name _____

Find the length of each segment.

1. $\overline{AD}$

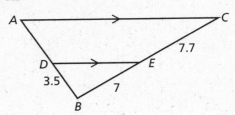

2. $\overline{PS}$

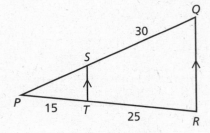

_____

_____

_____

_____

3. $\overline{FH}$

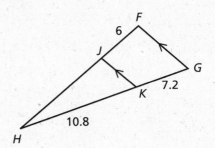

4. $\overline{WX}$

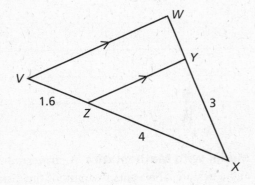

_____

_____

_____

_____

Determine if the segments are parallel. Explain your reasoning.

5. $\overline{AC}$ and $\overline{DE}$

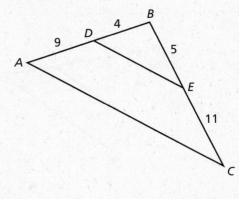

6. $\overline{MN}$ and $\overline{PQ}$

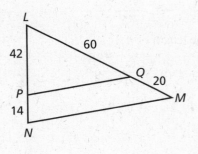

_____

_____

_____

_____

7. **Math on the Spot** Verify that the line segments are parallel. Show that $\overline{DE} \parallel \overline{BC}$.

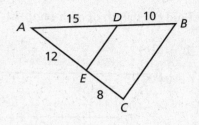

_____

_____

_____

8. **Use Structure** Sherry draws a triangle. The length of side $\overline{AC}$ is 8 inches. The length of side $\overline{AB}$ is 9 inches. She wants to draw a line $\overline{XY}$ that is parallel to $\overline{BC}$. If she draws point X 2 inches from B, how far from C does she need to draw point Y so that $\overline{XY} \parallel \overline{BC}$?

_____

_____

_____

_____

9. **Model with Mathematics** A farmer wants to build a new barn between her house and a pasture. She wants the ratio of the distance from the house to the barn and the barn to the pasture to be 7 to 1. She creates a map on a coordinate plane to represent her farm. She draws a point at $(-20, 2)$ to represent her house and a point at $(12, -6)$ to represent the pasture. At what point should she draw the point that represents the barn?

_____

_____

_____

10. Find the length of $\overline{AB}$.

Ⓐ 8

Ⓑ 12

Ⓒ 16

Ⓓ 36

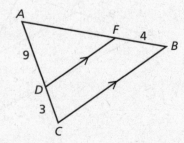

Name _____

Step It Out

Learn the Math

EXAMPLE 1 Write a paragraph proof of the first Geometric Mean Theorem.

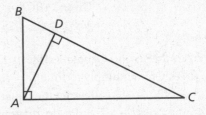

Given: Right triangle ABC with altitude $\overline{AD}$

Prove: $\dfrac{BD}{AD} = \dfrac{AD}{DC}$

You are given a right triangle ABC with an altitude $\overline{AD}$. By the Right Triangle Similarity Theorem, $\triangle ABD \sim \triangle CAD$. By the definition of similar triangles, you know that the corresponding sides of the triangles are proportional. Therefore, $\dfrac{BD}{AD} = \dfrac{AD}{DC}$.

Do the Math

Prove the first Geometric Mean Theorem without using the Right Triangle Similarity Theorem.

Learn the Math

EXAMPLE 2 Arthur builds a ramp to jump his remote control car. Some of the dimensions of the ramp are shown. What is the height of the ramp?

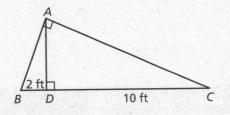

Use the Geometric Mean Theorem to write a proportion to find the height of the ramp, $\overline{AD}$. Let x be the length of $\overline{AD}$.

$\dfrac{2}{x} = \dfrac{x}{10}$

$x^2 = 20$

$x = 2\sqrt{5} \approx 4.5$

The ramp is about 4.5 feet tall.

Do the Math

Find WX.

$\dfrac{a}{\boxed{}} = \dfrac{\boxed{}}{\boxed{}}$

$\boxed{}\, a = \boxed{}$

$a = \boxed{}$

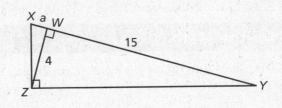

Learn the Math

> **EXAMPLE 3** Write a paragraph proof for the Pythagorean Theorem using geometric means.
>
> Given: ABC is a right triangle.
>
> Prove: $a^2 + b^2 = c^2$

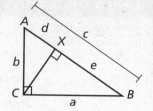

From the second Geometric Mean Theorem, you know that $\frac{e}{a} = \frac{a}{c}$ and $\frac{d}{b} = \frac{b}{c}$. Cross multiply to find $a^2 = ec$ and $b^2 = dc$. Add the equations, $a^2 + b^2 = ec + dc$. Rewrite the equation using the Distributive Property, $a^2 + b^2 = c(e + d)$. From the diagram, you know that $c = e + d$, so substitute, and you have $a^2 + b^2 = c(c)$. Multiply and you have the Pythagorean Theorem, $a^2 + b^2 = c^2$.

Do the Math

Prove the Pythagorean Theorem by finding the area of the square in two different ways and compare the results.

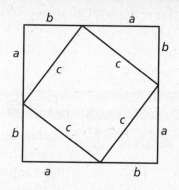

Learn the Math

> **EXAMPLE 4** Determine if 7, 24, 25 and 9, 12, 18 are Pythagorean Triples.

7, 24, 25

$7^2 + 24^2 \overset{?}{=} 25^2$

$49 + 576 \overset{?}{=} 625$

$\qquad 625 = 625$

9, 12, 18

$9^2 + 12^2 \overset{?}{=} 18^2$

$81 + 144 \overset{?}{=} 324$

$\qquad 225 \neq 324$

7, 24, 25 is a Pythagorean Triple. 9, 12, 18 is not a Pythagorean Triple.

Do the Math

Determine if 16, 30, 34 is a Pythagorean Triple.

Name _____

Find *x*, *y*, and *z*. Write your answer in simplest radical form.

1.

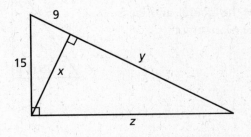

_____

_____

2.

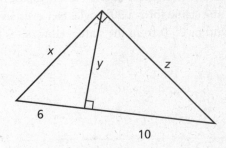

_____

_____

3.

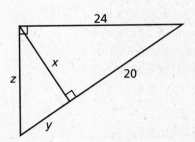

_____

_____

4.

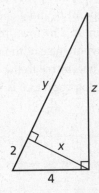

_____

_____

Tell whether the numbers form a Pythagorean triple. Explain.

5. 4, 5, 6

_____

_____

6. 8, 15, 17

_____

_____

7. 10, 24, 26

_____

_____

8. 9, 11, $\sqrt{202}$

_____

_____

9. **Math on the Spot** To estimate the height of a statue, Holly steps away from the statue until her line of sight to the top of the statue and her line of sight to the bottom of the statue form a 90° angle. Her eyes are 5 ft 6 in. above the ground, and she is standing 25 ft from the statue. How tall is the statue to the nearest foot?

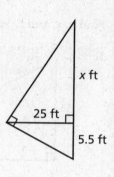

_____

_____

_____

10. **Use Structure** Three trees in a park form a right triangle. An ash tree is located at point *A*, a beech tree at point *B*, and a cherry tree at point *C*. The right angle of the triangle is located at point *A*. The town plants a dogwood tree at point *D*, which is at the intersection of the hypotenuse of the right triangle and the altitude from point *A*. If the distance from the beech tree to the dogwood tree is 60 feet, and the distance from the ash tree to the dogwood tree is 110 feet, what is the distance from the beech tree to the cherry tree?

_____

_____

_____

11. **Reason** Jana wants to find the length of $\overline{LN}$ but she is not sure if she has enough information to do so. Explain how she can find the length. What is the length of $\overline{LN}$?

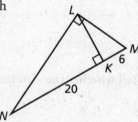

_____

_____

_____

12. Find the length of $\overline{AB}$.

Ⓐ $\dfrac{81}{16}$

Ⓑ $\dfrac{9\sqrt{337}}{16}$

Ⓒ $5\sqrt{7}$

Ⓓ $\sqrt{337}$

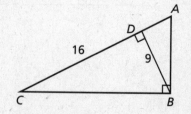

Step It Out

Learn the Math

EXAMPLE 1   Emily is looking at a flagpole 25 feet tall. From where she is standing, the angle made between the ground and the top of the flagpole is 40°. How far away from the flagpole is Emily?

Draw a diagram of the situation. Write the given information.

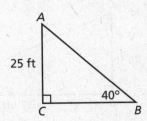

$m\angle B = 40°$

$AC = 25$ ft

$BC = x$

Write the tangent ratio.

$$\tan 40° = \frac{\text{length of side opposite } \angle B}{\text{length of side adjacent } \angle B} = \frac{25}{x}$$

Solve for the unknown distance. Be sure the calculator is in degree mode.

$\tan 40° = \dfrac{25}{x}$ Write the ratio using the identified values.

$x \cdot \tan 40° = \dfrac{25}{x} \cdot x$ Multiply both sides by x.

$x = \dfrac{25}{\tan 40°}$ Divide both sides by $\tan 40°$.

$x \approx 29.8$ Simplify. Round to the nearest tenth of a foot.

Emily is about 29.8 feet from the flagpole.

Do the Math

Cole is looking at a telephone pole 34 feet tall. From where he is standing, the angle made between the ground and the top of the telephone pole is 35°. How far away from the telephone pole is Cole?

$$\tan 35° = \frac{\boxed{}}{\boxed{}}$$

$$x = \frac{\boxed{}}{\boxed{}}$$

$$x \approx \boxed{}$$

Cole is about $\boxed{}$ feet from the telephone pole.

Learn the Math

EXAMPLE 2 A statue is 46 feet tall. Greg is standing 110 feet from the base of the statue. What is the measure of the angle made by the ground and the line to the top of the statue from where Greg is standing?

Draw a diagram of the situation.

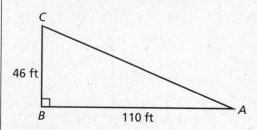

Write the given information.

Length of side opposite $\angle A$: 46 feet

Length of side adjacent $\angle A$: 110 feet

Write the tangent ratio.

$\tan A = \dfrac{46}{110} = \dfrac{23}{55}$

Solve using the inverse tangent.

$m\angle A = \tan^{-1}\dfrac{23}{55}$

$m\angle A \approx 22.7°$

The angle made by the ground and the top of the statue measures 22.7°.

Do the Math

Francisco is looking at a skyscraper. The skyscraper is 456 feet tall. Francisco is 140 feet from the base of the building. What is the angle formed by the ground and the line to the top of the skyscraper from where Francisco is standing?

Write the tangent ratio.

$\tan A = \dfrac{\boxed{}}{\boxed{}}$

Solve using the inverse tangent.

$m\angle A = \tan^{-1}\dfrac{\boxed{}}{\boxed{}}$

$m\angle A \approx \boxed{}°$

The angle made by the ground and the top of the statue measures $\boxed{}°$.

Name

LESSON 13.1
More Practice

ONLINE
Video Tutorials and
Interactive Examples

For each triangle, find the tangent of each given angle.

1. ∠Z

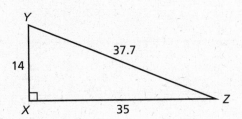

2. ∠J

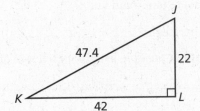

For each triangle, find the given side length. Round to the nearest tenth.

3. *PM*

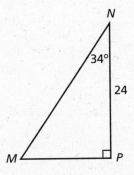

4. *RS*

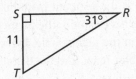

Use a calculator to find the measure of the given angle. Round the value to the nearest tenth of a degree.

5. ∠B

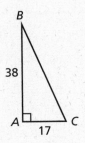

6. ∠F

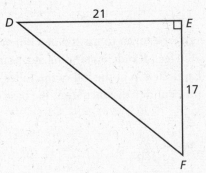

7. **Use Repeated Reasoning** Suppose $\triangle ABC$ and $\triangle XYZ$ are similar right triangles. For $\triangle ABC$, the length of the side opposite $\angle A$ is 13 ft, the length of the side opposite $\angle C$ is 9 ft, and $AC = 15.8$ ft.

   A. What are tan X and tan Z?

   _____

   B. What is a possible length of each side of $\triangle XYZ$?

   _____

8. A cell phone tower is 180 feet tall. A maintenance shed for the tower is 15 feet from the base of the tower. What is the measure of the angle located at the shed formed by the ground and the line to the top of the tower?

   _____

   _____

9. **Reason** Josh is at a park. He knows that the distance from the picnic table to a tree is 124 feet. Josh also knows the angle formed by a segment from his location to the picnic table and a segment from his position to the tree is 54° and that the triangle formed by his position, the picnic table, and the tree is a right triangle, with a right angle at the picnic table. Does Josh have enough to find how far he is from the picnic table? If so, find the distance. If not, explain what information he needs to find the distance.

   _____

   _____

   _____

10. Violet is standing next to a stream that flows under a bridge. The height of a tower that holds the bridge is 84 feet. Violet is 238 feet from the base of the tower. What is the measure of the angle formed by the ground and the top of the tower?

    _____

    _____

11. The height of a tower to the top of a hill on a roller coaster ride at an amusement park is 120 feet. Randy is standing at a point where the angle formed by the ground and the top of the hill of the roller coaster is 56°. Which equation can you use to find Randy's distance from the base of the tower?

    (A) $\tan 56° = \dfrac{120}{x}$

    (B) $\tan 56° = \dfrac{x}{120}$

    (C) $x = \dfrac{\tan 56°}{120}$

    (D) $56 = \dfrac{x}{120}$

Step It Out

Learn the Math

EXAMPLE 1 Find the perimeter of $\triangle LMN$.

Find LM.

$$\cos M = \frac{MN}{LM}$$ Use the cosine ratio.

$$\cos 40° = \frac{8}{LM}$$ Write the ratio using the given values.

$$LM \cdot \cos 40° = \frac{8}{LM} \cdot LM$$ Multiply both sides by LM.

$$LM = \frac{8}{\cos 40°}$$ Divide both sides by $\cos 40°$.

$$LM \approx 10.4 \text{ cm}$$ Use a calculator to evaluate the expression.

Find LN.

$$LN^2 + MN^2 = LM^2$$ Use the Pythagorean Theorem.

$$LN^2 + 8^2 = 10.4^2$$ Substitute.

$$LN^2 + 64 = 108.16$$ Simplify.

$$LN^2 = 44.16$$ Subtract 64 from both sides.

$$LN \approx 6.6 \text{ cm}$$ Take the square root. Round to the nearest tenth.

Calculate the perimeter of $\triangle LMN$.

Perimeter of $\triangle LMN = LM + MN + LN$ Write the perimeter equation.

$$= 10.4 + 8 + 6.6$$ Substitute the known information.

$$= 25$$ Simplify.

The perimeter of $\triangle LMN$ is approximately 25 cm.

Do the Math

Find the perimeter of $\triangle ABC$.

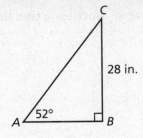

Learn the Math

EXAMPLE 2 A ladder is leaning against a building. The length of the ladder is 24 feet. The point where the ladder touches the side of the building is 23.1 feet above the ground. What is the measure of the angle formed by the ground and the ladder?

Draw a diagram of the situation.

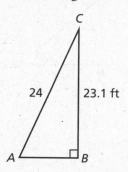

You are given the opposite side length and the hypotenuse, so use the sine ratio.

Solve using the inverse sine ratio. Use a calculator to solve.

$$\sin A = \frac{23.1}{24}$$

$$\sin^{-1}\left(\frac{23.1}{24}\right) = m\angle A$$

$$m\angle A \approx 74.3°$$

The angle made by the ground and the ladder measures 74.3°.

Do the Math

A new tree has been planted. Wires are attached to the tree to help support it. The length of the wire is 8 feet long, and the wires are buried in the ground 5 feet from the base of the tree. What is the measure of the angle A formed by the ground and the wire?

Which trigonometric ratio should you use to find the angle? _____

Use the trigonometric ratio and the inverse function to find the measure of the angle.

$$\underline{\hspace{1cm}} A = \frac{\boxed{}}{\boxed{}}$$

$$m\angle A \approx \boxed{}°$$

The measure of the angle is $\boxed{}°$.

Name _____

LESSON 13.2
More Practice

ONLINE
Video Tutorials and
Interactive Examples

Find each side length. Round to the nearest tenth.

1. *AC*

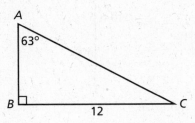

2. *DF*

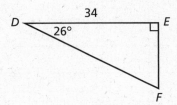

_____ _____

Use a calculator to find the measure of the given angle. Round the value to the nearest tenth of a degree.

3. ∠*K*

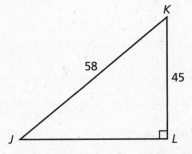

4. ∠*T*

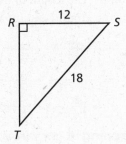

_____ _____

5. **Math on the Spot** Find each length. Round to the nearest hundredth.

A. *PQ*

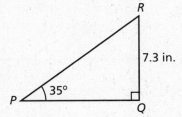

B. *AB*

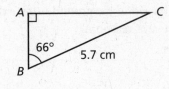

C. *YZ*

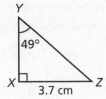

_____ _____ _____

6. Rhonda wants to build a fence around her triangular flower garden shown. Fencing can only be purchased in whole foot sections. How much fencing does she need to purchase to complete her fence?

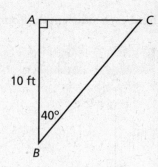

10 ft

_____

_____

_____

7. **Reason** Julio knows the measure of one of the non-right angles of a right triangle and the length of the side opposite the angle. Explain how he can find the length of the side adjacent to the angle without using the tangent ratio.

_____

_____

_____

8. Aki is building a ramp at a doorway to her house. The end of the ramp is 6 inches above the ground. The length of the ramp is 6 feet. What is the measure of the angle formed by the ground and the ramp?

_____

_____

_____

9. **Use Repeated Reasoning** A guy wire is attached to a communications tower at a height of 80 feet above the ground. The length of the guy wire is 130 feet.

A. What is the measure of the angle formed by the tower and the wire?

_____

B. What is the distance between the base of the tower and the point where the guy wire is buried in the ground? Use a trigonometric ratio to find the distance.

_____

C. Could you have found the distance between the base of the tower and the point where the guy wire is buried in the ground using a different trigonometric ratio? Explain your reasoning.

_____

_____

10. Use a calculator to find the measure of $\angle A$.

Ⓐ 0.41°

Ⓑ 24°

Ⓒ 29.3°

Ⓓ 66°

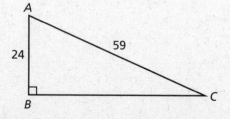

Step It Out

Learn the Math

EXAMPLE 1 ▶ Sketch a 30°-60°-90° triangle in which the shortest leg is 5. Then find the trigonometric ratios for the 30° and 60° angles.

Sketch the triangle.

The triangle is a 30°-60°-90° triangle, so you know the ratio of the side lengths is $x : x\sqrt{3} : 2x$. You know the shortest side is 5, so the side lengths are $5 : 5\sqrt{3} : 10$.

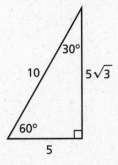

Write the trigonometric ratios of the 30° and 60° angles.

$$\sin 30° = \frac{\text{opp}}{\text{hyp}} = \frac{5}{10} = \frac{1}{2} \qquad\qquad \sin 60° = \frac{\text{opp}}{\text{hyp}} = \frac{5\sqrt{3}}{10} = \frac{\sqrt{3}}{2}$$

$$\cos 30° = \frac{\text{adj}}{\text{hyp}} = \frac{5\sqrt{3}}{10} = \frac{\sqrt{3}}{2} \qquad\qquad \cos 60° = \frac{\text{adj}}{\text{hyp}} = \frac{5}{10} = \frac{1}{2}$$

$$\tan 30° = \frac{\text{opp}}{\text{adj}} = \frac{5}{5\sqrt{3}} = \frac{\sqrt{3}}{3} \qquad\qquad \tan 60° = \frac{\text{opp}}{\text{adj}} = \frac{5\sqrt{3}}{5} = \sqrt{3}$$

Do the Math

Sketch a 45°-45°-90° triangle with a leg length of 8. Then find the trigonometric ratios for either 45° angle.

$$\sin 45° = \frac{\text{opp}}{\text{hyp}} = \frac{\square}{\square} = \frac{\square}{\square}$$

$$\cos 45° = \frac{\text{adj}}{\text{hyp}} = \frac{\square}{\square} = \frac{\square}{\square}$$

$$\tan 45° = \frac{\text{opp}}{\text{adj}} = \frac{\square}{\square} = \square$$

Learn the Math

EXAMPLE 2 Roberto is standing in a park. His position, the position of a picnic table, and the position of a grill form a 45°-45°-90° triangle as shown. The distance from Roberto to the grill is 250 feet. How far is Roberto from the picnic table?

The triangle is a 45°-45°-90°, so you know the ratio of a leg to the hypotenuse is $x : x\sqrt{2}$.

Write and solve an equation.

$x\sqrt{2} = 250$

$x = \dfrac{250}{\sqrt{2}}$

$x \approx 176.8$

Answer the question.

Roberto is about 177 feet from the picnic table.

Do the Math

The location of a bank, a post office, and a school form a 30°-60°-90° triangle as shown. The distance from the bank to the post office is 2300 feet. What is the distance from the bank to the school? What is the distance from the post office to the school?

The triangle is a 30°-60°-90°, so you know the ratio of the shorter leg to the

longer leg is $\boxed{} : \boxed{}$.

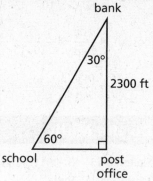

Write and solve an equation.

$\boxed{} = 2300$

$x = \dfrac{2300}{\boxed{}}$

$x \approx \boxed{}$

Answer the questions.

The distance from the bank to the school is $\boxed{}$ feet.

The distance from the post office to the school is $\boxed{}$ feet.

Determine whether each ratio of side lengths belongs to a
45°-45°-90° triangle, a 30°-60°-90° triangle, or neither.

1. $8 : 8 : 8\sqrt{2}$

2. $2\sqrt{3} : 6 : 4\sqrt{3}$

_____

Determine whether each triangle is possible. Show your work.

3.
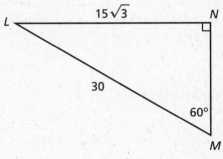

4.
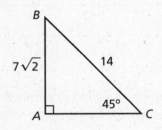

_____

Find the unknown side lengths in each triangle. Give an exact answer.

5.
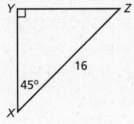

6.
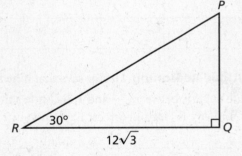

_____

7. **Math on the Spot** Use a trigonometric function to find the value of *x*.

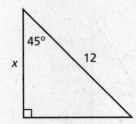

_____

8. **Critique Reasoning** Helen drew the triangle shown at the right. What error did she make in labeling the triangle? Is this a 30°-60°-90° triangle? Explain your reasoning.

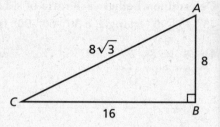

_____

_____

_____

9. **Reason** A window is shaped like the rhombus shown. What are the lengths of the diagonals of the rhombus? Explain your reasoning.

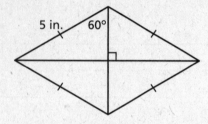

_____

_____

_____

10. **Critique Reasoning** Hector says that if he knows that the value of the sine of an acute angle is between $\frac{\sqrt{3}}{2}$ and 1, he knows that the measure of the angle is between 60° and 90°. Is Hector correct? Explain your reasoning.

_____

_____

_____

11. Find the value of x.

Ⓐ $x = \dfrac{27}{2}$

Ⓑ $x = \dfrac{27\sqrt{2}}{2}$

Ⓒ $x = \dfrac{27\sqrt{3}}{2}$

Ⓓ $x = 27\sqrt{3}$

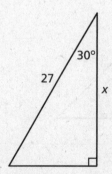

Step It Out

Learn the Math

EXAMPLE 1 Kwame is looking at a mural on the side of a building that is 32 feet tall. The angle formed by the ground and the top of the mural is 37°. Solve the right triangle that represents this situation.

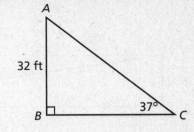

Find AC, BC, and $m\angle A$.

$\sin 37° = \dfrac{32}{AC}$ $\tan 37° = \dfrac{32}{BC}$

$\quad AC = \dfrac{32}{\sin 37°} \approx 53.2 \text{ ft}$ $BC = \dfrac{32}{\tan 37°} \approx 42.5 \text{ ft}$

$\quad m\angle A = 90° - 37° = 53°$

Do the Math

Kwame then looks at another building. This situation is represented by the right triangle. Solve the right triangle.

Learn the Math

EXAMPLE 2 Nancy sees a bird sitting in a tree. She uses a range finder to find that she is 94 feet away from the bird. The angle of elevation to the bird is 28°. How high off the ground is the bird?

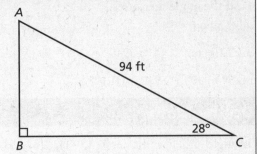

Use the sine function to find the height of the bird in the tree.

$\sin 28° = \dfrac{AB}{94}$

$\quad AB = 94 \cdot \sin 28° \approx 44.1$

The height of the bird in the tree is about 44 feet.

Do the Math

Frank is standing at the top of a hill. He looks down toward a town. He knows that the hill is 120 feet tall and the angle of depression is 8°. How far from the town is Frank?

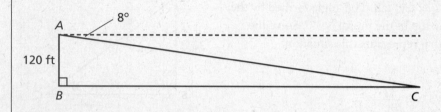

Learn the Math

EXAMPLE 3   Triangle LMN has vertices $L(-2, 3)$, $M(1, 3)$, and $N(-2, -2)$. Find the side lengths to the nearest tenth and the measures of each angle to the nearest degree.

Plot the coordinates on a graph.

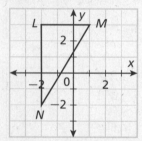

Find the side lengths.

$LM = 3, LN = 5$

$MN = \sqrt{\left(1 - (-2)\right)^2 + \left(3 - (-2)\right)^2} = \sqrt{3^2 + 5^2} = \sqrt{9 + 25} = \sqrt{34} \approx 5.8$

Find the angle measures.

$m\angle L = 90°$

$m\angle M = \tan^{-1}\left(\dfrac{5}{3}\right) \approx 59.0°$

$m\angle N \approx 90° - 59.0° \approx 31.0°$

Do the Math

Triangle XYZ has vertices $X(4, -1)$, $Y(6, -1)$, and $Z(6, -4)$. Find the side lengths to the nearest tenth and the measures of each angle to the nearest degree.

Name _____

LESSON 13.4
More Practice

ONLINE
Video Tutorials and
Interactive Examples

Find the area of each triangle. Round to the nearest tenth.

1.

25

44   49°

_____

2.

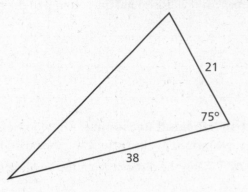

21

75°

38

_____

Solve each triangle. Round side lengths to the nearest tenth and angles to the nearest degree.

3.

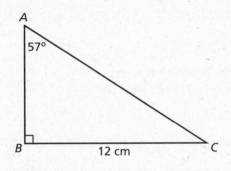

A

57°

B   12 cm   C

_____

_____

_____

4.

X

66°
Z   Y
13 ft

_____

_____

_____

The vertices of each triangle are given. Find the side lengths to the nearest tenth and the measures of each angle to the nearest degree.

5. $A(1, 5), B(1, -1), C(4, -1)$

_____

_____

_____

6. $R(-3, -6), S(2, -6), T(2, 1)$

_____

_____

_____

7. $X(-3, 2), Y(-3, -3), Z(5, -3)$

_____

_____

_____

8. $D(7, 5), E(2, 5), F(2, 1)$

_____

_____

_____

9. **Math on the Spot** If a hill has a percent grade of 52%, what angle does the hill make with a horizontal line? Round to the nearest degree.

_____

_____

_____

10. **Use Repeated Reasoning** An 8-foot-long board is leaning against a building. The angle formed by the ground and the board is 70°.

A. What is the distance from the building to the base of the board?

_____

_____

B. How far up the side of the building does the board reach?

_____

_____

11. Jason is on the ground looking at his friend who is at the top of an observation tower. The tower is 74 feet tall. The angle of elevation from Jason to his friend is 48°. How far is Jason from his friend?

_____

_____

_____

12. **Critique Reasoning** Sandra is standing on a balcony. A flower garden on the ground is 54 feet from her at an angle of depression of 49°. Sandra says that she can calculate her height above the ground by multiplying 54 by cos 49°. Is she correct? Explain your reasoning. Calculate Sandra's height above the ground.

_____

_____

_____

13. Find the measure of ∠A.

Ⓐ 18°

Ⓑ 70°

Ⓒ 72°

Ⓓ 90°

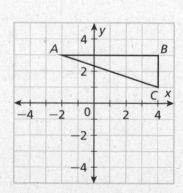

14.1

Step It Out

Learn the Math

EXAMPLE 1 ▶ Brenda and Camry are at points B and C. They are 120 feet apart, as shown. How far is each person from Amanda at point A? Round to the nearest foot.

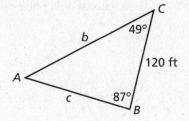

Find the unknown triangle measure.

$$m\angle A + m\angle B + m\angle C = 180° \qquad \text{Triangle Sum Theorem}$$
$$m\angle A + 87° + 49° = 180° \qquad \text{Substitute the known angle measures.}$$
$$m\angle A = 44° \qquad \text{Solve for the measure of } \angle A.$$

Use the Law of Sines to find the distances.

Find the value of b.

$$\frac{\sin B}{b} = \frac{\sin A}{a} \qquad \text{Law of Sines}$$

$$\frac{\sin 87°}{b} = \frac{\sin 44°}{120} \qquad \text{Substitute.}$$

$$b = \frac{120 \sin 87°}{\sin 44°} \qquad \text{Solve for unknown.}$$

$$b \approx 173 \qquad \text{Evaluate.}$$

Find the value of c.

$$\frac{\sin C}{c} = \frac{\sin A}{a}$$

$$\frac{\sin 49°}{c} = \frac{\sin 44°}{120}$$

$$c = \frac{120 \sin 49°}{\sin 44°}$$

$$c \approx 130$$

Brenda is about 130 feet from Amanda, and Camry is about 173 feet from Amanda.

Do the Math

Jackie is looking at a map of a zoo. He notices that the bears and the tigers are 455 feet apart as shown. How far are the bears and the tigers each from the lions? Round to the nearest foot.

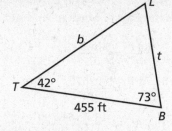

$$m\angle L = \boxed{}°$$

$$\frac{\sin \boxed{}°}{b} = \frac{\sin \boxed{}°}{\boxed{}} \qquad \text{Substitute.} \qquad \frac{\sin \boxed{}°}{t} = \frac{\sin \boxed{}°}{\boxed{}}$$

$$b = \frac{\boxed{} \sin \boxed{}°}{\sin \boxed{}°} \qquad \text{Solve for unknown.} \qquad t = \frac{\boxed{} \sin \boxed{}°}{\sin \boxed{}°}$$

$$b \approx \boxed{} \qquad \text{Evaluate.} \qquad t \approx \boxed{}$$

The bears are about $\boxed{}$ feet from the lions. The tigers are about $\boxed{}$ feet from the lions.

Learn the Math

EXAMPLE 2 In $\triangle ABC$, $AB = 11$ cm, $BC = 14$ cm, and m$\angle A = 57°$. What is AC? Round to the nearest tenth of a centimeter.

Determine how many triangles are possible.

$BC \geq AB$, so there is only one possible triangle.

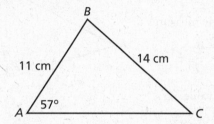

Use the Law of Sines to find the measure of $\angle C$.

$$\frac{\sin 57°}{14} = \frac{\sin C}{11} \qquad \text{Law of Sines}$$

$$\sin C = \frac{11 \sin 57°}{14}$$

$$m\angle C = \sin^{-1}\left(\frac{11 \sin 57°}{14}\right) \approx 41.220 \approx 41.2 \quad \text{Use the inverse sine function.}$$

Find the measure of $\angle B$.

$$m\angle B \approx 180° - 57° - 41.220° \approx 81.780° \approx 81.8°$$

Use the Law of Sines to find AC.

$$\frac{\sin B}{b} = \frac{\sin A}{a} \qquad \text{Law of Sines}$$

$$\frac{\sin 81.780°}{AC} \approx \frac{\sin 57°}{14} \qquad \text{Substitute.}$$

$$AC \approx \frac{14 \sin 81.780°}{\sin 57°} \qquad \text{Solve for } AC.$$

$$AC \approx 16.522 \approx 16.5 \text{ cm} \qquad \text{Evaluate.}$$

Do the Math

In $\triangle ABC$, $AB = 8$ m, $BC = 15$ m, and m$\angle A = 108°$. Round answers to the nearest tenth.

How many triangles are possible?

What is m$\angle C$?

What is m$\angle B$?

What is AC?

Name _____

LESSON 14.1
More Practice

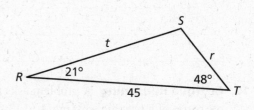

ONLINE
Video Tutorials and
Interactive Examples

Find the unknown measurements using the Law of Sines.
Round your answers to the nearest tenth if necessary.

1.

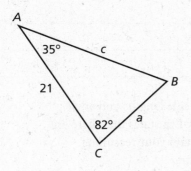

_____

_____

2.

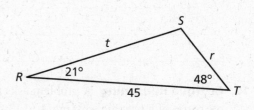

_____

_____

3.

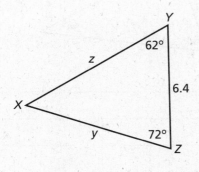

_____

_____

4.

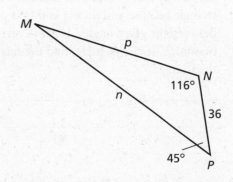

_____

_____

Use the given information to find the unknown angle measures and side lengths of each △ABC,
if possible. If more than one triangle is possible, find both sets of measures. Round to the nearest tenth.

5. m∠A = 43°, a = 24, b = 20

_____

_____

_____

6. m∠A = 62°, a = 15, b = 23

_____

_____

_____

7. m∠A = 34°, a = 31, b = 43

_____

_____

_____

8. m∠A = 98°, a = 15, b = 11

_____

_____

_____

9. **Math on the Spot** Bart is designing a quilt by using triangular patches of different shapes. Determine the number of triangles that he can form using the measurements. Then solve the triangle(s). Round to the nearest tenth.

$$a = 7 \text{ cm}, b = 10 \text{ cm}, \text{m}\angle A = 40°$$

_____

_____

_____

10. **Critique Reasoning** A problem asks to find the unknown side lengths and angle measures of a triangle with $\text{m}\angle A = 130°$, $a = 54$, and $b = 59$. Eva states that there are two possible triangles because $h < a < b$. Is Eva correct? Explain your reasoning. If Eva is not correct, state how many possible triangles there are.

_____

_____

11. **Critique Reasoning** Alex states that you cannot use the Law of Sines to find the unknown lengths of this triangle because you do not know the length of the side between the given angles. Is Alex correct? Explain your reasoning. If it is possible, find the missing measures of the triangle.

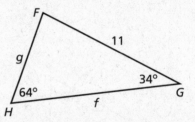

_____

_____

_____

12. Lucy, Monica, and Nathan are raking leaves. Their positions form the triangle shown. How far is Lucy from Monica? Round to the nearest tenth.

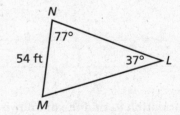

_____

_____

13. Find AB.

 55

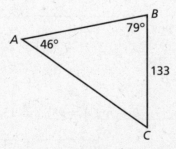

Ⓐ 55

Ⓑ 133

Ⓒ 151.5

Ⓓ 181.5

Step It Out

Learn the Math

EXAMPLE 1 In $\triangle FGH$, $f = 5$, $g = 2.6$, and $h = 4.6$. What are the angle measures of the triangle? Round the intermediate steps to three decimal places and the final answer to one decimal place.

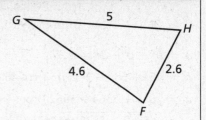

Use the Law of Cosines to find the measure of $\angle G$.

$$g^2 = f^2 + h^2 - 2fh \cos G$$

$$2.6^2 = 5^2 + 4.6^2 - 2(5)(4.6)\cos G$$

$$6.76 = 25 + 21.16 - 46 \cos G$$

$$-39.4 = -46 \cos G$$

$$\frac{39.4}{46} = \cos G$$

$$m\angle G \approx \cos^{-1}\left(\frac{39.4}{46}\right) \approx 31.072° \approx 31.1°$$

Use the Law of Sines to find the measure of $\angle F$.

$$\frac{\sin F}{f} = \frac{\sin G}{g}$$

$$\frac{\sin F}{5} \approx \frac{\sin 31.072°}{2.6}$$

$$\sin F \approx \frac{5 \sin 31.072°}{2.6}$$

$$m\angle F \approx \sin^{-1}\left(\frac{5 \sin 31.072°}{2.6}\right) \approx 82.992° \approx 83.0°$$

Use the Triangle Sum Theorem to find the measure of $\angle H$.

$$m\angle F + m\angle G + m\angle H = 180°$$

$$82.992° + 31.072° + m\angle H \approx 180°$$

$$m\angle H \approx 65.936° \approx 65.9°$$

In $\triangle FGH$, $m\angle F \approx 83.0°$, $m\angle G \approx 31.1°$, and $m\angle H \approx 65.9°$.

Do the Math

In $\triangle ABC$, $a = 5.8$, $b = 5.1$, and $c = 2$. What are the angle measures of the triangle? Round the intermediate steps to three decimal places and the final answer to one decimal place.

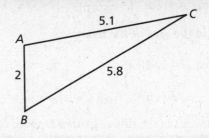

Learn the Math

EXAMPLE 2 Sofia, Claire, and Evelyn are playing catch. Sofia is 45 feet from Claire and 58 feet from Evelyn. The angle made by Claire, Sofia, and Evelyn is 46°. How far is Claire from Evelyn?

$a^2 = b^2 + c^2 - 2bc \cos A$

$a^2 = 45^2 + 58^2 - 2(45)(58)\cos 46°$

$a^2 = 2025 + 3364 - (5520)(\cos 46°)$

$a = \sqrt{5389 - 5520 \cos 46°}$

$a \approx 39.427 \approx 39.4$

Claire is about 39.4 feet from Evelyn.

Do the Math

Tommy, Christy, and Becky are kicking a ball to each other. Tommy is 66 feet from Christy and 51 feet from Becky. The angle made by Christy, Tommy, and Becky is 54°. How far is Christy from Becky?

Learn the Math

EXAMPLE 3 A triangular flower garden has the dimensions shown. Find the area of the garden. Round intermediate steps to three decimal places and the final answer to one decimal place.

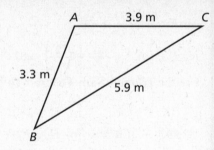

Find the measure of an angle.

$a^2 = b^2 + c^2 - 2bc \cos A$

$5.9^2 = 3.9^2 + 3.3^2 - 2(3.9)(3.3)\cos A$

$34.81 = 15.21 + 10.89 - 25.74 \cos A$

$8.71 = -25.74 \cos A$

$\dfrac{8.71}{-25.74} = \cos A$

$m\angle A \approx \cos^{-1}\left(\dfrac{8.71}{-25.74}\right) \approx 109.778° \approx 109.8°$

Find the area of the triangle.

$\text{Area} = \dfrac{1}{2} bc \sin A$

$\approx \dfrac{1}{2}(3.9)(3.3)\sin 109.778° \approx 6.055 \approx 6.1$

The area of the flower garden is about 6.1 square meters.

Do the Math

Find the area of a triangular piece of wood with side lengths of 34 inches, 24 inches, and 18 inches. Round intermediate steps to three decimal places and the final answer to one decimal place.

Solve each triangle. Round intermediate results to three decimal places and final answers to one decimal place.

1.
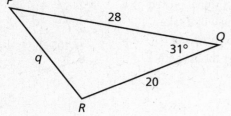

28
Q
31°
q
20
R
P

2.
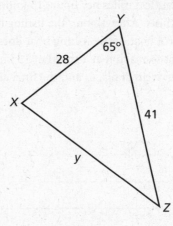

Y
65°
28
41
X
y
Z

_____

_____

_____

_____

3.
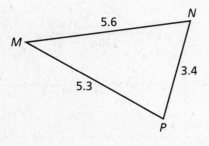

N
5.6
M
3.4
5.3
P

4.
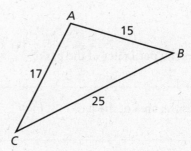

A
15
B
17
25
C

_____

_____

_____

_____

Find the area of each triangle. Round intermediate results to three decimal places and final answers to the nearest tenth of a square unit.

5.
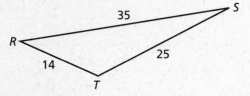

35
S
R
25
14
T

6.
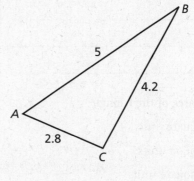

B
5
4.2
A
2.8
C

_____

_____

_____

_____

7. **Math on the Spot** A coast guard patrol boat and a fishing boat leave a dock at the same time on the courses shown. The patrol boat travels at a speed of 15 nautical miles per hour (15 knots), and the fishing boat travels at a speed of 2 knots. After 1 hour, the fishing boat sends a distress signal picked up by the patrol boat. If the fishing boat does not drift, how long will it take the patrol boat to reach it at a speed of 15 knots? Round the intermediate result to three decimal places and the final answer to the nearest thousandth.

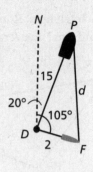

_____

_____

_____

8. **Use Repeated Reasoning** A park is shaped like a triangle. Samantha is standing at the intersection of two sides of the park. The length of one side is 320 yards and the length of the other side is 400 yards. The angle between these two sides is 112°. Round answers to the nearest whole yard.

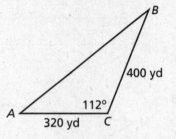

A. What is the perimeter of the park?

_____

B. What is the area of the park?

_____

9. **Critique Reasoning** Jillian states that to find the measures of the angles of the triangle, you can use the Law of Cosines to find the measure of one angle, then use the Law of Sines to find the measure of a second angle, then use the Triangle Sum Theorem to find the third angle. Michael states you can find the measures of each angle using only the Law of Cosines. Who is correct? Explain your reasoning.

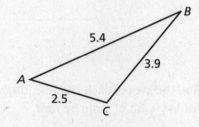

_____

_____

_____

10. Find the area of the triangle.

Ⓐ 9.2 square units

Ⓑ 13 square units

Ⓒ 14.3 square units

Ⓓ 15 square units

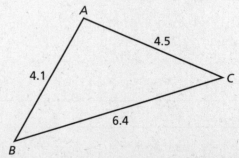

Step It Out

Learn the Math

EXAMPLE 1 Summarize the proof for the Inscribed Angle Theorem, using Case 2, which requires that the center of the circle is inside of the inscribed angle. Draw a diagram to support the summary.

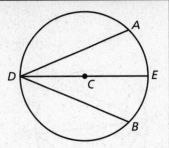

Given: $\angle ADB$ is inscribed in circle C. Point C is inside $\angle ADB$.

Prove: $m\angle ADB = \frac{1}{2}m\widehat{AB}$

Step 1: Draw diameter $\overline{DE}$.

Step 2: $m\angle ADB = m\angle ADE + m\angle EDB$ by the Angle Addition Theorem.

Step 3: $m\widehat{AB} = m\widehat{AE} + m\widehat{EB}$ by the Arc Addition Theorem. $\frac{1}{2}m\widehat{AB} = \frac{1}{2}m\widehat{AE} + \frac{1}{2}m\widehat{EB}$ by the Multiplication Property of Equality.

Step 4: $m\angle EDB = \frac{1}{2}m\widehat{EB}$ and $m\angle ADE = \frac{1}{2}m\widehat{AE}$ by Case 1 of the Inscribed Angle Theorem.

Step 5: $\frac{1}{2}m\widehat{AB} = m\angle ADE + m\angle EDB$ by Substitution of the last two steps.

Step 6: $\frac{1}{2}m\widehat{AB} = m\angle ADB$ by the Angle Addition Theorem.

Do the Math

Summarize the proof for the Inscribed Angle Theorem, using Case 3, which requires that the center of the circle is outside of the inscribed angle. Draw a diagram to support the summary.

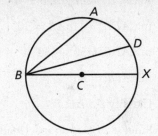

Given: $\angle ABD$ is inscribed in circle C. Point C is outside of $\angle ABD$.

Prove: $m\angle ABD = \frac{1}{2} m\widehat{AD}$

Step 1: Draw diameter $\overline{BX}$.

Step 2: $m\angle ABD = m\angle ABX - m\angle \boxed{}$ by the Angle Subtraction Theorem.

$m\widehat{AD} = m\boxed{} - m\widehat{DX}$ by the Arc Subtraction Theorem.

Step 3: $\frac{1}{2}m\widehat{AD} = \frac{1}{2}m\widehat{AX} - \frac{1}{2}m\widehat{DX}$ by the _____ Property of Equality.

Step 4: $m\angle \boxed{} = \frac{1}{2}m\widehat{AX}$ and $m\angle DBX = \frac{1}{2}m\boxed{}$ by Case 1 of the _____ Angle Theorem.

Step 5: $\frac{1}{2}m\widehat{AD} = m\angle \boxed{} - m\angle \boxed{}$ by Substitution of the last two steps.

Step 6: $\frac{1}{2}m\widehat{AD} = m\angle ABD$ by the Angle Subtraction Theorem.

Learn the Math	**Do the Math**

Learn the Math

> **EXAMPLE 2** ▷ Given the diagram below, find m$\widehat{BE}$ and m∠ADE. Next, classify △BDE, according to type of triangle and justify your answer.

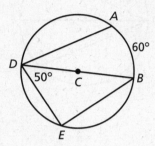

Find m$\widehat{BE}$.

$$m\angle BDE = \frac{1}{2}m\widehat{BE}$$

$$50° = \frac{1}{2}m\widehat{BE}$$

$$100° = m\widehat{BE}$$

Find m∠ADE.

$$m\angle ADE = m\angle BDE + m\angle ADB$$

$$m\angle ADB = \frac{1}{2}m\widehat{AB} = 30°$$

$$m\angle ADE = 50° + 30°$$

$$m\angle ADE = 80°$$

Classify △BDE.

Since ∠BED is an inscribed angle with endpoints that lie on the diameter, $\overline{DB}$, then ∠BED is a right angle. This means that △BDE is a right triangle.

Do the Math

Given the diagram below, find m$\widehat{BD}$ and m∠EAB. Next, classify △DBA, according to type of triangle and justify your answer.

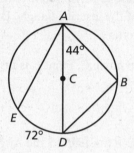

Find m$\widehat{BD}$.

$$m\angle DAB = \frac{1}{2}m\widehat{BD}$$

$$\boxed{}° = \frac{1}{2}m\widehat{BD}$$

$$\boxed{}° = m\widehat{BD}$$

Find m∠EAB.

$$m\angle EAB = m\angle EAD + m\angle DAB$$

$$m\angle EAB = \boxed{}° + \boxed{}°$$

$$m\angle EAB = \boxed{}°$$

Classify △DBA.

Since ∠DBA is an inscribed angle with endpoints that lie on the diameter, $\overline{AD}$, then ∠DBA is

a(n) _____ angle. This means

that △DBA is a(n) _____ triangle.

Name

LESSON 15.1
More Practice

ONLINE
Video Tutorials and
Interactive Examples

For Problems 1–4, use the diagram below to find each indicated measure. Show your work.

1. m$\widehat{DE}$

_____

2. m∠ABE

_____

3. m∠ABD

_____

4. m∠EDB

_____

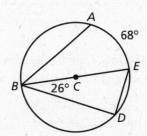

Find the value of x in each circle.

5.

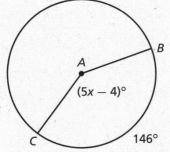

_____

6.

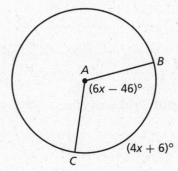

_____

7.

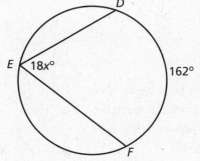

_____

8.

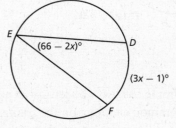

_____

Describe the measures of the arcs of each circle separated by the given inscribed figure. Show your work.

9. equilateral triangle *ABC*

_____

10. isosceles triangle *FGH*, m∠H = 90°

_____

11. **Open Ended** Write and solve a real-world problem that requires use of the Inscribed Angle Theorem to solve. Include a diagram that represents your problem.

_____

_____

_____

12. **Critique Reasoning** Camille describes how to solve the problem to the right by writing the following:

> Divide the measure of ∠DBE by 2. This will give the measure of the intercepted arc.

Given the diagram below, find m$\widehat{DE}$.

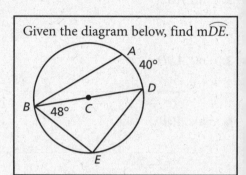

Explain the error in Camille's thinking. Then show the correct steps for solving and the correct answer.

_____

_____

_____

Math on the Spot Find each value.

13. w

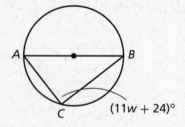

14. m∠JKM

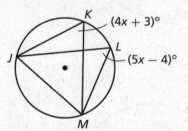

15. A circular frame has two wooden sticks placed inside the frame, with both sticks sharing a common endpoint on the frame. The other endpoints of the sticks touch the frame at two different points on the circle. The sticks form an inscribed angle measure of 58°. What is the measure of the intercepted arc formed by the sticks?

Ⓐ 19°

Ⓑ 29°

Ⓒ 116°

Ⓓ 122°

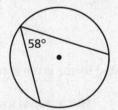

Name _____

Step It Out

Learn the Math

EXAMPLE 1 ▶ Find the measure of each interior angle in the inscribed quadrilateral *ABCD*.

Find the value of *x*.

$$m\angle A + m\angle C = 180°$$
$$(6x - 8)° + (8x - 22)° = 180°$$
$$14x - 30 = 180$$
$$14x = 210$$
$$x = 15$$

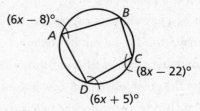

Substitute the value of *x* into the expression for each angle measure.

$$m\angle A = \left(6(15) - 8\right)° = (90 - 8)° = 82°$$
$$m\angle C = \left(8(15) - 22\right)° = (120 - 22)° = 98°$$
$$m\angle D = \left(6(15) + 5\right)° = (90 + 5)° = 95°$$

Find the fourth angle measure by subtracting the sum of the other three angles from the number of degrees found inside a quadrilateral.

$$m\angle B = \left(360 - (82 + 98 + 95)\right) = 85°$$

Do the Math

Find the measure of each angle in *ABCD*.

$$m\angle A + m\angle C = 180°$$

$$\left(\boxed{}a - \boxed{}\right)° + \left(\boxed{}a + \boxed{}\right)° = 180°$$

$$\boxed{}a - \boxed{} = 180$$

$$\boxed{}a = \boxed{}$$

$$a = \boxed{}$$

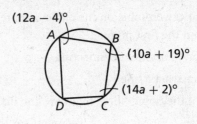

$$m\angle A = \left(12\boxed{} - 4\right)° = \boxed{}°$$

$$m\angle C = \left(14\boxed{} + 2\right)° = \boxed{}°$$

$$m\angle B = \left(10\boxed{} + 19\right)° = \boxed{}°$$

$$m\angle D = \left(\boxed{} - \left(80 + \boxed{} + 100\right)\right)° = \boxed{}°$$

Learn the Math

EXAMPLE 2 Maria is making a design. She wants to inscribe a trapezoid in a circle as part of her design. How can she construct an inscribed trapezoid?

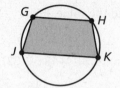

Use a compass to draw a circle.

Plot two points on a circle.

Draw a line segment connecting the points.

Draw a third point on the circle.

Construct a line parallel to the line segment through the third point.

Plot the point where that new line intersects the circle.

Draw two segments for the two legs of this trapezoid.

How do you know this figure is a trapezoid?

This figure is a trapezoid because it is a quadrilateral with exactly one pair of parallel sides.

Do the Math

Damien is making a design. How can he inscribe a kite in a circle as part of his design?

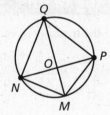

Use a compass to draw a circle.

Plot a point on the circle.

Mark two points on the circle that are _____ distance from the first point.

Draw a segment connecting _____ points.

Construct a line _____ to that segment through the _____ point.

Plot the point where that new line intersects the _____.

Draw _____ segments for the sides of this kite.

How do you know this figure is a kite?

This figure is a kite because it is a quadrilateral with one pair of congruent _____ sides and _____ diagonals.

Name _____

LESSON 15.2
More Practice

ONLINE
Video Tutorials and
Interactive Examples

Find the interior angles of each inscribed quadrilateral. Show your work.

1.

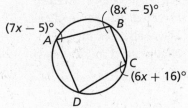

$(7x - 5)°$ A B $(8x - 5)°$
C $(6x + 16)°$
D

_____

_____

2.

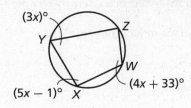

$(3x)°$ Z
Y
W
$(4x + 33)°$
$(5x - 1)°$ X

_____

_____

3.

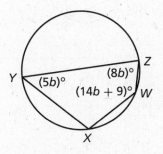

Y $(5b)°$ $(8b)°$ Z
$(14b + 9)°$ W
X

_____

_____

4.

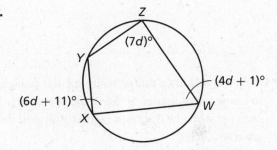

Z
$(7d)°$
Y
$(4d + 1)°$
$(6d + 11)°$ W
X

_____

_____

Find the measure of each chord or arc.

5. $\overline{AB}$

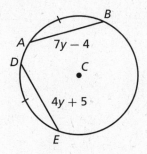

A B
D $7y - 4$
C
$4y + 5$
E

_____

6. $\overparen{AB}$

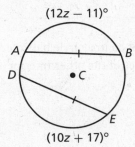

$(12z - 11)°$
A B
D
C
E
$(10z + 17)°$

_____

7. **Use Tools** Describe how to inscribe a rectangle within a circle.

_____

_____

_____

_____

8. **Critique Reasoning** Jackson summarizes the type of quadrilateral inscribed in a circle by writing the following:

Explain the error in Jackson's thinking.

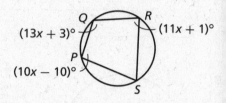

If a quadrilateral inscribed in a circle has perpendicular diagonals, then the quadrilateral must be square.

_____

_____

_____

9. **Math on the Spot** Find the angle measures of *PQRS*.

$(13x + 3)°$

$(10x − 10)°$

$(11x + 1)°$

_____

10. Steven is making a design using regular polygons inscribed in circles. He wants to know the measures of the smallest arcs on each circle. What is the measure of each arc when he inscribes regular polygons with 8, 9, 10, 12, and *n* sides in separate circles?

_____

11. Rhombus *ABCD* is inscribed in a circle. How else can *ABCD* be classified as a polygon? Explain.

_____

_____

_____

12. A quadrilateral inscribed in a circle has interior angle measures of 78° and 93°. What are the measures of the other interior angles?

Ⓐ 82° and 107°

Ⓑ 87° and 102°

Ⓒ 91° and 98°

Ⓓ 95° and 94°

Step It Out

Learn the Math

EXAMPLE 1 ▶ In the diagram below, *XA* is tangent to circle *C*. Describe what must be true, regarding ∠*CAX* and *XB*. Justify your statements.

Draw ∠*CAX*.

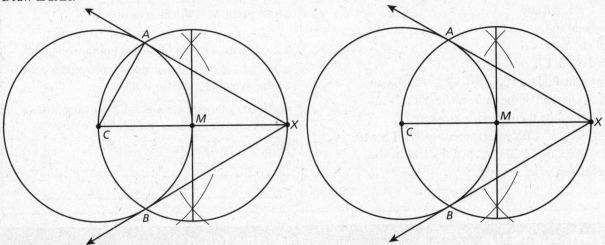

Notice that $\overline{CX}$ is the diameter of circle *M*. Also, notice that ∠*CAX* is an inscribed angle of circle *M*. According to the Inscribed Angle of a Diameter Theorem, ∠*CAX* must be a right angle.

Similarly, ∠*CBX* is also a right angle, meaning that $\overline{CB}$ is perpendicular to $\overline{XB}$. Then $\overline{XB}$ must also be tangent to circle *C* by the Converse of the Tangent-Radius Theorem.

Do the Math

Construct two tangents to a circle, using a compass and straightedge. Complete the steps needed to construct the tangents.

Step 1: Use a compass to draw a circle with center *C*.

Step 2: Mark a point, *P*, on the _____ of the circle.

Step 3: Connect the points ☐ and *P*.

Step 4: Bisect ☐ .

Step 5: Mark the midpoint of the bisected segment as *M*.

Step 6: Place the end of the compass at *M* and open the compass to a width equal to the distance

from ☐ to *M*.

Step 7: Draw a new circle *M* using this setting.

Step 8: Mark the points where the two circles intersect. Label these points *A* and *B*.

Step 9: Use a straightedge to connect *A* with ☐ and *B* with ☐ .

Step 10: ☐ and ☐ are tangents to circle *C*.

Learn the Math	Do the Math

Learn the Math

EXAMPLE 2 Prove *CAXB* is a kite.

Given: $\overrightarrow{XA}$ and $\overrightarrow{XB}$
are tangent to *C*.

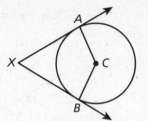

Prove: *CAXB* is a kite.

$\overrightarrow{XA}$ and $\overrightarrow{XB}$ are
tangent to *C* is
given. $\overrightarrow{XA} \perp \overline{CA}$
and $\overrightarrow{XB} \perp \overline{CB}$, by the
Tangent-Radius Theorem. $\overline{CB} \cong \overline{CA}$, because
they are radii of the same circle. Draw $\overline{CX}$.
$\overline{CX} \cong \overline{CX}$ by the Reflexive Property.
$\triangle CAX \cong \triangle CBX$ by Hypotenuse-Leg Theorem.
$\overline{AX} \cong \overline{BX}$ by CPCTC. *CAXB* is a kite by the
definition of a kite.

Do the Math

Describe how to prove the Two-Tangent Theorem by construction.

Plot a point *C*, and construct a circle centered at *C*. Plot a point *X* outside the circle. Draw $\overline{CX}$. Construct the _____ of $\overline{CX}$. Draw point *M* at the intersection of _____ and $\overline{CX}$. Construct a circle with a center at *M* that goes through _____. Label the intersection points of the two circles as *A* and *B*.

By the construction, $\overline{AX}$ and $\overline{BX}$ are tangents, so $\angle CAX$ and $\angle CBX$ are right angles.

How do you know that $\overline{AX} \cong \overline{BX}$?

_____

_____

Learn the Math

EXAMPLE 3 A circular air freshener is secured flush against the top of a wall. It is tangent to the ceiling at point *A*, and tangent to the wall at point *C*. The ceiling and wall meet at point *B*. What are *AB* and *BC*?

Find the value of *x*.

$AB = BC$

$x + 12 = 3x - 12$

$24 = 2x$

$12 = x$

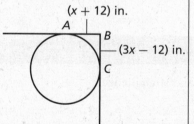

(x + 12) in.

(3x − 12) in.

Substitute 12 for *x* in each expression to check your work.

$AB = 12 + 12$ $BC = 3(12) - 12$

$\quad = 24$ in. $= 24$ in.

Do the Math

A circular drain is located at a corner of a floor. The drain is tangent to one wall at point *A*, and tangent to another wall at point *C*. The two walls meet at Point *B*. What are *AB* and *BC*?

Find the value of *y*.

$AB = BC$ (y + 10) cm

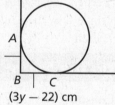

(3y − 22) cm

$y + \boxed{} = \boxed{} y - \boxed{}$

$\boxed{} = \boxed{} y$

$\boxed{} = \boxed{} y$

Substitute the value of *y* in each expression to check your work.

$AB = y + 10$

$\quad = \boxed{} + 10 \qquad BC = 3\left(\boxed{}\right) - 22$

$\quad = \boxed{}$ cm $\qquad\qquad = \boxed{}$ cm

Name

LESSON 15.3
More Practice

ONLINE
Video Tutorials and
Interactive Examples

The segments in each figure are tangent to the circle at the points shown. Find each length.

1.

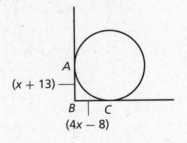

2.

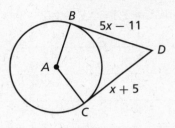

_____   _____

In each circle, *B* and *C* are points of tangency. Find the measures of the inscribed angle and the circumscribed angle.

3.

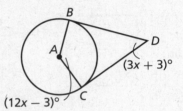

4.

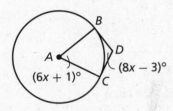

_____   _____

In circle *C*, *A* and *B* are points of tangency. Determine whether each statement is *always* or *sometimes* true. Explain your reasoning.

5. ∠*AXB* ≅ ∠*ACB*

_____

6. ∠*XAC* ≅ ∠*XBC*

_____

7. ∠*AXB* ≅ ∠*XBC*

_____

8. ∠*AXB* and ∠*XAC* are supplementary.

_____

9. ∠*XAC* and ∠*XBC* are supplementary.

_____

10. ∠*ACB* and ∠*AXB* are supplementary.

_____

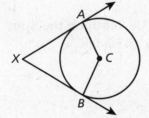

11. Reasoning

Given: Quadrilateral WXYZ is circumscribed about circle A.

Prove: $WX + YZ = XY + WZ$

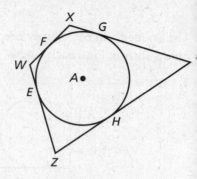

_____

_____

_____

_____

12. Critique Reasoning Marlon solves the problem to the right by writing the following:

$$AB = BC$$
$$x + 14 = 3x - 22$$
$$36 = 2x$$
$$18 = x$$
$$AB = 18 \text{ cm}$$

A circular dartboard is inscribed inside a square frame. The dartboard touches the top of the frame at point A. It touches the right side of the frame at point C. The sides of the square meet at point B. What is AB?

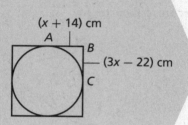

Explain the error in Marlon's work. Then show the correct solution steps and correct answer.

_____

_____

13. Math on the Spot $\overline{BC}$ and $\overline{DC}$ are tangent to A.
Find BC.

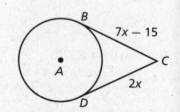

_____

14. Kim takes a small circular piece of construction paper and places two popsicle sticks at the top and right sides of the paper, where each stick touches the circle at a point of tangency, as shown to the right. What is BC?

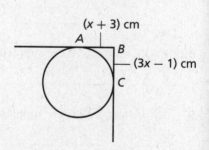

(A) 5 cm

(B) 6 cm

(C) 8 cm

(D) 9 cm

Name _____

Step It Out

Learn the Math

EXAMPLE 1 A circular track is located 2 miles east and 3 miles north of the school welcome sign. The track has a radius of 0.5 miles. Write an equation that represents the track on a coordinate plane with respect to the welcome sign.

Identify the center and radius of the circle.

The center of the circle is $(2, 3)$, and the radius is 0.5.

Write an equation for the circle.

The general form of the equation of a circle centered at (h, k) with radius r is $(x - h)^2 + (y - k)^2 = r^2$.

Substituting the given h, k, and r values into this general form results in the following equation:

$(x - 2)^2 + (y - 3)^2 = 0.5^2 = 0.25$

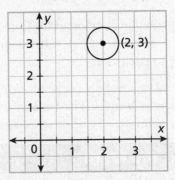

Do the Math

A circular garden is located 12 feet east and 8 feet north of a birdhouse. The garden has a radius of 4 feet. Write an equation that represents the garden on a coordinate plane with respect to the birdhouse.

Identify the center and radius of the circle.

The center of the circle is $\left(\boxed{}, \boxed{}\right)$, and the radius is $\boxed{}$.

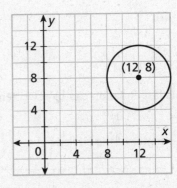

Write an equation for the circle.

The general form of the equation of a circle centered at (h, k) with radius r is $(x - h)^2 + (y - k)^2 = r^2$.

Substituting the given h, k, and r values into this general form results in the following equation:

$\left(x - \boxed{}\right)^2 + \left(y - \boxed{}\right)^2 = \boxed{}^2 = \boxed{}$

Learn the Math

EXAMPLE 2 Find the center and radius of the circle with equation $x^2 - 16x + y^2 + 6y = -48$.

Rewrite the equation in the form $(x - h)^2 + (y - k)^2 = r^2$ by completing the square twice.

$$x^2 - 16x + y^2 + 6y = -48$$

$$x^2 - 16x + \left(\frac{-16}{2}\right)^2 + y^2 + 6y + \left(\frac{6}{2}\right)^2 = -48 + \left(\frac{-16}{2}\right)^2 + \left(\frac{6}{2}\right)^2$$

$$x^2 - 16x + 64 + y^2 + 6y + 9 = -48 + 64 + 9$$

$$(x - 8)^2 + (y + 3)^2 = 25$$

This last equation can be rewritten as $(x - 8)^2 + (y - (-3))^2 = 25$ to clearly show the values of h and k. The center of a circle is the point (h, k). So, the center of this circle is the point $(8, -3)$. The radius is equal to the square root of 25, or 5.

Do the Math

Find the center and radius of the circle with equation $x^2 + 14x + y^2 - 8y = -16$.

Rewrite the equation in the form $(x - h)^2 + (y - k)^2 = r^2$ by completing the square twice.

$$x^2 + 14x + y^2 - 8y = -16$$

$$x^2 + 14x + \left(\frac{\boxed{}}{\boxed{}}\right)^2 + y^2 - 8y + \left(\frac{\boxed{}}{\boxed{}}\right)^2 = -16 + \left(\frac{\boxed{}}{\boxed{}}\right)^2 + \left(\frac{\boxed{}}{\boxed{}}\right)^2$$

$$x^2 + 14x + \boxed{} + y^2 - 8y + \boxed{} = -16 + \boxed{} + \boxed{}$$

$$\left(x + \boxed{}\right)^2 + \left(y - \boxed{}\right)^2 = \boxed{}$$

This last equation can be rewritten as $\left(x - \left(\boxed{}\right)\right)^2 + \left(y - \boxed{}\right)^2 = \boxed{}$.

The center of the circle is $\left(\boxed{}, \boxed{}\right)$. The radius is $\boxed{}$.

Learn the Math

EXAMPLE 3 Does $\left(\sqrt{7}, 3\right)$ lie on a circle that is centered at the origin and contains the point $(0, 4)$?

Write an equation for the circle.

$$x^2 + y^2 = 16$$

Substitute the given point in the equation.

$$\left(\sqrt{7}\right)^2 + (3)^2 = 16$$

$$7 + 9 = 16$$

$$16 = 16$$

Since the statement is true, the point $\left(\sqrt{7}, 3\right)$ does lie on the circle.

Do the Math

Does $\left(\sqrt{21}, 10\right)$ lie on a circle that is centered at the origin and contains the point $(0, -11)$?

Name

LESSON 15.4
More Practice

ONLINE
Video Tutorials and
Interactive Examples

Write the equation of the circle, with the given center and radius.

1. center: $(3, 5)$; radius: 4

2. center: $(-8, 2)$; radius: 3

3. center: $(1, -9)$; radius: 2

4. center: $(-7, -6)$; radius: 5

Find the center and radius of the circle given by the equation, by completing the square.

5. $x^2 + 4x + y^2 - 10y = 35$

6. $x^2 - 18x + y^2 + 6y = -41$

7. $x^2 - 8x + y^2 + 12y = 48$

8. $x^2 + 14x + y^2 - 20y = -68$

Write the equation of each circle.

9.

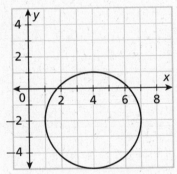

10.

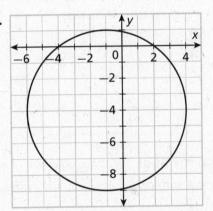

11.

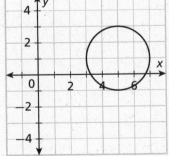

12.

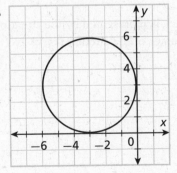

13. State whether or not $\left(\sqrt{11}, 5\right)$ is a point on a circle that is centered at the origin and passes through $(0, 6)$. Show your work.

_____

_____

14. State whether or not $\left(\sqrt{14}, 6\right)$ is a point on a circle that is centered at the origin and passes through $(-7, 0)$. Show your work.

_____

_____

15. Critique Reasoning Andy solves the problem to the right by writing the following solution:

$$\left(\sqrt{23}\right)^2 + (11)^2 \neq 12$$

$$23 + 121 \neq 12$$

$$144 \neq 12$$

> A circle is centered at the origin and contains the point $(0, -12)$. Is $\left(\sqrt{23}, 11\right)$ a point on the circle? Explain.

Explain the error in Andy's work. Then show the correct solution steps and correct answer.

_____

_____

_____

_____

16. Math on the Spot Write the equation of each circle.

A. Circle A with center $A(-1, 5)$ and radius 4

_____

B. Circle B that passes through $(-2, 3)$ and has a center $B(2, 0)$

_____

17. A circular track is represented by the equation $x^2 - 18x + y^2 - 22x = -177$. What is the center of the circular track?

- Ⓐ $(3, 11)$
- Ⓑ $(6, 9)$
- Ⓒ $(9, 11)$
- Ⓓ $(3, 9)$

Step It Out

Learn the Math

EXAMPLE 1 What is the value of x?

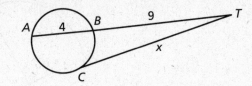

$AT \cdot BT = CT^2$

$13 \cdot 9 = x^2$	Substitute the given values.
$117 = x^2$	Multiply.
$\sqrt{117} = x$	Take the square root of both sides.
$10.8 \approx x$	Simplify.

Do the Math

What is the value of x? Round to the nearest tenth.

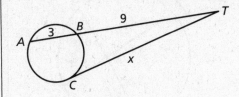

$AT \cdot BT = CT^2$

$\boxed{} \cdot \boxed{} = \boxed{}^2$

$\boxed{} = \boxed{}^2$

$\sqrt{\boxed{}} = x$

$\boxed{} \approx x$

Learn the Math

EXAMPLE 2 Amelia designs a circular garden. She divides the garden into four sections using boards, as shown in the diagram. What is the length of $\overline{BD}$?

$$AX \cdot XC = DX \cdot XB$$
$$4 \cdot 4.5 = DX \cdot 6$$
$$18 = DX \cdot 6$$
$$3 = DX$$

To find the length of $\overline{BD}$, add the lengths of $\overline{DX}$ and $\overline{XB}$.

$$BD = 3 + 6 = 9$$

So, the length of $\overline{BD}$ is 9 feet.

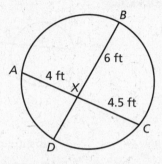

Do the Math

A circular swimming pool is divided into sections, using two ropes from A to C and from B to D, as shown in the diagram below. What is the length of the rope represented by $\overline{AC}$?

$$AX \cdot XC = DX \cdot XB$$

$$AX \cdot \boxed{} = \boxed{} \cdot \boxed{}$$

$$AX \cdot \boxed{} = \boxed{}$$

$$AX = \boxed{}$$

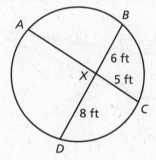

To find the length of $\overline{AC}$, add the lengths of $\overline{AX}$ and $\overline{XC}$.

$$AC = \boxed{} + 5 = \boxed{}$$

So, the length of $\overline{AC}$ is $\boxed{}$ feet.

Name _____

LESSON 16.1
More Practice

ONLINE
Ed Video Tutorials and
Interactive Examples

In Problems 1–4, find each value of *x*.
Round to the nearest tenth. Show your work.

1.

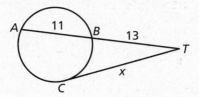

2.

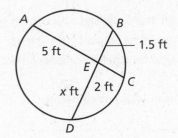

_____

3.

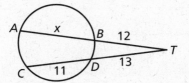

4.

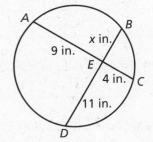

_____

In Problems 5–8, find each indicated segment length.
Round to the nearest tenth. Show your work.

5. *EF, FD, ED, BC, BD,* and *CD*

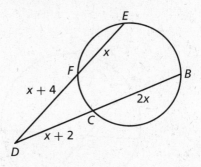

6. *AD, BD,* and *CD*

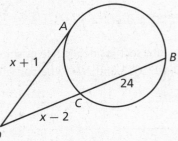

_____

7. *IJ, IL,* and *KL*

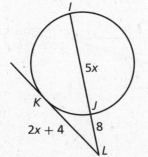

8. *NQ, RQ, NM,* and *RP*

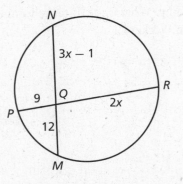

_____

9. **Critique Reasoning** Jackson summarizes the procedure for applying the Secant-Tangent Product Theorem as:

> Given a secant in a circle and a tangent to the circle, multiply the interior portion of the secant by the exterior portion and set this product equal to the square of the tangent.

Explain the error in Jackson's thinking.

_____

_____

_____

_____

10. **Math on the Spot** Find the value of x and the length of each chord.

_____

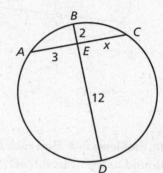

11. **Reason** Would the Secant-Secant Product Theorem be true if the word *circle* is replaced by the word *sphere* in the statement of the theorem? Explain your answer.

_____

_____

_____

_____

12. Two chords intersect inside a circle as shown here. Is it possible for the lengths AD, BD, GD, and HD to be consecutive even integers? Explain.

_____

_____

_____

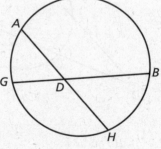

13. Two construction workers stand at two different points on a circular opening. A third construction worker stands at a point outside of the circular opening. What is the distance from Construction Worker B to Construction Worker C?

Ⓐ 9 ft

Ⓑ 10 ft

Ⓒ 12 ft

Ⓓ 16 ft

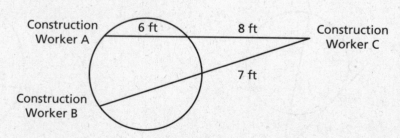

Step It Out

Learn the Math

EXAMPLE 1 ▶ Write a paragraph proof of the Tangent-Secant Exterior Angle Measure Theorem for two secants.

Given the two secants, $\overrightarrow{AC}$ and $\overrightarrow{AE}$, you can draw a chord between B and E and then show that the measure of $\angle CBE$, an exterior angle of $\triangle BAE$, is equal to the sum of $m\angle CAE$ and $m\angle BEA$ by the Exterior Angle Theorem. You can isolate $m\angle CAE$ by subtracting $m\angle BEA$ from both sides of the equation. By the

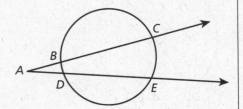

Inscribed Angle Theorem, you know that $m\angle BEA = \frac{1}{2}m\widehat{BD}$. You also know that $m\angle CBE = \frac{1}{2}m\widehat{CE}$. By substituting these values into the equation for $m\angle CAE$, you get the equation $m\angle CAE = \frac{1}{2}m\widehat{CE} - \frac{1}{2}m\widehat{BD}$. Factoring out $\frac{1}{2}$ results in $m\angle CAE = \frac{1}{2}\left(m\widehat{CE} - m\widehat{BD}\right)$.

Do the Math

Complete the paragraph proof to prove the Tangent-Secant Exterior Angle Measure Theorem for two tangents.

The tangents are $\overrightarrow{CB}$ and ☐. You can draw a chord from B to D. Next,

use the _____ to show that the measure of the exterior angle equals the sum of the measures of the opposite interior angles. Next, isolate $m\angle BCD$ to show that it is equal to the difference of the measures of the exterior angle and the other interior angle. Use the _____ to show that each of these angle measures is equal to one-half the measure of the _____. By substitution

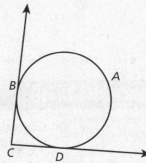

and factoring out $\frac{1}{2}$, you have $m\angle BCD = \frac{1}{2}\left(m\boxed{} - m\boxed{}\right)$.

Learn the Math

EXAMPLE 2 ▸ Find m∠DTC.

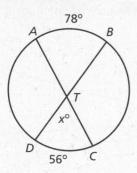

Apply the Intersecting Chords Angle Measure Theorem.

$$m\angle DTC = \frac{1}{2}\left(m\widehat{AB} + m\widehat{DC}\right)$$

$$= \frac{1}{2}\left(78° + 56°\right)$$

$$= \frac{1}{2}\left(134°\right)$$

$$= 67°$$

Do the Math

Find m∠ATB.

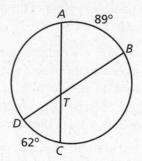

Apply the Intersecting Chords Angle Measure Theorem.

$$m\angle ATB = \frac{1}{2}\left(m\widehat{AB} + m\widehat{DC}\right)$$

$$= \frac{1}{2}\left(\boxed{}° + \boxed{}°\right)$$

$$= \frac{1}{2}\left(\boxed{}°\right)$$

$$= \boxed{}°$$

Learn the Math

EXAMPLE 3 ▸ Given the graphic design for a logo, what is m∠AVB?

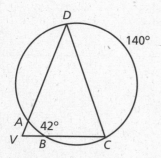

Apply the Intersecting Chords Angle Measure Theorem.

$$m\angle AVB = \frac{1}{2}\left(m\widehat{DC} - m\widehat{AB}\right)$$

$$= \frac{1}{2}\left(140° - 42°\right)$$

$$= \frac{1}{2}\left(98°\right)$$

$$= 49°$$

Do the Math

Given the graphic design for a logo, what is m∠APB?

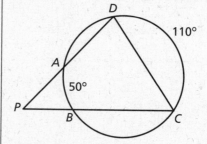

Apply the Intersecting Chords Angle Measure Theorem.

$$m\angle APB = \frac{1}{2}\left(m\widehat{DC} - m\widehat{AB}\right)$$

$$= \frac{1}{2}\left(\boxed{}° - \boxed{}°\right)$$

$$= \frac{1}{2}\left(\boxed{}°\right)$$

$$= \boxed{}°$$

Name

LESSON 16.2
More Practice

ONLINE
Ed Video Tutorials and
Interactive Examples

In Problems 1–6, find the measure of the indicated angles and arcs.
Round to the nearest tenth. Show your work.

1. m∠*ATB*

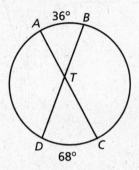

2. m∠*BCD*

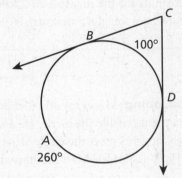

_____

_____

3. m∠*KNM*

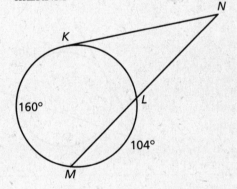

4. m∠*EJF*

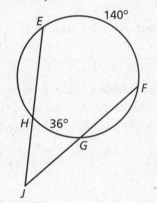

_____

_____

5. m$\widehat{AC}$

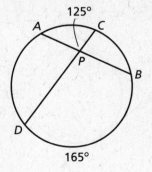

6. m$\widehat{KM}$

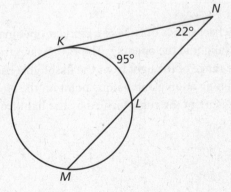

_____

_____

7. **Reasoning** Use the diagram to write formulas.

   A. Write a formula for the measure of $\angle RPQ$ formed by two tangents to a circle, where the given measure is $\overparen{RQ}$.

   B. Write a formula for the measure of $\angle RPQ$ formed by two tangents to a circle, where the given measure is arc $\overparen{RTQ}$.

   _____

   _____

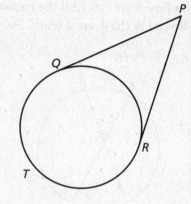

8. **Critique Reasoning** Mario says that he drew two tangents to a circle that meet at a point outside the circle. He also says that the two points where the two tangents meet the circle separate the circle into two semicircles. Is it possible for Mario to have drawn this figure? Explain.

   _____

   _____

   _____

9. **Math on the Spot** Find the value of x.

   _____

10. Two chords intersect inside a circle, forming vertical angles. The intercepted arc measures for one pair of vertical angles are 32° and 56°. What is the measure of each of these vertical angles? Show your work.

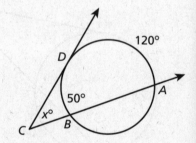

   _____

11. **Open Ended** Draw a circle, its center, and two secants that intersect outside the circle. Use a protractor to measure the angle that is formed by the two secants. Draw central angles that intercept the same arcs as the secants. Compare the measures of the central angles to the measure of the angle between the secants.

   _____

12. Michael stands outside of a circular opening. He points a flashlight at the opening. The two rays in the diagram represent the range of the light from the flashlight. Each ray touches the opening at only one unique point on the circle. What is the measure of the angle formed by the light from the flashlight?

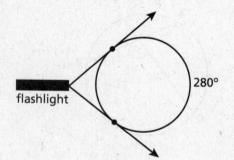

   Ⓐ 80°

   Ⓑ 100°

   Ⓒ 120°

   Ⓓ 140°

Step It Out

Learn the Math

EXAMPLE 1 ▶ A grounds crew is marking out a circular logo at the center of a football field. The logo will have a circumference of 141.3 feet. What will be the diameter length of the logo in yards?

Since the problem asks for the diameter of the circle, use this circumference formula:

$C = \pi d$

Substitute the known values into the formula and solve for d.

$C = 141.3$

$141.3 = \pi d$

$\dfrac{141.3}{\pi} = \dfrac{\pi d}{\pi}$

$45 = d$

The problem asks for the diameter in yards. Divide by 3 to convert the diameter from feet to yards.

$45 \div 3 = 15$

The logo will have a diameter of 15 yards.

Do the Math

Jamison is restoring an old western-style wooden wagon wheel. The wheel is circular and is designed to have 12 wooden spokes that are radii of the circle. There are five spokes missing. The wagon wheel has a circumference of 176 inches. What is the approximate length of the radius to the nearest inch? What is the approximate total length of wood needed to replace the five missing spokes to the nearest whole inch?

Use the circumference formula to find the value of the radius.

$C = 2\pi r$

$\boxed{} = 2\left(\boxed{}\right) r$

$r = \dfrac{\boxed{}}{2\pi}$

$r \approx \boxed{}$

The radius of the wheel is approximately $\boxed{}$ inches.

Use the length of the radius to find the total length of wood needed for the five missing spokes.

The length of one spoke is inches.

$\boxed{} \cdot 28 = \boxed{}$

Jamison will need about $\boxed{}$ inches of wood.

Learn the Math

EXAMPLE 2 A circular swimming pool has a diameter of 20 feet. A 3-foot-wide tile walkway is being installed around the pool. Rounded to the nearest tenth of a square foot, what is the area of the walkway?

Use the formula for the area of a circle: $A = \pi r^2$

First, find the area of the swimming pool and walkway together.

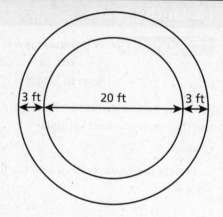

3 ft | 20 ft | 3 ft

Use the radius of the swimming pool and walkway together.

diameter = 20 ft + 3 ft + 3 ft = 26 ft

radius = 13 feet

Substitute into the area formula and solve.

$A = \pi r^2$

$A = (\pi)(13)^2$

$A = (\pi)(169)$

$A \approx 530.9 \text{ ft}^2$

Next, find the area of the swimming pool.

diameter = 20 ft   radius = 10 ft

Substitute into the area formula and solve.

$A = \pi r^2$

$A = (\pi)(10)^2$

$A = (\pi)(100)$

$A \approx 314.2 \text{ ft}^2$

Subtract the area of the swimming pool from the area of the swimming pool and walkway together to find the area of the walkway only.

$$530.9 - 314.2 = 216.7$$

The area of the walkway is approximately 216.7 square feet.

Do the Math

Janice is creating a design that is part of a logo consisting of a small and a large circle. The diameter of the small circle is $\frac{1}{3}$ of the diameter of the large circle. The diameter of the large circle is 27 centimeters. To the nearest tenth of a centimeter, what is the area of the smaller circle?

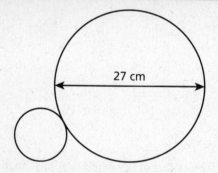

27 cm

Use the diameter of the large circle to find the diameter and radius of the small circle.

$d = \frac{1}{3}\left(\boxed{}\right) = \boxed{}$

$r = \frac{1}{2}(9) = \boxed{}$

The radius of the small circle is $\boxed{}$ cm.

Substitute into the area formula and solve.

$A = \pi r^2$

$A = (\pi)\left(\boxed{}\right)^2$

$A = (\pi)(20.25)$

$A \approx \boxed{}$

The area of the small circle is about $\boxed{}$ cm².

Name _____

LESSON 17.1
More Practice

🙂 Ed **ONLINE**
Video Tutorials and
Interactive Examples

**Find the circumference of the circle with the given radius _r_ or diameter _d_.
Round answers to the nearest tenth.**

1. $r = 4$ mm

2. $d = 4$ cm

_____   _____

3. $r = 20$ ft

4. $d = 35$ yd

_____   _____

Find the area of the circle with radius _r_ or diameter _d_. Round answers to the nearest tenth.

5. $r = 18$ ft

6. $d = 8$ yd

_____   _____

7. $r = 24$ mm

8. $d = 40$ cm

_____   _____

**Find the circumference of the circle with the given area. Round answers to the nearest
tenth.**

9. $A = 36\pi$ cm^2

10. $A = 64\pi$ ft^2

_____   _____

11. **Reason** One circle has a radius that is three times the length of a smaller circle. Explain the relationship between the areas of the circles.

_____

_____

_____

12. Dian is designing a silver chain necklace that consists of three circles as shown. The diameter of the smallest circle is 10 inches, the second circle has a diameter of 12 inches, and the third circle has a diameter of 14 inches. What is the total length of silver chain in the necklace? Show your work. Round the answer to the nearest tenth.

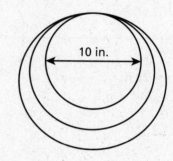

_____

13. **Math on the Spot** A bicycle odometer recorded 254 revolutions of a wheel with a diameter of $\frac{5}{4}$ ft. How far did the bicycle travel? Round the answer to the nearest tenth.

_____

14. **Model with Mathematics** The diameter of a circular oil spill from a leaking pipe in the ocean is increasing by a rate of 4 feet per hour. The diameter is currently 28 feet. In how many hours will the area of the oil spill be 3630 square feet? Show your work. Round the answer to the nearest whole hour.

_____

15. The area of a circle is given by the formula $A = \pi r^2$. Which shows the area formula written in terms of the diameter d?

Ⓐ $A = \dfrac{\pi d^2}{2}$

Ⓑ $A = \dfrac{\pi d^2}{4}$

Ⓒ $A = 2\pi d^2$

Ⓓ $A = 4\pi d^2$

Step It Out

Learn the Math

EXAMPLE 1 A 14-inch diameter circular pizza is cut through its center into 8 equal-sized pieces. What is the arc length of the outside edge of one piece to the nearest tenth inch?

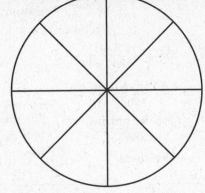

Find the radius. The radius is half the diameter.

$d = 14$ $r = 7$

Find the arc measure.

The pizza is divided into 8 sections. Divide 360° by 8 to find the arc measure for one section.

$\frac{360}{8} = 45$

Find the arc length.

Substitute the known values into the formula and solve for s.

$s = \frac{x°}{360°} \cdot 2\pi r$ $x = 45$ $r = 7$

$s = \frac{45}{360} \cdot 2\pi(7)$

$s = \frac{1}{8} \cdot 2\pi(7)$ $s = \frac{7}{4}\pi$ $s \approx 5.5$

The arc length is about 5.5 inches.

Do the Math

Jonathan is designing a circular face for a watch. He wants the arc around the outside of the face from the 12 o'clock position to the 3 o'clock position to be bright orange. If the diameter of the watch face is 1.8 centimeters, what is the length of the bright orange arc? Round to the nearest hundredth of a centimeter.

Find the radius. The radius is half the diameter.

$d = 1.8$ $r = \boxed{}$

Find the arc measure.

The watch face is divided into twelve sectors. From

12 o'clock to 3 o'clock is $\boxed{}$ of a complete rotation.

$\frac{3}{12}(360°) = \boxed{}°$

The arc measure is $\boxed{}°$.

Find the arc length.

Substitute the known values into the formula and solve for s.

$s = \frac{x°}{360°} \cdot 2\pi r$ $x = 90$ $r = 0.9$

$s = \frac{\boxed{}}{360} \cdot 2\pi\left(\boxed{}\right)$

$s = \frac{1}{4} \cdot 2\pi(0.9)$

$s = \frac{\boxed{}}{2}\pi$ $s \approx \boxed{}$

The arc length is about $\boxed{}$ centimeters.

Learn the Math

EXAMPLE 2 Convert 135° to radian measure. Multiply the degree measure by $\frac{\pi \text{ radians}}{180°}$ and simplify the fraction.

$$135° = 135° \left(\frac{\pi \text{ radians}}{180°} \right)$$

$$= \frac{135° \cdot \pi \text{ radians}}{180°}$$

$$= \frac{135° \cdot \pi \text{ radians}}{180°}$$

$$= \frac{3\pi}{4} \text{ radians}$$

> The measurement unit degrees cancels, leaving just radians.

Do the Math

Convert 240° to radian measure. Multiply the degree measure by $\frac{\pi \text{ radians}}{180°}$ and simplify the fraction.

$$240° = \boxed{}° \left(\frac{\pi \text{ radians}}{180°} \right)$$

$$= \frac{\boxed{}° \cdot \pi \text{ radians}}{180°}$$

$$= \boxed{} \text{ radians}$$

Learn the Math

EXAMPLE 3 Convert $\frac{5\pi}{6}$ radians to degree measure.

Multiply the radian measure by $\frac{180°}{\pi \text{ radians}}$ and simplify the fraction.

$$\frac{5\pi}{6} = \left(\frac{5\pi}{6} \text{ radians} \right)\left(\frac{180°}{\pi \text{ radians}} \right)$$

$$= \left(\frac{5\pi}{6} \text{ radians} \right)\left(\frac{180°}{\pi \text{ radians}} \right)$$

$$= \frac{(5)(180°)}{6}$$

$$= 150°$$

> The measurement unit radians cancels, leaving just degrees.

Do the Math

Convert $\frac{2\pi}{5}$ radians to degree measure. Multiply the radian measure by $\frac{180°}{\pi \text{ radians}}$ and simplify the fraction.

$$\frac{2\pi}{5} = \left(\boxed{} \text{ radians} \right)\left(\frac{180°}{\pi \text{ radians}} \right)$$

$$= \frac{\left(\boxed{} \right)(180°)}{\boxed{}}$$

$$= \boxed{}°$$

Find the length of $\overset{\frown}{AB}$ using the given measure of $\overset{\frown}{AB}$ in a circle with a diameter of 9 feet. Round to the nearest hundredth.

1. $m\overset{\frown}{AB} = 45°$

_____

2. $m\overset{\frown}{AB} = 125°$

_____

3. $m\overset{\frown}{AB} = 240°$

_____

4. $m\overset{\frown}{AB} = 80°$

_____

Convert each angle from degree measure to radian measure. Write the answer in terms of π.

5. $25°$

_____

6. $75°$

_____

7. $200°$

_____

8. $140°$

_____

Convert each angle from radian measure to the nearest whole degree measure.

9. $\frac{\pi}{12}$ radians

_____

10. $\frac{5\pi}{8}$ radians

_____

11. $\frac{11\pi}{12}$ radians

_____

12. $\frac{17\pi}{9}$ radians

_____

13. **Reasoning** One circle has a radius that is four times the radius of a smaller circle. An arc that measures 40° is marked on each circle. What is the relationship between the arc lengths of the two circles? Explain.

_____

_____

_____

14. The pendulum of a grandfather clock is 1.2 meters long. It swings back and forth through an angle of 36°. Through what distance does the end of the pendulum swing? Show your work. Round the answer to the nearest hundredth of a meter.

_____

15. A two-inch safety label is placed on the outer edge of a circular weight-lifting weight. The weight has an 8-inch diameter. An identical two-inch safety label is also placed on the outer edge of a larger circular weight with a 15-inch diameter. What is the difference between the arc measures that the safety label covers on the weights? Show your work. Round answers to the nearest tenth of a degree if necessary.

_____

16. **Model with Mathematics** A piece of a circle-shaped ornamental plate is discovered during an archeological dig. The piece has part of the circular edge of the plate with an arc measurement of 80° and an arc length of about 20 centimeters. What was the diameter of the complete plate? Round the answer to the nearest tenth.

_____

17. Which is the radian equivalent of three full rotations of a circle?

Ⓐ 6π

Ⓑ 3π

Ⓒ 2π

Ⓓ 12π

Step It Out

Learn the Math

EXAMPLE 1 A sector of a circular corral is fenced off to separate five sheep from the rest of the flock. The radius of the circle is 40 feet and the central angle is 160°. What is the area of the sector? Round the answer to the nearest tenth.

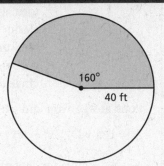

160°
40 ft

Substitute the known values into the formula for the area of a sector and solve.

$$A = \frac{x°}{360°} \cdot \pi r^2$$

$x = 160°$ $r = 40$ ft

$$A = \frac{160}{360} \cdot \pi(40)^2$$
$$= \frac{4}{9} \cdot \pi(1600)$$
$$= \frac{6400}{9}\pi$$
$$\approx 2234.0 \text{ ft}^2$$

Do the Math

A water sprinkler set in the corner of a soccer field sweeps through a central angle of 90° and has a range of 20 yards. What area of the field is covered by a sweep of the sprinkler? Round to the nearest yard.

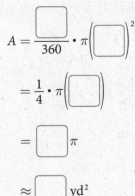

20 yd

90°

Substitute the known values into the formula for the area of a sector and solve.

$$A = \frac{x°}{360°} \cdot \pi r^2$$

$x = \boxed{}°$ $r = \boxed{}$ yd

$$A = \frac{\boxed{}}{360} \cdot \pi \left(\boxed{}\right)^2$$

$$= \frac{1}{4} \cdot \pi \left(\boxed{}\right)$$

$$= \boxed{}\pi$$

$$\approx \boxed{} \text{ yd}^2$$

The sprinkler covers about $\boxed{}$ square yards.

Learn the Math

EXAMPLE 2 A high school marching band is in a circular formation on a football field. The flute and clarinet sections form a central angle with a measure of 30°. The area of the sector formed is 12π square yards. What is the radius of the circle formed by the band?

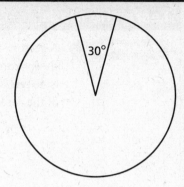

Look at what you know from the given information.

$A = 12\pi$ yd^2 $x° = 30°$

Use the formula for area of a sector.

$A = \dfrac{x°}{360°} \cdot \pi r^2$	Write the formula.
$12\pi = \dfrac{30°}{360°} \cdot \pi r^2$	Substitute the given values.
$\dfrac{360°}{30°} \cdot 12\pi = \dfrac{30°}{360°} \cdot \pi r^2 \cdot \dfrac{360°}{30°}$	Multiply to clear the fraction.
$144\pi = \pi r^2$	Simplify.
$144 = r^2$	Divide both sides by π.
$12 = r$	Take the square root of both sides.

The radius of the circle created by the band is 12 yards.

Do the Math

A sector of a circle with a central angle of 200° has an area of 320π square meters. What is the length of the radius of the circle?

Use the formula for area of a sector.

$A = \dfrac{x°}{360°} \cdot \pi r^2$	Write the formula.
$\boxed{} = \dfrac{\boxed{}}{360°} \cdot \pi r^2$	Substitute the given values.
$\dfrac{360°}{200°} \cdot 320\pi = \dfrac{200°}{360°} \cdot \pi r^2 \cdot \dfrac{360°}{200°}$	Multiply to clear the fraction.
$\boxed{} = \pi r^2$	Simplify.
$\boxed{} = r^2$	Divide both sides by π.
$\boxed{} = r$	Take the square root of both sides.

The radius of the circle is $\boxed{}$ meters.

Name _____

Find the approximate area of each sector with the given measure $x°$ in a circle with diameter d or radius r. Round to the nearest hundredth.

1. $x° = 35°, d = 14$ cm

2. $x° = 125°, r = 10$ m

_____

_____

3. $x° = 95°, d = 24$ ft

4. $x° = 225°, r = 3$ yd

_____

_____

Estimate the radius r to the nearest tenth of each sector with the given measure $x°$ in a circle with the given area.

5. $x° = 45°$, area = 250 in^2

6. $x° = 75°$, area = 180.5 ft^2

_____

_____

7. $x° = 200°$, area = 280.5 cm^2

8. $x° = 135°$, area = 1345 m^2

_____

_____

Find the exact area of each sector, leaving the answer in terms of π.

9.

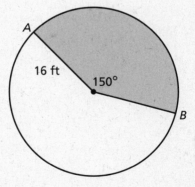

10.

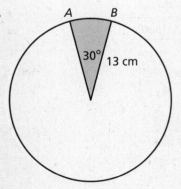

_____

_____

11. **Reasoning** Rachel is comparing the areas of sectors of two circles that have the same central angle measure. The larger area is four times the size of the smaller area. Rachel states that the radius of the larger circle must be twice the radius of the smaller circle. Is Rachel correct? Explain.

_____

_____

_____

12. **Model with Mathematics** A windshield wiper on a car rotates through an angle of 120°. The inside radius of its path is 3 inches and the wiper blade is 18 inches long. What area does the wiper blade clean on a single pass? Show your work. Round the answer to the nearest tenth.

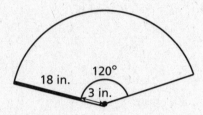

18 in.   120°

3 in.

_____

13. **Math on the Spot** A circular plot with a 400-foot diameter is watered by a spray irrigation system. To the nearest square foot, what is the area that is watered as the sprinkler rotates through an angle of 60°?

_____

14. **Model with Mathematics** The minute hand on a circular clock moves from 12:05 a.m. to 12:20 a.m. The area of the sector of the clock that the minute hand sweeps through is 25.1 square inches. What is the length of the minute hand? Show your work. Round the answer to the nearest tenth.

_____

15. Which shows the formula for finding the radius r given the area A and central angle measure x of a sector of a circle?

Ⓐ $r = \sqrt{\dfrac{360°}{x°A\pi}}$

Ⓑ $r = \sqrt{\dfrac{(A)(360°)}{x°\pi}}$

Ⓒ $r = \sqrt{\dfrac{(\pi)(360°)}{Ax°}}$

Ⓓ $r = \dfrac{(A)(360°)}{x°\pi}$

Step It Out

Learn the Math

EXAMPLE 1 ▸ A large cube of dry ice is cut in half from the top left edge to the bottom right edge. What is the area of the newly exposed cross section? Round to the nearest tenth of a square inch.

The cross section is a rectangle. The length of the cross section forms the hypotenuse of an isosceles right triangle with legs of 11 inches. Use the Pythagorean Theorem to find the length of the cross section.

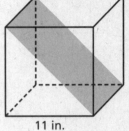

11 in.

$11^2 + 11^2 = c^2$

$242 = c^2$

$11\sqrt{2} = c$

The width of the cross section is the same as the width of the cube of dry ice, 11 inches. Use the length and the width to find the area of the cross section.

$A = lw$

$A = (11\sqrt{2})(11)$

$A = 121\sqrt{2}$

$A \approx 171.1$

The area of the cross section of the dry ice is approximately 171.1 square inches.

Do the Math

Raquel finds the limb of a large tree in her backyard after a storm. The limb is shaped like a cylinder with a diameter of 6.35 centimeters. She cuts eight congruent cross sections parallel to the base of the limb to make a trivet. How much area does the trivet cover? Round to the nearest tenth of a square centimeter.

6.35 cm

A cross section cut parallel to the base of a cylinder is a _____.

The formula for the area of a _____ is $A = \boxed{}$.

The radius of one cross section is $\boxed{}$ centimeters.

The area of one cross section is $A = \boxed{}$, or approximately $\boxed{}$ square centimeters.

The area of the trivet is about $\boxed{} \cdot \boxed{}$, or $\boxed{}$ square centimeters.

Learn the Math

EXAMPLE 2 Hannah has always wanted a four-poster bed. She wants the tops of the vertical support posts to resemble the figure shown. She needs to draw a profile of the tops so she can have them made to her specifications. Draw the two-dimensional profile that would form the top of the post when rotated around an axis.

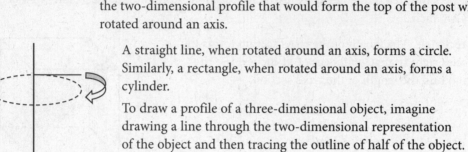

A straight line, when rotated around an axis, forms a circle. Similarly, a rectangle, when rotated around an axis, forms a cylinder.

To draw a profile of a three-dimensional object, imagine drawing a line through the two-dimensional representation of the object and then tracing the outline of half of the object.

Do the Math

When Hannah's friends see her four-poster bed, they each decide they want one, too. Draw a two-dimensional profile for the designs that her friends create for the tops of their vertical support posts.

Mariah's post   Kaylin's post

Sketch the figure created by rotating each given figure about the axis.

1.

2.

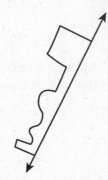

Describe each cross section.

3.

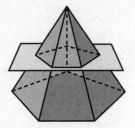

_____

4.

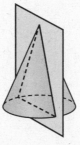

_____

5.

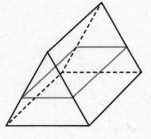

_____

6.

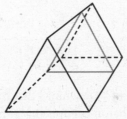

_____

7. **Math on the Spot** Describe and then sketch the figure that is generated by each rotation in three-dimensional space.

A. A right triangle rotated around a line containing one of its legs

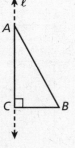

B. A rectangle rotated around a line containing one of its sides

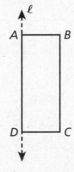

_____

_____

8. A plane intersects a triangular pyramid perpendicular to its base. What is true about the cross section?

_____

9. Critique Reasoning A plane intersects a cylinder. Mario says the cross section is a circle, and Jeremiah says the cross section is a rectangle. Who is correct? Explain.

_____

_____

Find the area of the cross section created by each slice.

10.

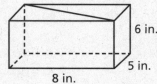

6 in.

5 in.

8 in.

11.

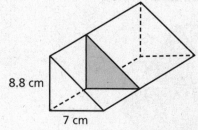

8.8 cm

7 cm

_____

_____

12. Open Ended Explain one way a cube can be sliced so that the cross section is an equilateral triangle.

_____

_____

13. Critique Reasoning Lucy thinks that rotating the given figure about the x-axis will create a cone. Sharon believes that rotating the figure about the x-axis will yield a diamond-like three-dimensional object. Who is correct? Explain your reasoning.

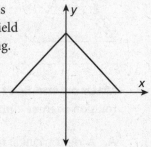

_____

_____

14. What are the length and the width of the cross section of the cube shown?

Ⓐ length = 15 m; width = 15 m

Ⓑ length = $15\sqrt{2}$ m; width = 15 m

Ⓒ length = $15\sqrt{2}$ m; width = $15\sqrt{2}$ m

Ⓓ length = 7.5 m; width = $15\sqrt{2}$ m

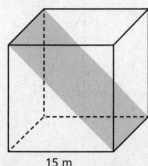

15 m

Step It Out

Learn the Math

EXAMPLE 1 Ashley makes a ramp out of wood for her deck. Find the surface area of the composite figure.

First, calculate the surface area of the rectangular prism, excluding the side attached to the ramp.

$S = 2\ell w + 2\ell h + wh$

$\quad = 2(5)(4) + 2(5)(3) + (4)(3)$

$\quad = 82 \text{ ft}^2$

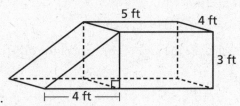

5 ft   4 ft

3 ft

4 ft

Calculate the hypotenuse of the triangle that forms the ramp. The ramp is made of a 3-4-5 triangle, so the hypotenuse is 5 feet.

Calculate the surface area of the triangular prism, excluding the side attached to the deck.

$S = (5)(4) + (4)(4) + 2\left(\dfrac{1}{2}(4)(3)\right)$

$\quad = 48 \text{ ft}^2$

The total surface area is the sum of the surface areas of both prisms.

$S = 82 + 48 = 130 \text{ ft}^2$

Do the Math

Find the surface area of the composite figure. Round your answer to the nearest square millimeter.

Calculate the surface area of the rectangular prism.

$S = 6s^2$

$\quad = 6\left(\boxed{}\right)^2 = \boxed{} \text{ mm}^2$

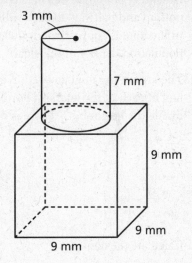

3 mm

7 mm

9 mm

9 mm

9 mm

You could subtract the area of the bottom base of the cylinder from the surface area of the rectangular prism. But that same area would be added back in as the top of the cylinder. Imagine that you can push the cylinder down flat. Then the area of the top base would be part of the surface area of the rectangular prism already calculated. So, rather than subtracting and then adding the same amount, you can disregard the area of the circular bases of the cylinder.

Calculate the lateral area of the cylinder.

$L = 2\pi rh$

$\quad = 2\pi\left(\boxed{}\right)\left(\boxed{}\right) \approx \boxed{} \text{ mm}^2$

The total surface area is the sum of the surface areas of the prism and the cylinder.

$\boxed{} + \boxed{} \approx \boxed{} \text{ mm}^2$

Learn the Math

EXAMPLE 2 Max studies bacteria. He has a cylindrical petri dish with a population of 12,000 bacteria. The dish has an inside radius of 5 centimeters and a height of 2 centimeters. The bacteria grow on the inside of the dish with no lid. What is the population density of the bacteria?

Calculate the lateral area of the dish.

$L = 2\pi rh$

$= 2\pi(5)(2) \approx 62.8 \text{ cm}^2$

Calculate the area of the base of the dish.

$A = \pi r^2$

$= \pi(5)^2 \approx 78.5 \text{ cm}^2$

The total surface area is the sum of the lateral area and the area of the base.

$S \approx 62.8 + 78.5 \approx 141.3 \text{ cm}^2$

Calculate the population density.

$D \approx \dfrac{12,000}{141.3} \approx 84.9$

There are about 85 bacteria per square centimeter in the dish.

Do the Math

An empty pool in disrepair has algae growing on the entire bottom and halfway up each side. The population of algae in the pool is approximately 400,000,000,000 cells. What is the population density of the algae?

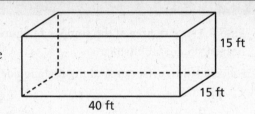

The area of the pool covered in algae includes the bottom and half of each of the lateral sides. To calculate the lateral area, divide the height by 2. There is no top on the pool.

$S = \ell w + 2\ell h + 2wh$

$= \left(\boxed{}\right)(15) + 2\left(\boxed{}\right)(7.5) + 2(15)\left(\boxed{}\right)$

$= \boxed{} \text{ ft}^2$

Calculate the density.

$D = \dfrac{400,000,000,000}{\boxed{}} = \boxed{}$

There are about $\boxed{}$ cells of algae per square foot in the pool.

Name _____

Find the surface area of each figure.

1.

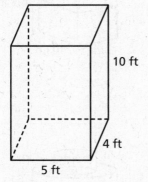

10 ft

4 ft

5 ft

2.

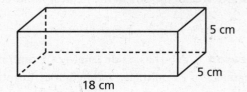

5 cm

5 cm

18 cm

3.

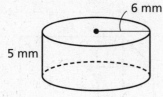

5 cm

12 cm

14 cm

4.

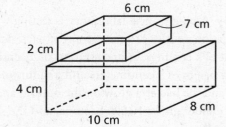

6 cm

7 cm

2 cm

4 cm

10 cm

8 cm

Find the surface area of each cylinder. Leave your answer in terms of π.

5.

6 mm

5 mm

6.

1 ft

10 ft

7.

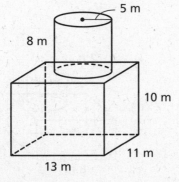

5 m

8 m

10 m

11 m

13 m

8.

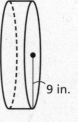

4 in.

9 in.

9. **Math on the Spot** The jewelry box is a composite figure. What is the surface area of the box to the nearest hundredth of an inch?

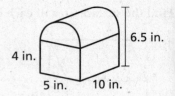

6.5 in.
4 in.
5 in.   10 in.

_____

10. **Reason** A cube has a side length of 1 centimeter, and a cylinder has a diameter of 1 centimeter and height of 1 centimeter. Which has greater surface area, the cube or the cylinder?

_____

11. Jim is baking a cake with three layers. One ounce of frosting will cover 10 square inches of cake. How many ounces of frosting are needed to cover the cake, not including the bottom? Round to the nearest ounce.

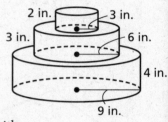

2 in.   3 in.
3 in.   6 in.
4 in.
9 in.

_____

12. **Apply** A biochemical laboratory is testing which surface allows for greater population density of a new strain of bacteria. The first surface is a cylinder with a height of 2 centimeters and a radius of 4 centimeters. The second surface is a cylinder with a height of 2 centimeters and a radius of 5 centimeters. Both cylinders have open tops, and the bacteria grow on the bottom and the inside walls of the cylinders. The first cylinder grows 10,000 bacteria, and the second grows 12,000 bacteria.

   A. What is the population density of the bacteria on each cylinder?

   _____

   B. Which cylinder should they use?

   _____

13. A metal manufacturing company makes a cubic part with a cylindrical hole through it. It is later coated with a sealant that is 0.1 centimeter thick. The sealant costs $1.50 per cubic centimeter.

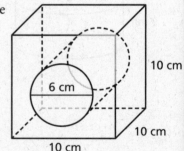

10 cm
6 cm
10 cm
10 cm

   A. What is the surface area of the part?

   _____

   B. Volume is the product of surface area and thickness. What is the volume of the sealant used to cover the part?

   _____

   C. How much does it cost to seal one part?

   _____

14. What is the surface area of the composite figure rounded to the nearest square foot?

   Ⓐ 235 ft²   Ⓒ 200 ft²

   Ⓑ 222 ft²   Ⓓ 215 ft²

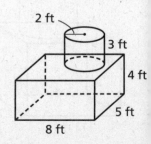

2 ft
3 ft
4 ft
5 ft
8 ft

Step It Out

Learn the Math

EXAMPLE 1   Sal designs a figure consisting of two cones attached at the base. What is the surface area of the figure? Round your answer to the nearest tenth.

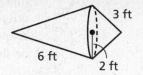

The variable ℓ represents the slant height of a cone. Find the lateral area of the larger cone.

$L = \pi r \ell$

$\quad = \pi(2)(6)$

$\quad \approx 37.7 \text{ ft}^2$

Find the lateral area of the smaller cone.

$L = \pi r \ell$

$\quad = \pi(2)(3)$

$\quad \approx 18.8 \text{ ft}^2$

The surface area of the figure is the sum of the lateral areas, $S \approx 37.7 + 18.8 \approx 56.5 \text{ ft}^2$.

Do the Math

Tammy plans to paint the outside of a box she bought at a yard sale. The box is made of a rectangular prism with a regular pyramid on top. What is the surface area of the box? Round your answer to the nearest tenth.

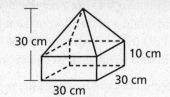

Find the surface area of the rectangular prism.

$S = 4\left(\boxed{} \cdot \boxed{} \right) + 30 \cdot \boxed{} = \boxed{} \text{ cm}^2$

Find the height of the pyramid.

$30 - \boxed{} = \boxed{} \text{ cm}$

Find the slant height of the pyramid.

$\ell = \sqrt{\boxed{}^2 + 15^2} = \boxed{} \text{ cm}$

Find the lateral area of the pyramid.

$L = \dfrac{1}{2}P\ell$

$\quad = \dfrac{1}{2}\left(\boxed{} \right)\left(\boxed{} \right)$

$\quad = \boxed{} \text{ cm}^2$

The surface area of the figure is the sum of the surface area of the prism and the

lateral area of the pyramid, $\boxed{} + \boxed{} = \boxed{} \text{ cm}^2$.

Learn the Math

EXAMPLE 2 Ian is baking a cake that looks like a castle. He plans to place four congruent cones on top of the castle and cover them with crisped rice. Ian uses all of a bag that contains 8000 pieces of crisped rice. What is the surface density of the crisped rice on the cones? Round to the nearest square inch.

8 in.

3 in.

Because the bottoms of the cones are on the cake, find only the lateral area of one cone.

$L = \pi r \ell$

$\quad = \pi(3)(8) \approx 75.4 \text{ in}^2$

Multiply by 4 to find the total lateral area of the cones.

$L \approx 4(75.4) \approx 301.6 \text{ in}^2$

Calculate the density.

$D \approx \dfrac{8000}{301.6} \approx 26.5$

Ian uses about 27 pieces of crisped rice per square inch to cover all the cones.

Do the Math

Abigail is making a regular pyramid for an art class. She will cover the entire pyramid with sand to make it look like a pyramid in the desert. She will use about 100,000 grains of sand. What is the surface density of the sand on the pyramid? Round to the nearest square inch.

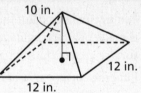

10 in.

12 in.

12 in.

Find the slant height of the pyramid.

$\ell = \sqrt{10^2 + \boxed{}^2} \approx \boxed{} \text{ in.}$

Find the surface area of the pyramid.

$S = \dfrac{1}{2}P\ell + B$

$\quad \approx \dfrac{1}{2}\left(\boxed{}\right)\left(\boxed{}\right) + \left(\boxed{} \cdot 12\right)$

$\quad \approx \boxed{} \text{ in}^2$

Calculate the density.

$D = \dfrac{100,000}{\boxed{}} \approx \boxed{}$

There will be about _____ grains of sand per square inch on the pyramid.

Find the surface area of each regular pyramid. Round to the nearest tenth, if necessary.

1.

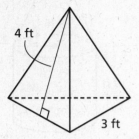

4 ft

3 ft

_____

2.

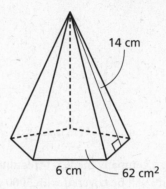

14 cm

6 cm   62 cm²

_____

3.

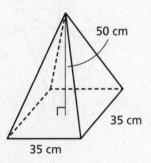

50 cm

35 cm

35 cm

_____

4.

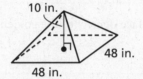

10 in.

48 in.

48 in.

_____

Find the surface area of each right cone. Leave your answer in terms of π.

5.

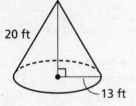

20 ft

13 ft

_____

6.

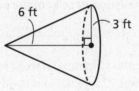

6 ft   3 ft

_____

7.

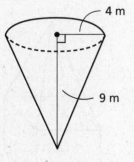

4 m

9 m

_____

8.

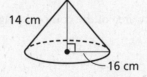

14 cm

16 cm

_____

9. **Math on the Spot** Find the surface area of the composite figure. Round to the nearest tenth.

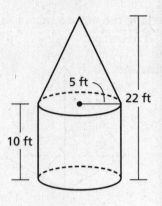

_____

10. A graphic design company made a three-dimensional figure for a client. The figure will be covered with 3000 golden flakes.

    A. What is the surface area of the figure? Round to the nearest tenth.

    _____

    B. What is the surface density of the golden flakes? Round to the nearest tenth.

    _____

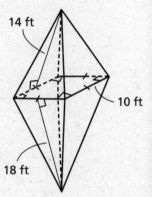

11. A square portion of a counter has a length of 10 centimeters. There are 25 right cones with radii of 0.5 centimeter and a slant height of 1 centimeter spread evenly over the counter. A colony of 10,000 bacteria lives on the surface.

    A. What is the surface area of the counter, including the cones on it? Round to the nearest tenth.

    _____

    B. What is the population density of the bacteria? Round to the nearest tenth.

    _____

12. The Rockefeller Center Christmas Tree is set up and decorated every year in New York City. One year, the tree was 72 feet tall and the diameter was 45 feet. The tree was decorated with 50,000 lights. The lateral area of the tree can be modeled using the formula for a right cone. What is the surface density of the lights?

    _____

13. What is the surface area of the composite figure rounded to the nearest square foot?

    (A) 680 ft²

    (B) 780 ft²

    (C) 880 ft²

    (D) 660 ft²

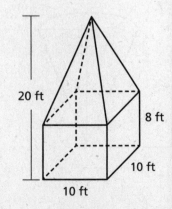

Name _____

Step It Out

Learn the Math

EXAMPLE 1 Morgan is painting a large sphere for a local theater. The thickness of the paint is 0.2 centimeter. Given that one gallon is approximately 3785.41 cubic centimeters, how many gallons of paint will Morgan need to cover the sphere?

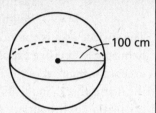
100 cm

Calculate the surface area of the sphere.

$S = 4\pi r^2$

$\quad = 4\pi(100)^2$

$\quad \approx 125,664 \text{ cm}^2$

Calculate the volume of paint.

$125,664 \text{ cm}^2 \cdot 0.2 \text{ cm} \approx 25,133 \text{ cm}^3$

Determine how many gallons of paint it will take to cover 25,133 cubic centimeters.

$25,133 \text{ cm}^3 \cdot \dfrac{1 \text{ gal}}{3785.41 \text{ cm}^3} \approx 6.64 \text{ gal}$

Morgan will need 7 gallons of paint to cover the sphere.

Do the Math

A restaurant serves a sugar bubble for dessert. The sugar is 2 millimeters thick. How much sugar does the restaurant use to create each bubble? Given that sugar costs $1.00 for 500,000 cubic millimeters, how much does it cost to make one bubble?

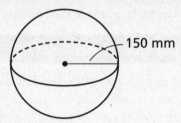
150 mm

Calculate the surface area of the bubble.

$S = 4\pi r^2$

$\quad = 4\pi \left(\boxed{} \right)^2$

$\quad \approx \boxed{} \text{ mm}^2$

Calculate the volume of sugar.

$\boxed{} \text{ mm}^2 \cdot 2 \text{ mm} = \boxed{} \text{ mm}^3$

Determine the cost of one sugar bubble.

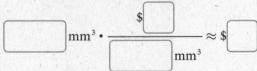

$\boxed{} \text{ mm}^3 \cdot \dfrac{\$ \boxed{}}{\boxed{} \text{ mm}^3} \approx \$ \boxed{}$

It costs $\boxed{}$ to make one sugar bubble.

Learn the Math

EXAMPLE 2 ▸ A building is made of a rectangular prism topped by a hemisphere as shown. Find the surface area of the building to the nearest square foot.

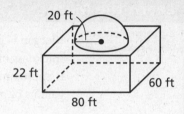

The surface area is composed of the spherical part of the hemisphere and five exposed faces of the rectangular prism, except for the part of the top face covered by the flat surface of the hemisphere. You will need to subtract that area in the calculation of the surface area of the building.

Calculate the surface area of the five exposed faces of the rectangular prism.

$S = 2(22 \cdot 80) + 2(22 \cdot 60) + 80 \cdot 60 = 10{,}960 \text{ ft}^2$

Calculate the surface area of the spherical part of the hemisphere.

$S = \frac{1}{2}\left(4\pi(20)^2\right) \approx 2513.27 \text{ ft}^2$

Calculate the area of the flat surface of the hemisphere.

$S = \pi(20)^2 \approx 1256.64 \text{ ft}^2$

Calculate the surface area of the building.

$S \approx 10{,}960 + 2513.27 - 1256.64 \approx 12{,}216.63 \text{ ft}^2$

The surface area of the building is approximately 12,217 square feet.

Do the Math

An engineering firm builds a custom metal part and coats it with a rust-resistant material. The amount of coating depends on the surface area of the part. What is the surface area, to the nearest square centimeter, of the part shown?

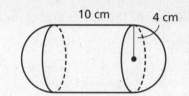

The surface area is composed of two hemispheres and the lateral area of a cylinder. Because two hemispheres equal one sphere, you can use the formula for the surface area of a sphere.

$S = 4\pi\left(\boxed{}\right)^2 \approx \boxed{} \text{ cm}^2$

Calculate the lateral area of the cylinder.

$L = 2\pi\left(\boxed{}\right)\left(\boxed{}\right) \approx \boxed{} \text{ cm}^2$

Calculate the surface area of the part.

$\boxed{} + \boxed{} \approx \boxed{} \text{ cm}^2$

The surface area of the part is approximately $\boxed{}$ square centimeters.

Find the surface area of each figure. Leave answers in terms of π.

1.

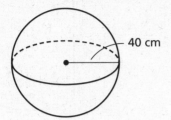

40 cm

_____

2.

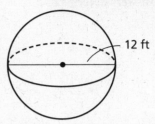

12 ft

_____

3.

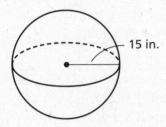

15 in.

_____

4.

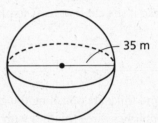

35 m

_____

5.

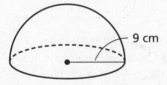

9 cm

_____

6.

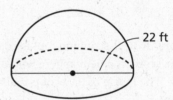

22 ft

_____

Find the surface area of each composite figure. Round answers to the nearest tenth.

7.

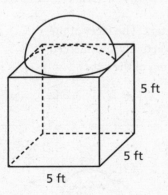

5 ft

5 ft

5 ft

_____

8.

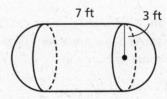

7 ft   3 ft

_____

9. A cone has a diameter and slant height equal to the diameter of a sphere. Which has more surface area? Explain.

_____

_____

10. **Math on the Spot** Find the surface area of the composite figure. Leave answers in terms of π.

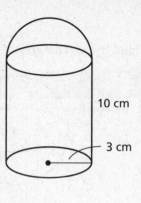

10 cm

3 cm

_____

11. Sara wraps a spherically shaped melon in plastic wrap. She considers whether she should cut the melon in half before wrapping it. How much more plastic wrap would she need if she cut it in half? Explain.

_____

_____

12. Alex and Mike are polishing the golden spheres on the tops of basketball trophies. Mike polishes three trophies with diameters of 12 inches each. Alex polishes six trophies with diameters of 6 inches each. Who polishes the larger surface area?

_____

_____

13. **Apply** A steel-scooping tool is coated with a metal alloy to prevent rust. The outside of the scoop is a hemisphere with a radius of 2 centimeters. The steel is 0.2 centimeter thick. The inside of the scoop is also a hemisphere. What is the surface area of the scoop?

_____

_____

_____

14. **Reason** A six-sided number cube has a side length of 3 centimeters. The faces of the cube represent the numbers 1 through 6 using "dots." Each dot is actually an indented hemisphere with a radius of 0.1 centimeter. What is the surface area of the cube?

_____

_____

15. What is the surface area of the composite figure?

Ⓐ $(90 + 4\pi)$ ft^2

Ⓑ $(90 + 3\pi)$ ft^2

Ⓒ $(90 + \pi)$ ft^2

Ⓓ $(40 + 4\pi)$ ft^2

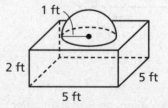

1 ft

2 ft

5 ft

5 ft

Name _____

Step It Out

Learn the Math

EXAMPLE 1 Ariel is making a box out of sheet metal to contain her rock collection. The sheet of metal is 20 inches long and 30 inches wide. She cuts squares out of each corner and folds up the sides to build the box. What dimensions, to the nearest inch, maximize the volume of the box?

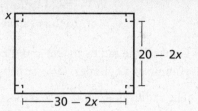

Write the equation for the volume of the box.

Squares of side length x inches are cut from each corner. So the height of the box after it is folded is x inches. Once the sides are folded up, the length of the box is given by $\ell = 20 - 2x$ and the width is given by $w = 30 - 2x$.

The volume is the product of the length, the width, and the height: $V = (20 - 2x)(30 - 2x)x$.

The value of x must be between 0 and 10 to ensure that none of the dimensions are negative.

Use a graphing calculator to find the height. Use the value of x to find the length and the width of the box. Then determine the maximum volume.

From the graph, $x \approx 4$ inches. So the length is approximately $20 - 2(4)$, or 12 inches, and the width is approximately $30 - 2(4)$, or 22 inches.

The maximum volume is $(12)(22)(4)$, or 1056 cubic inches.

Do the Math

Caleb is making a box out of cardboard to hold his tools. The piece of cardboard is 12 inches long and 15 inches wide. He cuts squares out of each corner and folds up the sides to build the box. What dimensions, to the nearest inch, maximize the volume of the box?

Write the equation for the volume of the box. Let ☐ represent the height of the box.

The length of the box is given by $l = $ ☐ $-$ ☐, and the width is given by

$w = $ ☐ $-$ ☐. The volume is given by $V = \left(\text{☐} - \text{☐}\right)\left(\text{☐} - \text{☐}\right)\left(\text{☐}\right)$.

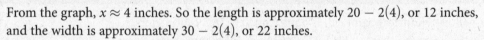

Use a graphing calculator to graph the volume function. Set the values of x between

☐ and ☐ to ensure that none of the dimensions are negative.

From the graph, $x \approx$ ☐ inches. The length is approximately ☐ inches, and the

width is approximately ☐ inches. The maximum volume is $\left(\text{☐}\right)\left(\text{☐}\right)\left(\text{☐}\right)$,

or ☐ cubic inches.

Learn the Math

EXAMPLE 2 ▸ Dimitri bought a cylindrical clay flowerpot that holds approximately 15 gallons of dry soil $\left(1 \text{ gallon} \approx 0.15 \text{ cubic foot}\right)$. The radius of the pot is 9 inches. What is the height, to the nearest tenth of a foot, of the flowerpot?

Convert the radius to feet and the volume to cubic feet. Then use the formula for the volume of a cylinder: $V = \pi r^2 h$.

The radius is $\frac{9}{12}$, or 0.75 foot. Solve the proportion $\frac{1 \text{ gal}}{0.15 \text{ ft}^3} = \frac{15 \text{ gal}}{V}$ to convert the volume to cubic feet: $V = 15(0.15) = 2.25 \text{ ft}^3$.

$$V = \pi r^2 h$$
$$2.25 = \pi(0.75)^2 h$$
$$2.25 = 0.5625\pi h$$
$$\frac{2.25}{0.5625\pi} = h$$
$$h \approx 1.3 \text{ ft}$$

The height of the flowerpot is approximately 1.3 feet.

Do the Math

The diameter of a one-gallon cylindrical paint can is approximately 16.5 centimeters. Manufacturing specifications require there to be 1.27 centimeters of empty space above the level of the paint to allow for tinting and mixing. What height, to the nearest hundredth of a centimeter, must the paint can be?

$\left(1 \text{ gallon} \approx 3785.4 \text{ cubic centimeters}\right)$

Calculate the radius of the can, and substitute known values into the formula for the volume of a cylinder.

The radius is $\dfrac{\Box}{\Box}$, or $\boxed{}$ centimeters.

$$V = \pi r^2 h$$
$$\boxed{} = \pi\left(\boxed{}\right)^2 h$$
$$\boxed{} = \boxed{}\,\pi h$$
$$\frac{\boxed{}}{\boxed{}\,\pi} = h$$
$$h \approx \boxed{} \text{ ft}$$

To account for the extra space above the paint, add $\boxed{}$ centimeters to the height. The height of the can must be $\boxed{}$ centimeters.

Name _____

Find the volume of each figure. Round your answer to the nearest hundredth.

1.

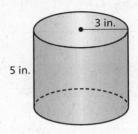

3 in.

5 in.

2.

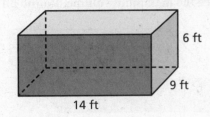

6 ft

9 ft

14 ft

_____   _____

3.   Math on the Spot Give exact answers in terms of π.

A. Find the volume of the cylinder.

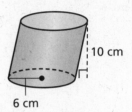

10 cm

6 cm

B. Find the volume of a cylinder with a base area of 25π in^2 and a height equal to the radius.

_____   _____

Find the missing dimension of each figure. Round your answer to the nearest tenth.

4. $V = 100$ in^3

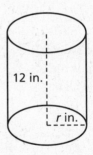

12 in.

r in.

5. $V = 252$ ft^3

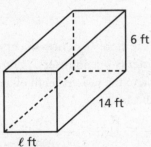

6 ft

14 ft

ℓ ft

_____   _____

Find the volume of each composite figure. Round your answer to the nearest tenth.

6.

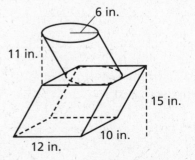

6 in.

11 in.

15 in.

10 in.

12 in.

7.   A cylindrical-shaped hole is cut from the center of a cube.

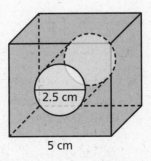

2.5 cm

5 cm

_____   _____

Find the maximum volume of each box and the dimensions, in inches, that produce the maximum volume. Round all answers to the nearest hundredth.

8.

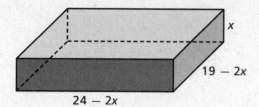

$19 - 2x$

$24 - 2x$

x

9.

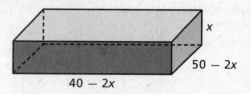

$50 - 2x$

$40 - 2x$

x

_____

_____

10. Critique Reasoning Eugene believes that a prism with a square base of 14 centimeters and a height of 9 centimeters will have the same volume as a cylinder with a diameter of 14 centimeters and a height of 9 centimeters. Is Eugene correct? Explain your reasoning.

_____

_____

11. Reason A rectangular in-ground pool with a uniform depth measures 36 feet long by 18 feet wide. The fill line is 1.5 feet below the pool deck. The pool is filled with approximately 24,236.88 gallons of water $\left(1 \text{ gallon} \approx 0.1337 \text{ cubic feet}\right)$. How far underground is the bottom of the pool?

_____

_____

12. Jerra wants to store 16 ounces of coffee beans in a cylindrical canister. The radius of the canister is 7 centimeters. $\left(1 \text{ ounce} \approx 29.57 \text{ cubic centimeters}\right)$ What is the least height, to the nearest tenth of a centimeter, the canister can be to hold all of the coffee beans?

_____

_____

13. Open Ended Give the dimensions of a rectangular prism and of a cylinder so that the two figures have approximately the same volume.

_____

_____

14. The quarter is a circular coin with a diameter of 24.26 millimeters and a thickness of 1.75 millimeters. What is the volume of a stack of 20 quarters to the nearest cubic millimeter?

(A) 8090

(C) 32,357

(B) 16,179

(D) 64,714

Step It Out

Learn the Math

EXAMPLE 1 A ski resort creates a three-dimensional model of its logo consisting of two cones. One of the cones has a radius of 6 feet and a height of 12 feet, and the other has a radius of 5 feet and is $\frac{2}{3}$ the height of the first. What is the volume of the model? Round to the nearest hundredth.

Find the height of the second cone: $12 \cdot \frac{2}{3} = 8$ feet.

Use the formula $V = \frac{1}{3}\pi r^2 h$ for the volume of each cone. Substitute the values for the radius and the height of each cone into the formula. Remember that volume is measured in cubic units.

First Cone:

$V = \frac{1}{3}\pi r^2 h$

$V = \frac{1}{3}\pi(6)^2(12)$

$V = 144\pi$

$V \approx 452.39 \text{ ft}^3$

Second Cone:

$V = \frac{1}{3}\pi r^2 h$

$V = \frac{1}{3}\pi(5)^2(8)$

$V = \frac{200\pi}{3}$

$V \approx 209.44 \text{ ft}^3$

Add the volumes of the two cones together to find the volume of the model.

$144\pi + \frac{200\pi}{3}$

The total volume of the model is approximately 661.83 ft³.

Do the Math

An Egyptian pyramid with a square base with a side length of 230 meters once stood at 146 meters tall. Due to erosion, it is now only 139 meters tall but the base is unchanged. How much volume did the pyramid lose due to erosion? Round to the nearest whole.

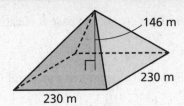

Calculate the area of the base B.

$230 \cdot 230 = \boxed{}$

Use the equation for volume of a pyramid, $V = \frac{1}{3}Bh$.

Find the volume of the pyramid before and after erosion.

Volume Before:

$V = \frac{1}{3}\left(\boxed{}\right)(146)$

$V \approx \boxed{}$

Volume After:

$V = \frac{1}{3}\left(\boxed{}\right)\left(\boxed{}\right)$

$V \approx \boxed{}$

Subtract the volumes to find how much was lost.

$\boxed{} - \boxed{} = \boxed{}$ m³ was lost due to erosion.

Learn the Math

EXAMPLE 2 A plastic cone has a radius of 7 centimeters and a height of 20 centimeters. The cone has a mass of 900 grams. What is the density of the plastic? Round to the nearest hundredth.

Find the volume of the cone using the formula $V = \frac{1}{3}\pi r^2 h$.

$V = \frac{1}{3}\pi r^2 h$

$V = \frac{1}{3}\pi (7)^2 (20)$

$V \approx 1026.25 \text{ cm}^3$

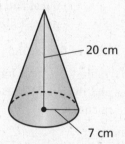

20 cm

7 cm

Find the density using the formula $\text{density} = \frac{\text{mass}}{\text{volume}}$.

$d = \frac{900}{1026.25} \approx 0.88$

The density of the plastic is about 0.88 gram per cubic centimeter.

Do the Math

The head of a steel meat tenderizer is a cube with a side length of 5 centimeters. One face of the cube contains 25 square pyramids that protrude from the surface. The side length of the base of each square pyramid is 0.5 centimeter, and the height of each is 0.5 centimeter. The mass of the head of the tenderizer is 1000 grams. What is the density of the steel? Round to the nearest hundredth.

Find the volume of the cube using the formula $V = s^3$.

$V = \boxed{}^3 = \boxed{}$

Find the area of the base B of each pyramid.

$B = \left(\boxed{}\right)^2 = \boxed{}$

Find the volume of one pyramid using the formula $V = \frac{1}{3}Bh$.

$V = \frac{1}{3}\left(\boxed{}\right)\left(\boxed{}\right) \approx \boxed{}$

Multiply the volume of one pyramid by the number of pyramids. Then add the volume of the cube to find the total volume.

$25\left(\boxed{}\right) + \boxed{} \approx \boxed{}$

Find the density using the formula $\text{density} = \frac{\text{mass}}{\text{volume}}$.

$d = \frac{1000}{\boxed{}} \approx \boxed{}$

The density of the steel is about $\boxed{}$ grams per cubic centimeter.

1. Find the volume of the pyramid.

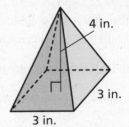

4 in.

3 in.

3 in.

2. Find the volume of a cone with a height of 3 feet and a radius of 1 foot. Round to the nearest hundredth.

3. Find the volume of a triangular pyramid with a height of 10 centimeters. The base of the pyramid has a height of 14 centimeters and a base length of 12 centimeters.

4. Find the volume of the cone shown. Round to the nearest hundredth.

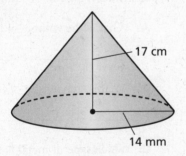

17 cm

14 mm

5. Find the density of a metal cone with a height of 20 centimeters and a radius of 5 centimeters. The mass is 2500 grams. Round to the nearest hundredth.

6. Find the density of the wooden square pyramid shown. The mass is 100,000 grams. Round to the nearest hundredth.

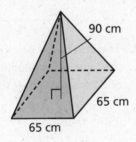

90 cm

65 cm

65 cm

7. Find the density of a plastic triangular pyramid with a height of 5 feet. The base of the pyramid has a height of 4 feet and a base length of 3 feet. The mass is 55 kilograms.

8. Find the density of a wooden cone with a height of 100 centimeters and a radius of 25 centimeters. The mass is 18,000 grams. Round to the nearest hundredth.

9. **Math on the Spot** Find the volume of the composite figure. Round to the nearest hundredth.

A. Find the volume of the cylinder.

B. Find the height of the cone.

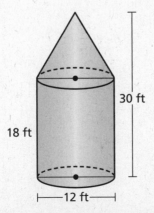

30 ft

18 ft

12 ft

C. Find the volume of the cone.

D. Find the total volume.

10. Reason A rubber ball consists of a sphere with 150 small cones protruding from the surface. The volume of the sphere is 50 cubic centimeters. Each cone has a radius of 0.2 centimeter and a height of 0.4 centimeter.

A. Write the formula for the total volume of the ball.

_____

B. What is the volume of the ball? Round to the nearest hundredth.

_____

11. A square pyramid made of metal is at the peak of the Washington Monument in Washington, DC. It was constructed of the metal considered to be most precious at the time. The side length of the base of the pyramid is 11.37 centimeters, and the height is 22.86 centimeters. The mass of the pyramid is about 2835 grams. The following are approximate densities of various metals in grams per cubic centimeter: lead 11.36; aluminum 2.70; silver 10.49; gold 19.32; zinc 7.13.

A. What is the volume of the pyramid?

_____

B. What is the density of the pyramid?

_____

C. Which type of metal is the pyramid made of?

_____

12. The area of the base of a hexagonal pyramid is 200 square inches. The volume of the pyramid is double the volume of a cone with a radius of 6 inches and a height of 8 inches. What is the height of the pyramid to the nearest inch?

Ⓐ 3 inches

Ⓑ 5 inches

Ⓒ 9 inches

Ⓓ 27 inches

Step It Out

Learn the Math

EXAMPLE 1 When a spaceship is orbiting Earth, water can be suspended in the air and it will form a sphere. Amaya measures a water sphere on her spaceship that has a radius of 5 centimeters. Find the volume and the mass of the water. To find the mass, use the fact that the density of water is 1 gram per cubic centimeter. Round answers to the nearest tenth.

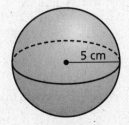

Use the formula for volume of a sphere, $V = \frac{4}{3}\pi r^3$.

$$V = \frac{4}{3}\pi(5)^3$$
$$= \frac{500}{3}\pi$$
$$\approx 523.6 \text{ cm}^3$$

Use the formula for density, $d = \frac{m}{V}$, to calculate the mass.

$$m = dV$$
$$\approx (1)(523.6)$$
$$\approx 523.6 \text{ g}$$

Do the Math

When a substance has a density that is less than the density of water, it floats. A wooden sphere has a radius of 4 centimeters and a mass of 250 grams. Will the wooden sphere float? Round answers to the nearest hundredth.

Calculate the volume of the wooden sphere.

$$V = \frac{\Box}{\Box}\pi r^3 = \frac{\Box}{\Box}\pi \Box^3 = \frac{\Box}{3}\pi$$

$$\approx \Box \text{ cm}^3$$

Calculate the density of the wooden sphere.

$$d = \frac{\Box}{V} \approx \frac{250}{\Box}$$

$$\approx \Box \text{ g/cm}^3$$

Because the density of the wooden sphere is _____ than the density of water, it _____ .

Learn the Math

EXAMPLE 2   Planets are nearly spherical. They are not perfectly spherical because their equatorial diameters are greater than their polar diameters. The equatorial diameter of Earth is 7926 miles. The equatorial diameter of Mars is 4222 miles. Estimate how many times as great the volume of Earth is as the volume of Mars.

Use the formula for the volume of a sphere to estimate the volumes of the two planets.

Earth	Mars
$V = \dfrac{4}{3}\pi(3963)^3$	$V = \dfrac{4}{3}\pi(2111)^3$
$\approx 2.61 \times 10^{11}$ mi^3	$\approx 3.94 \times 10^{10}$ mi^3

Divide the volumes to determine how many times as large Earth is as Mars.

$$\frac{2.61 \times 10^{11}}{3.94 \times 10^{10}} \approx 6.6$$

The volume of Earth is about 6.6 times as great as the volume of Mars.

Do the Math

Kelly has a Granny Smith apple with a diameter of 7.5 centimeters and a Honeycrisp apple with a diameter of 9 centimeters. The apples are nearly spherical. Estimate how many times as great the volume of the Honeycrisp apple is as the volume of the Granny Smith apple. Round to the nearest tenth.

Learn the Math

EXAMPLE 3   A storage shed is composed of a cube with a hemisphere on top, as shown. The diameter of the hemisphere is equal to the side length of the cube. What is the volume of the shed to the nearest cubic foot?

Use the formula $V = s^3$ to calculate the volume of the cube.

$V = 50^3 = 125{,}000$ ft^3

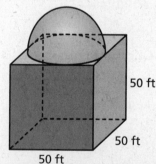

A hemisphere is half a sphere, so use the formula $V = \dfrac{2}{3}\pi r^3$ to calculate the volume of the hemisphere.

$V = \dfrac{2}{3}\pi(25)^3$

$\approx 32{,}725$ ft^3

The volume of the shed is about $125{,}000 + 32{,}725$, or $157{,}725$ ft^3.

Do the Math

A gas tank is composed of a cylinder with a hemisphere on each end. The height of the cylinder is 10 feet, and the radius is 2 feet. The bases of the hemispheres are congruent to the base of the cylinder. What is the volume of the gas tank to the nearest cubic foot?

Name _____

LESSON 19.3
More Practice

ONLINE
Video Tutorials and
Interactive Examples

Find the volume of each figure. Round your answer to the nearest tenth.

1.

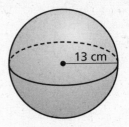

13 cm

_____

2.

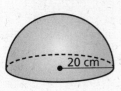

20 cm

_____

3. a sphere with a radius of 7 feet

_____

4. a sphere with a diameter of 18 inches

_____

5. a sphere with a diameter of 12 meters

_____

6. a hemisphere with a diameter of 8 feet

_____

Find the volume of each composite figure. Round your answer to the nearest tenth.

7.

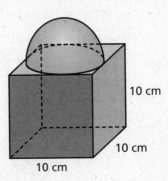

10 cm

10 cm

10 cm

_____

8.

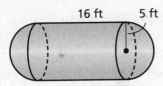

16 ft   5 ft

_____

9.

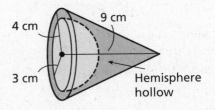

4 cm   9 cm

3 cm   Hemisphere
hollow

_____

10.

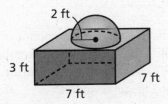

2 ft

3 ft   7 ft

7 ft

_____

11. **Math on the Spot** Find the volume of the composite figure. Round to the nearest cubic inch.

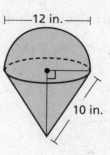

12 in.

10 in.

12. **Reason** The diameter of Earth's moon is about 2159 miles. Like Earth, it is nearly spherical. Use the information given in Example 2 to estimate how many moons could fit inside Earth.

_____

13. Tyler is designing a bouncy object for his toy manufacturing company. The object consists of a cube with hemispheres protruding from each face. The side length of the cube and the diameters of the hemispheres all measure 6 inches. What is the volume of the object to the nearest cubic inch?

_____

14. A cylindrical container holds three tennis balls, each with a radius of 3.3 centimeters. The radius of the container is 3.5 centimeters, and the length is 20.2 centimeters. What is the volume of the empty space in the container to the nearest tenth?

_____

15. **Critique Reasoning** Students are making jewelry in art class. Andi is drilling through the center of holes wooden spheres to make beads for a necklace. (Note: because the sphere is round, the holes drilled through it are not quite cylinders because the "bases" are not flat.) Clara is drilling cylindrical holes into wooden cylinders to make beads for a bracelet. Clara says the volumes of their beads are the same, but Andi says the volume of her beads is greater than the volume of Clara's beads. The holes have radius 0.25 centimeter. Who is correct? Explain.

Clara's bead

Andi's bead

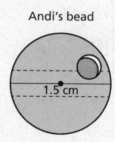

1.5 cm

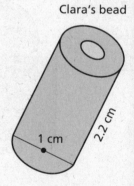

1 cm

2.2 cm

_____

16. Patrick has to calculate the volume of 16 hemispheres with the same radius. To simplify the calculations, he computes the volume of one sphere with the given radius. By what number does Patrick need to multiply the volume of the sphere to determine the total volume?

Ⓐ 2

Ⓒ 8

Ⓑ 4

Ⓓ 16

Step It Out

Learn the Math

> **EXAMPLE 1** In a carnival contest, participants are asked to draw a marble from a bag that contains 7 red marbles, 11 green marbles, 9 blue marbles, and 3 silver marbles. Anyone who draws a silver marble is considered a winner. Tim decides to try the contest. What is the probability that Tim is not a winner?

For Tim to *not* be a winner, he must draw a red, a green, or a blue marble. In other words, he must draw a *non-silver* marble. It is easier to use the complement of drawing a silver marble to calculate the probability of Tim *not* being a winner.

The probability of drawing a silver marble $P(S)$ is $\frac{3}{30}$ or $\frac{1}{10}$.

The probability that Tim is not a winner is $P(S^C)$.

$$P(S^C) = 1 - P(S)$$
$$= 1 - \frac{1}{10}$$
$$= \frac{9}{10}$$

The probability that Tim is not a winner is $\frac{9}{10}$.

Do the Math

Siri spins the spinner shown once. The spinner is divided into 20 equal sections. Find the probability that the pointer lands on an odd number.

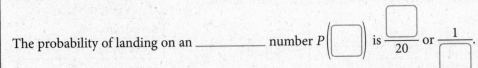

There are fewer _____ numbers than _____ numbers.

Therefore, it is easier to use the complement of drawing

an _____ number to calculate the probability that the

pointer lands on an _____ number.

The probability of landing on an _____ number $P\left(\boxed{}\right)$ is $\dfrac{\boxed{}}{20}$ or $\dfrac{1}{\boxed{}}$.

The probability that the pointer lands on an _____ number is $P\left(\boxed{}^C\right)$.

$$P\left(\boxed{}^C\right) = 1 - P\left(\boxed{}\right)$$

$$= 1 - \frac{1}{\boxed{}} = \frac{\boxed{}}{\boxed{}}$$

The probability that the pointer lands on an _____ number is $\dfrac{\boxed{}}{\boxed{}}$.

Learn the Math

EXAMPLE 2 A DJ knows the best way to keep the dance floor crowded is to play songs with an average of 120 beats per minute. He also knows that people occasionally prefer a break and that he should include slower songs for couples' dances. The DJ creates a playlist with 500 songs, 60 of which average 50 beats per minute. The DJ sets the playlist to play songs randomly. What is the probability that the first song will be a fast song?

To find the probability that the first song will be a fast song, find the probability of the complement of the event that the first song is a slow song.

Let S be the event that the first song is a slow song.

$$P(S) = \frac{\text{number of slow songs}}{\text{total number of songs}} = \frac{60}{500}$$

Find the probability that the first song is a fast song.

$$P(S^C) = 1 - \frac{60}{500} = \frac{440}{500} = \frac{22}{25}$$

The probability that the first song will be a fast song is $\frac{22}{25}$.

Do the Math

There are 300 members in a marching band. The table shows the number of members in the band that play each type of instrument. What is the probability that the band member chosen to be the drum major plays a brass or woodwind instrument?

To find the probability that the drum major plays a brass or woodwind

instrument, find the probability of the _____ of the event that the

drum major plays a _____ instrument.

Let P be the event that the drum major plays a _____ instrument.

$$P(P) = \frac{\text{number of} \underline{\hspace{3cm}}}{\text{total number of} \underline{\hspace{2cm}}} = \frac{\boxed{}}{\boxed{}}$$

Brass	
Piccolo	20
Trombone	42
Trumpet	54
Tuba	28
Woodwind	
Clarinet	49
Flute	35
Saxophone	27
Percussion	
Bass drum	8
Cymbals	13
Snare drum	24

Find the probability that the drum major plays a brass or woodwind instrument.

$$P(P^C) = 1 - \frac{\boxed{}}{\boxed{}} = \frac{\boxed{}}{\boxed{}} = \frac{\boxed{}}{\boxed{}}$$

The probability that the band member chosen to be the drum major plays a brass or

woodwind instrument is $\frac{\boxed{}}{\boxed{}}$.

Let *A* be the set of factors of 20, *B* be the set of factors of 30,
C be the set of factors of 40, and *D* be the set of factors of 50.
The universal set is {1, 2, 3, 4, 5, 6, 8, 10, 15, 20, 25, 30, 40, 50}.

1. Write sets *A* through *D* using set notation.

_____

_____

_____

_____

2. Is $A \subset C$? Explain.

_____

_____

3. What is $B \cap C$?

_____

4. What is $D \cap A$?

_____

5. What is $A \cup B$?

_____

6. What is $C \cup D$?

_____

7. What is D^C?

_____

8. What is $A \cap C$?

_____

9. What is $B \cup C$?

_____

10. What is B^C?

_____

A set of 26 cards contains the letters of the alphabet. The letter Y is considered both a vowel
and a consonant. Event *A* is choosing a vowel. Event *B* is choosing one of the first
12 letters of the alphabet. Event *C* is choosing a consonant. Calculate each probability.

11. $P(A)$ _____

12. $P(A^C)$ _____

13. $P(A \cup B)$ _____

14. $P(A \cap B)$ _____

15. $P(B^C)$ _____

16. $P(C)$ _____

17. $P(B \cap C)$ _____

18. $P(B \cup C)$ _____

19. **Math on the Spot** A floor is covered with 50 square-foot tiles. All the tiles are purple except for those listed in the table. If you toss a quarter onto the floor at random, what is the probability that it will land on a purple tile?

Floor Tiles	
Color	**Number of tiles**
Blue	4
Green	1
Red	2
Yellow	3

_____

20. **Model with Mathematics** At the end of the day, a roadside stand has 5 tomatoes, 3 cucumbers, 4 summer squash, and 3 peppers still left for sale. Use set notation to represent the universal set in this situation.

_____

21. **Critique Reasoning** A set of 10 cards is numbered 1 to 10. A card is chosen at random. Event A is choosing a card less than 7. Event B is choosing a card greater than 3. Mira says $P(A \cap B) = \frac{6}{13}$. What mistake did Mira make? What is $P(A \cap B)$?

_____

_____

_____

22. **Open Ended** In a standard bingo game, the numbers 1 to 15 are in column B, 16 to 30 are in column I, 31 to 45 are in column N, 46 to 60 are in column G, and 61 to 75 are in column O. Write a problem for this situation that can be solved by finding the complement of an event. Then write the solution for your problem.

_____

_____

23. Liam has a bag with 30 marbles in it. There are 5 white marbles and 3 red marbles. The rest of the marbles are silver. If he chooses a marble at random from the bag, use the complement of the event to find each probability.

A. He chooses a silver marble. _____

B. He chooses a silver or red marble. _____

C. He does not choose a red marble. _____

24. A six-sided number cube is rolled once. Which events have probability $\frac{2}{3}$? Select all that apply.

   (A) $P(\text{rolls a number} < 5)$ (D) $P(\text{rolls a number} > 3)$

   (B) $P(\text{rolls a number} \geq 2)$ (E) $P(\text{rolls a factor of 6})$

   (C) $P(\text{rolls a number} \geq 1)$ (F) $P(\text{rolls a number} \leq 4)$

Step It Out

Learn the Math

EXAMPLE 1 Bailey randomly chooses a card from a standard deck of 52 playing cards. What is the probability that she chooses a card that is red or an even number?

Let A be the event that the card is red. Let B be the event that the card is an even number.

The events are overlapping because a card may be red and contain an even number. Because the events are overlapping, use the Addition Rule to find the probability.

First, make a table to organize the different probabilities.

Use the Addition Rule to find the probability.

$P(A \text{ or } B) = P(A) + P(B) - P(A \text{ and } B)$

$= \dfrac{26}{52} + \dfrac{20}{52} - \dfrac{10}{52} = \dfrac{36}{52} = \dfrac{9}{13}$

Answer the question.

The probability that Bailey chooses a card that is red or an even number is $\dfrac{9}{13}$.

Probability	Value
$P(A)$	$\dfrac{26}{52} = \dfrac{1}{2}$
$P(B)$	$\dfrac{20}{52} = \dfrac{5}{13}$
$P(A \text{ and } B)$	$\dfrac{10}{52} = \dfrac{5}{26}$

Do the Math

Reno spins a spinner once that has 8 equal sections. Two sections are blue, one section is yellow, three sections are red, and two sections are green. What is the probability that the result is red or blue?

Let A be the event that the section is red. Let B be the event that the section is blue.

The events are disjoint because the spinner cannot land on red and blue at the same time. So, $P(A \text{ or } B) = P\left(\boxed{}\right) + P\left(\boxed{}\right)$. You can also use the Addition Rule to find

the probability because $P(A \text{ and } B) = \boxed{}$.

Make a table to organize the different probabilities.

Use the Addition Rule to find the probability.

$P(A \text{ or } B) = P\left(\boxed{}\right) + P\left(\boxed{}\right) - P\left(\boxed{}\right)$

$= \dfrac{\boxed{}}{8} + \dfrac{\boxed{}}{8} - \dfrac{\boxed{}}{8} = \dfrac{\boxed{}}{8}$

The probability that the result is red or blue is $\dfrac{\boxed{}}{8}$.

Probability	Value
$P(A)$	$\dfrac{\boxed{}}{8}$
$P(B)$	$\dfrac{\boxed{}}{8} = \dfrac{\boxed{}}{4}$
$P(A \text{ and } B)$	$\boxed{}$

Learn the Math

EXAMPLE 2 Students were asked in a survey if they preferred baseball/softball, tennis, basketball, swimming, or dance. The results are shown in the table. What is the probability that a randomly selected student is a sophomore or prefers basketball?

	Baseball/ softball	Tennis	Basketball	Swimming	Dance	Total
Freshman	15	18	16	23	13	85
Sophomore	27	25	28	33	20	133
Junior	26	12	15	11	5	69
Senior	44	13	39	17	24	137
Total	112	68	98	84	62	424

Let A be the event that a student is a sophomore. Let B be the event that a student prefers basketball. Find $P(A)$, $P(B)$, and $P(A \text{ and } B)$. Then use the Addition Rule to find $P(A \text{ or } B)$.

$$P(A) = \frac{133}{424}; P(B) = \frac{98}{424} = \frac{49}{212}; P(A \text{ and } B) = \frac{28}{424} = \frac{7}{106}$$

$$P(A \text{ or } B) = P(A) + P(B) - P(A \text{ and } B)$$

$$= \frac{133}{424} + \frac{98}{424} - \frac{28}{424} = \frac{203}{424}$$

The probability that the student is a sophomore or prefers basketball is $\frac{203}{424}$.

Do the Math

The table shows the results of a survey of different ages of people who were asked whether they prefer spaghetti, chicken, steak, or vegetable stir-fry for dinner. What is the probability that a randomly selected person is between 15 and 30 or prefers spaghetti?

	Spaghetti	Chicken	Steak	Vegetable stir-fry	Total
15 and under	31	21	15	9	76
Between 15 and 30	20	16	16	13	65
30 and over	15	25	19	23	82
Total	66	62	50	45	223

Let A be the event that the person is between 15 and 30. Let B be the event that the person prefers spaghetti. Use the Addition Rule to find $P(A \text{ or } B)$.

$$P(A \text{ or } B) = P(A) + P(B) - P(A \text{ and } B) = \frac{\square}{223} + \frac{\square}{223} - \frac{\square}{223} = \frac{\square}{223}$$

The probability that the person is between 15 and 30 or prefers spaghetti is $\frac{\square}{223}$.

Carrie randomly chooses a marble out of a bag that contains 5 yellow marbles, 6 orange marbles, 4 blue marbles, and 5 purple marbles.

1. What is the probability that Carrie chooses a marble that is purple and blue? Are these disjoint or overlapping events? Explain.

_____

_____

2. What is the probability that Carrie chooses a yellow or an orange marble? Are these disjoint or overlapping events? Explain.

_____

_____

A spinner has eight same-sized sections numbered 1 through 8. Sections 2 and 3 are yellow. Sections 4, 5, and 6 are blue. Section 7 is red. Sections 1 and 8 are purple. The spinner is spun one time. Find each probability. Show your work.

3. P(purple and even)

_____

4. P(yellow or multiple of 3)

_____

5. P(blue and less than 4)

_____

6. P(red or odd)

_____

7. P(blue or factor of 8)

_____

8. P(purple and greater than 1)

_____

At a family picnic, family members split into teams wearing purple, maroon, teal, and pink shirts. The teams have a water balloon-toss competition. The table shows the results of the competition.

	Purple	Maroon	Teal	Pink	Total
Wins	6	4	0	2	12
Losses	0	2	6	4	12
Total	6	6	6	6	24

9. What is the probability that a team is wearing a teal shirt or loses the water balloon toss? Show your work.

_____

10. What is the probability that a team is wearing a maroon shirt or wins the water balloon toss? Show your work.

_____

11. **Open Ended** Devin is rolling a six-sided number cube. Write and solve a probability problem about two overlapping events using the number cube.

_____

_____

12. **Math on the Spot** A carnival gives a prize to each customer. Upon entrance, each customer receives a scratch-off card that says one of four things: "free popcorn," "free corn dog," "free game," or "free drink." A card has a $\frac{4}{15}$ probability of being labeled "free drink" and a $\frac{3}{10}$ probability of being labeled "free corn dog." What is the probability that a ticket is "free drink" or "free corn dog?"

_____

_____

13. **Model with Mathematics** The table shows some of the results of a survey of people who were asked what activity they prefer. Can you determine the probability that a person chosen at random is out of school or prefers to exercise? If so, what is the probability? Explain your reasoning.

	Reading	Exercising	Sleeping	Watching TV	Total
High school student	10	12	13	15	50
College student	11	15	17		51
Out of school	18		10		53
Total	39	41	40	34	154

_____

_____

_____

14. There are 20 rows (labeled 1–20) with 15 seats (labeled 1–15) in each row in a theater. What is the probability that a person chosen at random is sitting in an odd-numbered row or in an odd-numbered seat?

   Ⓐ $\frac{21}{30}$

   Ⓑ $\frac{23}{30}$

   Ⓒ $\frac{25}{30}$

   Ⓓ $\frac{27}{30}$

Name _____

Step It Out

Learn the Math

EXAMPLE 1 ▶ A survey was conducted to determine whether people prefer summer or winter and whether they prefer to be outside or inside. What is the probability that a person prefers winter given that he or she prefers to be outside? What is the probability that a person prefers to be outside given that he or she prefers winter?

	Winter	Summer	Total
Outside	13	19	32
Inside	9	9	18
Total	22	28	50

The formula for conditional probability is $P(B \mid A) = \dfrac{P(A \cap B)}{P(A)}$.

Let W be the event that a person prefers winter and U be the event that a person prefers to be outside.

The probability that a person prefers winter given that he or she prefers to be outside is the same as the probability that a person prefers winter and being outside divided by the probability that he or she prefers to be outside. There are 13 people who prefer winter and being outside and 32 people who prefer being outside.

$$P(W \mid U) = \frac{\left(\frac{13}{50}\right)}{\left(\frac{32}{50}\right)} = \frac{13}{32} \approx 40.6\%$$

The probability that a person prefers to be outside given that he or she prefers winter is the same as the probability that a person prefers being outside and winter divided by the probability that he or she prefers winter. There are 13 people who prefer being outside and winter and 22 people who prefer winter.

$$P(U \mid W) = \frac{\left(\frac{13}{50}\right)}{\left(\frac{22}{50}\right)} = \frac{13}{22} \approx 59.1\%$$

Do the Math

A survey was conducted to determine whether people prefer carrots or celery and whether they prefer soup or salad. What is the probability that a person prefers soup given that he or she prefers celery? Let P be the event that a person prefers soup. Let Y be the event that a person prefers celery.

	Soup	Salad	Total
Carrot	7	6	13
Celery	4	3	7
Total	11	9	20

The probability that a person prefers soup given that he or she prefers _____ is the same as the probability that a person prefers _____ and _____ divided by the probability that he or she prefers _____. There are ☐ people who prefer soup and celery and ☐ people who prefer _____.

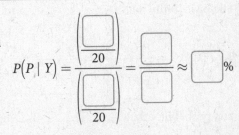

$$P(P \mid Y) = \frac{\left(\dfrac{\Box}{20}\right)}{\left(\dfrac{\Box}{20}\right)} = \frac{\Box}{\Box} \approx \Box\%$$

Learn the Math

EXAMPLE 2 A restaurant owner is working hard at having less food waste. On any given night, she knows the probability that more than 10% of prepared food goes to waste is 22%. She also knows that the probability that it is Monday and more than 10% of food is wasted is 6.8%.

A. What is the probability that it is Monday given that more than 10% of food is wasted?

B. What is the probability that more than 10% of food is wasted given that it is Monday?

Let W be the probability that more than 10% of food is wasted. Let M be the probability that it is Monday.

Identify the given probabilities: $P(W) = 0.22$ and $P(W \cap M) = 0.068$. There are 7 days in a week, so $P(M) = \frac{1}{7} \approx 0.143$.

A. $P(M \mid W) = \dfrac{P(W \cap M)}{P(W)} = \dfrac{0.068}{0.22} \approx 30.9\%$

The probability that it is Monday given that more than 10% of food is wasted is about 30.1%.

B. $P(W \mid M) = \dfrac{P(W \cap M)}{P(M)} = \dfrac{0.068}{0.143} \approx 47.6\%$

The probability that more than 10% of food is wasted given that it is Monday is about 47.6%.

Do the Math

In the town of Deep Creek, there is a probability of 66% that the temperature is above 50 °F. The probability that it is above 50 °F and is sunny is 45%. It is sunny in Deep Creek 57% of the time.

A. What is the probability that it is sunny in Deep Creek given that the temperature is greater than 50 °F?

B. What is the probability that the temperature is greater than 50 °F given that it is sunny in Deep Creek?

Let G be the probability that the temperature is greater than 50 °F. Let S be the probability that it is sunny.

Identify the given probabilities: $P(G) = \boxed{}$, $P(G \cap S) = \boxed{}$, and $P(S) = \boxed{}$.

A. $P(S \mid G) = \dfrac{P(G \cap S)}{P\left(\boxed{}\right)} = \dfrac{\boxed{}}{\boxed{}} \approx \boxed{}\%$

The probability that it is _____ in Deep Creek given that _____ is about $\boxed{}$%.

B. $P(G \mid S) = \dfrac{P(G \cap S)}{P\left(\boxed{}\right)} = \dfrac{\boxed{}}{\boxed{}} \approx \boxed{}\%$

The probability that _____ in Deep Creek given that it is _____ is about $\boxed{}$%.

Campers collected either pinecones or acorns for an art project.
Then they got to choose between paints or string to complete their
projects. Use the results in the table to answer the questions about
the campers' choices. Let A be the event that the camper collected
acorns. Let S be the event that the camper chose string to finish the
project. Round answers to the nearest tenth of a percent.

	Pinecone	Acorn	Total
Paints	18	16	34
String	39	27	66
Total	57	43	100

1. What does $P(S \mid A)$ represent? What is $P(S \mid A)$?

_____

2. What does $P(A \mid S^C)$ represent? What is $P(A \mid S^C)$?

_____

3. Explain the difference between $P(A \mid S)$ and $P(S \mid A)$. What is $P(A \mid S)$?

_____

Dog owners of popular breeds completed a survey. Let W be the event that a dog prefers
to take walks and F be the event that a dog prefers to play fetch. Let S be the event that
the breed is a German shepherd, R be the event that the breed is a golden retriever, and
B be the event that the breed is a beagle.

4. What is the missing value in each row? What does the value represent?

Calculate each probability to the nearest tenth of a percent.

	German shepherd	Golden retriever	Beagle	Total
Walks		0.32	0.08	0.59
Fetches	0.12	0.24		0.41
Total	0.31		0.13	1.00

5. $P(B \mid W)$

_____

6. $P(W \mid R)$

_____

7. $P(F \mid S)$

_____

8. $P(W \mid S)$

_____

9. $P(R \mid F)$

_____

10. $P(F \mid B^C)$

_____

11. Open Ended A drawer is filled with unmatched black and white socks. Thaila and Stephano take turns pulling a sock out of the drawer. What are two probabilities that can be asked about this scenario?

_____

_____

12. Math on the Spot Joe throws three types of pitches. His coach records whether each pitch is a strike or ball for 100 randomly chosen pitches. The record for the 100 pitches is shown here. Use conditional probabilities to determine the type of pitch that is most likely to be a strike.

	Strike	Ball
Fastball	ＨＴ ＨＴ ＨＴ ＨＴ ＨＴ Ｉ	ＨＴ ＨＴ ＩＩＩＩ
Breaking ball	ＨＴ ＨＴ ＩＩ	ＨＴ ＨＴ ＨＴ ＨＴ ＩＩＩ
Changeup	ＨＴ ＨＴ	ＨＴ ＨＴ ＨＴ

_____

_____

_____

13. Critique Reasoning Grace surveyed her neighbors who own fish or cats and whether they go on road trips. Grace concluded $P(\text{cats} \mid \text{no road trips}) = \frac{3}{11} \approx 27\%$. What was Grace's error? What is the correct probability?

	Fish	Cats	Total
Road trips	6	3	9
No road trips	8	8	16
Total	14	11	25

_____

_____

_____

14. Carla and Katelin are on vacation. During the week, Katelin goes in the ocean 76% of the time they are on the beach while Katelin and Carla go in 46% of the time. What is the probability that Carla will go in the ocean given that Katelin also goes in that day? Round to the nearest percent.

Ⓐ 30%   Ⓒ 60%

Ⓑ 46%   Ⓓ 61%

Step It Out

Learn the Math

EXAMPLE 1 Several cards with different shapes on them are shown. You select a card, return it, and then select another card. What is the probability that you select a card with a triangle first and a card with a shaded shape second? Let T be the event of selecting a triangle first and S be the event of selecting a shaded shape second.

Find $P(T)$ and $P(S)$.

There are ten cards to select from, five of which have triangles.

So, $P(T) = \dfrac{5}{10} = \dfrac{1}{2}$.

There are six cards with shaded shapes, so $P(S) = \dfrac{6}{10} = \dfrac{3}{5}$.

Because the first card is replaced before the second card is drawn, events T and S are independent. Therefore, $P(T \cap S) = P(T) \cdot P(S)$.

$P(T \cap S) = \dfrac{1}{2} \cdot \dfrac{3}{5} = \dfrac{3}{10}$

Do the Math

You roll a standard number cube twice. What is the probability that you roll a two first and an odd number second? Let T be the event that you roll a two first and D be the event that you roll an odd number second.

Find $P(T)$ and $P(D)$.

There are _____ numbers on a standard number cube, _____ of which is $\boxed{}$.

So, $P(T) = \dfrac{\boxed{}}{\boxed{}}$. There are _____ odd numbers on a standard number cube, so

$P(D) = \dfrac{\boxed{}}{\boxed{}} = \dfrac{\boxed{}}{\boxed{}}$.

Because one roll has _____ on another roll, events T and D are _____. Therefore,

$P(T \cap D) = \boxed{} \cdot \boxed{} = \dfrac{\boxed{}}{\boxed{}} \cdot \dfrac{\boxed{}}{\boxed{}} = \dfrac{\boxed{}}{\boxed{}}$.

Learn the Math

EXAMPLE 2 Mr. DeFranco wants to determine whether the event that a student is in 10th grade is independent of the event that the student likes action movies. Let T be the event a student is in 10th grade and A be the event the student likes action movies.

	Likes action movies	Does not like action movies	Total
9th grade	120	40	160
10th grade	180	60	240
Total	300	100	400

Method A: Compare $P(T)$ and $P(T \mid A)$.

There are 400 students total, and 240 of them are in 10th grade.

$P(T) = \dfrac{240}{400} = 0.6 = 60\%$

There are 300 students who like action movies, and 180 of them are in 10th grade.

$P(T \mid A) = \dfrac{180}{300} = 0.6 = 60\%$

Because $P(T) = P(T \mid A)$, events T and A are independent.

Method B: Compare $P(T \cap A)$ and $P(T) \cdot P(A)$.

There are 400 students total, and 180 of them are 10th graders who like action movies.

$P(T \cap A) = \dfrac{180}{400} = \dfrac{9}{20}$

There are 400 students total, and 240 of them are in 10th grade, so $P(T) = \dfrac{240}{400} = \dfrac{3}{5}$.

There are 400 students total, and 300 of them like action movies, so $P(A) = \dfrac{300}{400} = \dfrac{3}{4}$.

$P(T) \cdot P(A) = \dfrac{3}{5} \cdot \dfrac{3}{4} = \dfrac{9}{20}$

Because $P(T \cap A) = P(T) \cdot P(A)$, events T and A are independent.

Do the Math

The school nurse wants to determine whether the event that a person is left-handed is independent of the event that the person wears glasses. Let L be the event a person is left-handed and G be the event that the person wears glasses. Are the two events independent? Explain.

	Wears glasses	Does not wear glasses	Total
Left-handed	39	26	65
Right-handed	261	174	435
Total	300	200	500

Name _____

LESSON 21.2
More Practice

ONLINE
Video Tutorials and
Interactive Examples

Determine each probability. Assume events *A* and *B* are independent.

1. $P(A) = \frac{2}{3}$; $P(B) = \frac{1}{5}$

Find $P(B \mid A)$. _____

2. $P(B \mid A) = \frac{4}{7}$; $P(A) = \frac{2}{9}$

Find $P(B)$. _____

3. $P(A) = \frac{1}{8}$; $P(B) = \frac{2}{3}$

Find $P(A \cap B)$. _____

4. $P(A \cap B) = \frac{9}{35}$; $P(B) = \frac{3}{7}$

Find $P(A)$. _____

5. **Math on the Spot** Find the probabilities. Justify your reasoning.

  A. Spinning 1 and then 1 again on the spinner

  _____

  B. Spinning shaded, then hatched, and then 5 on the spinner

  _____

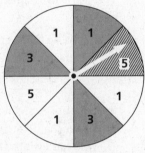

6. A sock drawer contains 12 black socks, 21 white socks, and 7 gray socks. You randomly select socks from the drawer. Each time you select a sock, you replace it before selecting another. Let *B* be the event that a black sock is drawn, let *W* be the event that a white sock is drawn, and let *G* be the event that a gray sock is drawn. Find each probability.

  A. A black sock is drawn first, and a gray sock is drawn second.

  B. Two white socks are drawn.

  C. A gray sock is drawn first, and a white sock is drawn second.

  D. Two gray socks are drawn.

7. Tiles containing each letter of the alphabet are placed in a bag. You randomly select tiles from the bag. Each time you select a tile, you replace it before selecting another. The letter Y is considered both a vowel and a consonant. Find each probability.

  A. The letter A is drawn first, and a vowel is drawn second.

  B. Either X, Y, or Z is drawn first, and J is drawn second.

  C. The letter A is drawn first, B is drawn second, and C is drawn third.

  D. A consonant is drawn first, K or L is drawn second, and a vowel is drawn third.

8. Open Ended A bag of marbles contains 5 green marbles, 10 purple marbles, and 7 orange marbles. Let A be the event a purple marble is randomly chosen first. Let B be the event a purple marble is randomly chosen second. What has to be true for the two events to be independent? How do you know?

_____

_____

_____

9. Make Sense of Problems Arsha asks students at her school whether they prefer math or language arts. She asks the same students whether they prefer action movies or comedies. The two-way frequency table shows the survey results.

	Math	Language arts	Total
Action movies	8	17	25
Comedies	16	34	50
Total	24	51	75

A. Let M be the event that a student prefers math. Let C be the event that a student prefers comedies. Determine whether M and C are independent. Show your work.

_____

B. Suppose Arsha does another survey, but this time she asks students whether they prefer math, language arts, or world studies. Would the process for determining whether events M and C are independent change? Explain.

_____

_____

10. A principal gathers data on the grade-point averages (GPAs) of students. Is the event that a student is an athlete independent of the event that the student has a GPA greater than 3.4? Show your work.

	GPA > 3.4	GPA ≤ 3.4	Total
Athlete	54	32	86
Not an athlete	138	133	271
Total	192	165	357

11. A standard number cube is rolled three times. What is the probability that the first roll is 5, the second roll is an even number, and the third roll is a number greater than 2?

Ⓐ $\frac{1}{24}$

Ⓑ $\frac{5}{18}$

Ⓒ $\frac{5}{72}$

Ⓓ $\frac{1}{18}$

Step It Out

Learn the Math

> **EXAMPLE 1** A bag contains 12 red stars, 5 blue stars, and 3 green stars. Marcy selects a star from the bag, then selects another star without replacing the first.

A. What is the probability that Marcy selects a blue star and then a green star?

There are 20 stars in the bag. Because Marcy does not replace the first star she selects, there are only 19 stars left in the bag when she selects a second star. So, the probability of drawing a second star of any color depends on the first star that was selected.

For dependent events, probability is calculated with the Multiplication Rule:

$P(A \cap B) = P(A) \cdot P(B \mid A).$

Let B be the event that Marcy selects a blue star first and G be the event that she selects a green star second.

$$P(B \cap G) = P(B) \cdot P(G \mid B) = \frac{5}{20} \cdot \frac{3}{19} = \frac{3}{76}$$

B. What is the probability that Marcy selects a red star and then another red star?

Let R_1 be the event that Marcy selects a red star first and R_2 be the event that she selects a red star second.

$$P(R_1 \cap R_2) = P(R_1) \cdot P(R_2 \mid R_1) = \frac{12}{20} \cdot \frac{11}{19} = \frac{33}{95}$$

Do the Math

A box contains 14 striped balls, 8 solid-colored balls, and 4 dotted balls. Amir selects a ball from the box, then selects another ball without replacing the first.

A. What is the probability that Amir selects a striped ball and then a dotted ball?

Let S be the event that Amir selects a _____ ball first and D be the event that he selects a _____ ball second.

$$P(S \cap D) = P\left(\boxed{}\right) \cdot P\left(\boxed{} \middle| \boxed{}\right)$$

$$= \frac{\boxed{}}{26} \cdot \frac{\boxed{}}{25}$$

$$= \frac{\boxed{}}{\boxed{}}$$

B. What is the probability that Amir selects a solid-colored ball and then another solid-colored ball?

Let S_1 be the event that Amir selects a _____ ball first and S_2 be the event that he selects a _____ ball second.

$$P(S_1 \cap S_2) = P\left(\boxed{}\right) \cdot P\left(\boxed{} \middle| \boxed{}\right)$$

$$= \frac{8}{\boxed{}} \cdot \frac{\boxed{}}{\boxed{}}$$

$$= \frac{\boxed{}}{\boxed{}}$$

Learn the Math

EXAMPLE 2 ▶ Aliyah selects three cards from a standard deck of playing cards, each time without replacement. There are four suits in a standard deck of playing cards: hearts and diamonds (which are red), clubs and spades (which are black). There are 13 cards per suit, including number cards from 2 to 10, a jack, a queen, a king, and an ace.

A. What is the probability that Aliyah selects an ace, then a jack, and finally a queen?

Because Aliyah does not replace any of the cards she selects, the events are dependent. The Multiplication Rule can be extended to three or more dependent events:

$P(A \cap B \cap C) = P(A) \cdot P(B \mid A) \cdot P(C \mid A \cap B)$.

Let A be the event that Aliyah selects an ace first, J be the event that she selects a jack second, and Q be the event that she selects a queen third.

$$P(A \cap J \cap Q) = P(A) \cdot P(J \mid A) \cdot P(Q \mid A \cap J)$$
$$= \frac{4}{52} \cdot \frac{4}{51} \cdot \frac{4}{50}$$
$$\approx 0.000483$$

B. What is the probability that Aliyah selects three spades in a row?

Let S_1 be the event that Aliyah selects a spade first, S_2 be the event that she selects a spade second, and S_3 be the event that she selects a spade third.

$$P(S_1 \cap S_2 \cap S_3) = P(S_1) \cdot P(S_2 \mid S_1) \cdot P(S_3 \mid S_1 \cap S_2)$$
$$= \frac{13}{52} \cdot \frac{12}{51} \cdot \frac{11}{50}$$
$$\approx 0.012941$$

Do the Math

What is the probability that Aliyah selects a king, then a black 5, and finally the 2 of hearts?

Let K be the event that Aliyah selects a _____ first, B_5 be the event that she selects a _____ second, and let 2_H be the event that she selects a _____ third.

$$P(K \cap B_5 \cap 2_H) = P\left(\boxed{}\right) \cdot P\left(\boxed{} \mid K\right) \cdot P\left(2_H \mid \boxed{} \cap \boxed{}\right)$$

$$= \frac{\boxed{}}{\boxed{}} \cdot \frac{\boxed{}}{\boxed{}} \cdot \frac{\boxed{}}{\boxed{}}$$

$$\approx \boxed{}$$

Name _____

LESSON 21.3
More Practice

⊙ Ed **ONLINE**
Video Tutorials and
Interactive Examples

A basket contains 6 yellow eggs, 10 blue eggs, and 12 green eggs.
Jermaine reaches into the basket and takes an egg. Then William reaches
into the basket and takes an egg.

1. What is the probability that Jermaine takes a yellow egg and William takes a green egg?

_____

2. What is the probability that Jermaine takes a green egg and William takes a green egg?

_____

3. What is the probability that Jermaine takes a green egg and William takes an egg that is not green?

_____

4. What is the probability that Jermaine takes a blue egg and William takes a purple egg?

_____

A bag contains 4 red marbles, 3 yellow marbles, and 5 white marbles. Three marbles are
selected in a row at random, each time without replacement.

5. What is the probability that the first two marbles are white and the third is red?

_____

6. What is the probability that none of the marbles are red?

_____

7. What is the probability that the first marble is yellow, the second marble is white, and the third marble is not yellow?

_____

8. What is the probability that the first marble is red, the second marble is white, and the third marble is yellow?

_____

9. There are nine fish in a tank at a pet store. Four of them are goldfish, three of them are guppies, and two of them are koi. Sai reaches into the tank with a net and selects three fish to purchase. He selects one at a time without looking and without replacement. What is the probability Sai selects a koi first and then two goldfish?

_____

10. Math on the Spot Two cards are drawn from a deck of 52. Determine whether the events are independent or dependent. Find the probability of

   A. selecting two red cards when the first card is replaced.

_____

   B. selecting a queen or jack and then an ace without replacement.

_____

11. A survey asked students whether they have a library membership and whether they read at least 5 hours per week. The two-way frequency table shows the results. Let M be the event that the student has a library membership and let F be the event the student reads at least 5 hours per week.

	Has a library membership	Has no library membership	Total
Reads < 5 hours	107	125	232
Reads ≥ 5 hours	91	43	134
Total	198	168	366

A. Are events M and F independent or dependent? Explain how you know.

_____

B. Find $P(M \mid F)$ and $P(F \mid M)$.

_____

12. Critique Reasoning Rachel draws a card from a standard deck of cards, then selects another without replacing the first. What is the probability that Rachel draws two queens?

Alex solves the problem as follows.

$P(\text{queen and queen}) = \dfrac{4}{52} \cdot \dfrac{4}{51} = \dfrac{16}{2652} = \dfrac{4}{663}$

Explain the error in Alex's thinking.

_____

13. A shipment of 100 computers contains three that are defective. Three computers are randomly selected. Find the probability that they are all defective if they are selected with replacement. Then find the probability that they are all defective if they are selected without replacement. What do you notice about the probabilities?

_____

_____

14. Open Ended Explain the Multiplication Rule, as applied to three events, in your own words.

_____

_____

15. The letters of the word PROBABILITY are written on slips of paper and placed in a bag. Three letters are randomly selected without replacement. Let A be the event that the first letter selected is an A, B be the event that the second letter selected is a B, and I be the event that the third letter selected is an I. Find $P(A \cap B \cap I)$.

Ⓐ $\dfrac{4}{1331}$ Ⓒ $\dfrac{2}{1331}$

Ⓑ $\dfrac{2}{495}$ Ⓓ $\dfrac{4}{495}$